CASTAWAY MOUNTAIN

CASTAWAY MOUNTAIN

LOVE AND LOSS AMONG THE WASTEPICKERS OF MUMBAI

Saumya Roy

ASTRA HOUSE | NEW YORK

For information about permission to reproduce selections from this book, please
contact permissions@astrahouse.com.

Astra House
A Division of Astra Publishing House
astrahouse.com
Printed in the United States of America

Publisher's Cataloging-in-Publication Data

Names: Roy, Saumya, author.
Title: Castaway mountain : love and loss among the wastepickers of Mumbai /
    Saumya Roy.
Description: Includes bibliographical references. | New York, NY: Astra House,
    2021.
Identifiers: LCCN: 2021909406 | ISBN: 9781662600951 (hardcover) |
    9781662600968 (ebook)
Subjects: LCSH Ragpickers—India—Mumbai—Economic conditions. |
    Ragpickers—India—Mumbai—Social conditions. | Plastic scrap—
    Economic aspects—India. | Refuse and refuse disposal—Social aspects—
    India—Mumbai. | Poor—India—Mumbai. | Slums—India—Mumbai. |
    Mumbai (India)—Social conditions. | Mumbai (India)—Economic conditions. |
    BISAC SOCIAL SCIENCE / Sociology / Urban | SOCIAL SCIENCE /
    Ethnic Studies / Asian Studies | POLITICAL SCIENCE / Public Policy /
    Environmental Policy
Classification: LCC HD9975.I43 R69 2021 | DDC 363.728/209—dc23

First edition
10 9 8 7 6 5 4 3 2 1

Design by Richard Oriolo
The text is set in Adobe Caslon Pro.
The titles are set in Akzidenz Grotesk BQ.

To,

My grandmother, professor and poet, who wrote –
have you seen, my friend?
on the peaks of inky, dark, rain cloud topped-mountains,
snowy white illuminating clouds appear sometimes?

and Prashant Kant, my uncle,
who could not see but showed me how to spot the
illuminating clouds.

CONTENTS

CASTAWAY MOUNTAIN

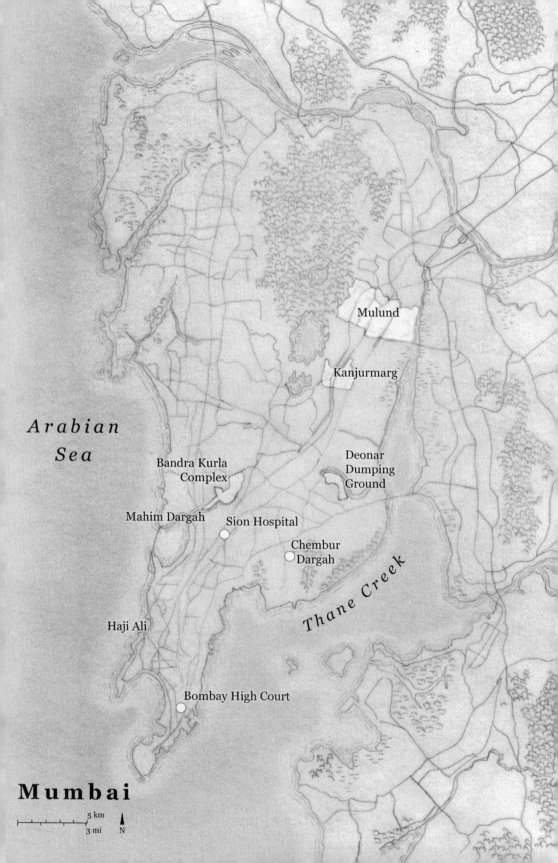

Arabian
Sea

Mulund

Kanjurmarg

Deonar
Dumping
Ground

Bandra Kurla
Complex

Mahim Dargah   Sion Hospital

Chembur
Dargah

Thane Creek

Haji Ali

Bombay High Court

Mumbai

5 km

3 mi   N

CAST OF PRINCIPAL CHARACTERS

AT THE MOUNTAINS

Hyder Ali Shaikh: Wastepicker at the Deonar garbage mountains and father of Farzana and her eight siblings.

Shakimun Ali Shaikh: Hyder Ali's wife.

Jehana Shaikh: Hyder Ali and Shakimun's daughter and the eldest of the nine children.

Jehangir Shaikh: Hyder Ali's oldest son and the second oldest of the children.

Rakila Shaikh: Jehangir's wife. Mother of their three children.

Alamgir Shaikh: Hyder Ali's second oldest son, drives garbage trucks.

Yasmeen Shaikh: Alamgir's wife and mother of their two children.

Sahani Shaikh: Second oldest of the Shaikh daughters.

Ismail Shaikh: Sahani's husband. Does odd jobs around the mountains.

Afsana Shaikh: The third oldest sister and the only one who married and moved away from the mountains. Does tailoring work and is a mother of two.

FARZANA SHAIKH: Hyder Ali and Shakimun's daughter. Sixth of the nine children.

Farha Shaikh: The sister after Farzana. The two often pick together.

Jannat Shaikh: The youngest of the daughters.

Ramzan Shaikh: Hyder Ali's son and youngest child.

Moharram Ali Siddiqui: Picker, known for working night shifts and finding treasures in mountain trash.

Yasmin Siddiqui: Moharram Ali's wife.

Hera Siddiqui: Moharram Ali's oldest child. Hera is beautiful, imperious, and of the few girls from these lanes to have made it to high school.

Sharib Siddiqui: Older of Moharram Ali's two sons. Often missing school to pick on the mountains.

Sameer Siddiqui: Younger of Moharram Ali's sons.

Mehrun Siddiqui: Moharram Ali and Yasmin's middle daughter.

Ashra Siddiqui: The youngest of the Siddiqui children.

Salma Shaikh: Picker who came to work on the mountains more than three decades ago with a toddler son and hundred-day-old baby son wrapped to her back, after her husband had died.

Aslam Shaikh: Salma's older son, married to Shiva, father of four sons and a daughter.

Arif Shaikh: One of Aslam's four sons.

Vitabai Kamble: Said to be one of the oldest pickers on the mountains. She came to live at the mountains' rim in the mid-seventies with her husband and children.

Nagesh Kamble: Vitabai's oldest son. Came to pick at the mountains as a ten-year-old and turned middle-aged and potbellied on them.

Babita Kamble: Vitabai's daughter.

Rafique Khan: Garbage trader.

Atique Khan: Rafique's younger brother.

IN THE COURT

Dr. Sandip Rane: Doctor who lives in a genteel neighborhood near the mountains' rim and runs a cardiology hospital. Filed for contempt in 2008 when the municipality did not close the mountains per court directions, following a case filed in 1996.

Justice Dhananjaya Chandrachud: Adjudicated on Dr. Rane's case in the Bombay High Court.

Raj Kumar Sharma: Grew up and lives in a leafy area not far from the mountains. Filed a court case in December 2015 asking for the mountains to get mended.

Justice Abhay Oka: Judge who heard Sharma's case for several years.

INTRODUCTION

VITABAI KAMBLE FIRST ARRIVED at my office on a warm April afternoon in 2013. She worked on the garbage mountains at the edge of the city and needed a loan from the foundation I had set up with my father in 2010 to provide small, low-interest loans to grow the city's poorest residents' businesses. I had worked as a reporter for nearly a decade before that and wanted to do more than write about India's rising economy and its lengthening shadow of slums and waste. While India's economy was fueled by people buying, and even taking loans for, new gadgets, holiday travel, and weddings, I had written about how telemarketers from banks often hung up when they reached people in slums.

We set up our office at the end of interminable, undrying clotheslines in a residential lane in the Sion area of the city. At first, the only sounds were of trains passing by on the tracks behind it, but, as word of our operation spread, the city's fish, fruit, and street food sellers, lunch makers, cobblers, and tailors filled our office, drowning out the train sounds.

As I met vendors who exchanged garlic for household waste that they then resold and others who made the city's shoes, clothes, and toys, my brain slowly got rewired. I saw a city different from the one I had lived in for years. I asked about how they made a profit on their meager, and often several, businesses, eliciting blank stares. They were not sure.

But hardly anyone I had met through the foundation had fascinated me as Vitabai did that summer afternoon. She huddled close to the thin mattress I sat on, revealing hands and feet covered in fading scars, which mapped memories of the nearly four decades she had spent on rising trash. The mountains had lightened her hair and I saw the thrill of chasing forgotten treasures dance in her silver-rimmed eyes. Her plucky energy and memories of her life on the growing mountains had lit up my languorous afternoon.

I fretted about how she would repay our loan, with her odd business. "If you can only sell what you collect with your hands, how will our loans help you grow?" I asked her in Marathi. "*Kachra kadhi kami honar ka?*" Vitabai quickly countered. *Will trash ever reduce?* She worked in one of Mumbai's fastest-growing industries, she said, offering to show me the unending hills they mined. What she could not collect herself, she would use our loans to buy from others and sell to garbage traders. She quickly became my introduction to the world of the Deonar township, a place I knew nearly nothing about before her arrival, but would soon become addicted to.

Soon after she took a loan, Vitabai brought her daughter, Babita, for one. Weeks later, I saw Hyder Ali Shaikh's lean shoulders and deep eyes rising behind her diminutive frame, as they walked through the long waiting area I had fashioned out of a car garage. She had brought Hyder Ali, Moharram Ali Siddiqui, and Aftab Alam, who lived nearby, to form a group, which would take on a loan with her son, Nagesh. If one of them could not pay weekly installments, the others would.

Hyder Ali stretched languidly on the thinly matted floor, across from me. With the sun streaming on his face, he began, saying, *"Hamara gaon, Laluji ke bagal ka hai,"* making a reference to the former chief minister of the eastern state of Bihar. He belonged to the village next to that of Lalu Yadav, who was known for his humor and easy laughter, often at himself. I looked up from reading his loan application form. *"Aap jante the?"* I asked. *Did you know him?* He nodded sideways to say no. *"Mile The?"* I tried again. *Have you met him?* He nodded sideways again, breaking into a bony grin. But I understood that this was what he wanted to say about himself, the thing that the lengthy form, filled with personal details, did not ask. I came to associate humor and unfettered laughter with Hyder Ali, too.

Unlike Vitabai and her family, Hyder Ali said he did not want to stay in the trash business. He leaned back, resting his hand on the lime green floor mat, barely noticing the stripes it pressed into his reddened palm, and told me of his journey into the mountains' shade and his dreams of stepping out. He wanted to use the money to set up an embroidery work-shop, of the sort he had spent his youth in. He would bring embroiderers from his village to make bridal outfits to sell, in the city, for a commis-sion. He hoped it would take him away from the hills, inching up his family's fortunes.

I followed Vitabai, Nagesh, Hyder Ali, and the others back to the garbage mountains, to see if their odd businesses would lead to unpaid loans for us. But I also went to see this strange place, which I had heard of but, like most Mumbaikars, never seen. I found a vast township of trash growing invisibly in plain sight, mountains that were more than 120 feet high, surrounded on one side by the Arabian Sea and on the other by a sequence of settlements.

This began my more than eight-year entanglement with the Deonar mountains and its denizens. I watched the lives and businesses of four families unfold in their shadow. Most of all, I had watched Hyder Ali's teenaged daughter, Farzana Shaikh, grow into a life that seemed as unlikely as the mountains that I also watched rising precipitously with desires that had flickered and died in the city. This book is Farzana's story, her family's and neighbors' story, and I am grateful for their permission to write about it.

I came to see the mountains as the pickers did: bringing the city's used luck, depositing its fading wealth on the township's tricky passes. I attended hundreds of hours of court proceedings that aimed to control the city's waste, thinking every time that the mountains were about to move. I collected archival documents to unravel the rumors I heard from pickers. "*Kachra train ni yaycha,*" Vitabai had told me in one of my earlier walks on the mountains. *Garbage once came here by train.* It felt unreal, like many of the legends and lives around the tricky mountain slopes: a train service just for garbage? And yet, it was true: years later, I found myself at Oxford University's storied Bodleian Library, reading colonial records of how Bombay's garbage had indeed come to Deonar by a special train.

IN THE SUMMER of 2016, we had begun reducing and soon stopped our lending in the lanes around the mountains. I visited only to meet pickers, hear of their lives, and write about them. Some were uninterested in conversations that did not end in our low-interest loans, but most chatted endlessly, cried, or steamed up as they spoke. "*Bolne se nahi samjhega ham khaadi pe kaise jiye, video le ke aao,*" Salma Shaikh, who had worked there for nearly forty years, told me. *Just speaking won't explain how we lived on the dumping grounds. You'll have to bring a video camera.*

My own affection, frustration, and bonds formed with these people over the course of eight years. But the world of the Deonar garbage mountains is a world of its own, where I was only passing through, even if as a long-term visitor. In these pages, I have stepped away in order to take readers into a world they created but never visited, so they can step into this mirror image of their own lives.

Deonar's mountainous township of trash has a unique history and yet, wherever I went in the world, the pull of desire was just as unyielding, and as transient, throwing up waste mountains much like Deonar. A journalist friend had written of the "waste Everest," outside Moscow. The mountains in Delhi were said to be nearly as tall as the Taj Mahal, and had tumbled down in avalanches, as had others in Colombo, Addis Ababa, and Shenzhen, killing people, while I researched Deonar's more stable ones. One of the great urban legends of New York, I heard, was of the barge that floated off its coast, filled with the city's trash, no state willing to accept it for burial. Then I met the former city official who had cut short a vacation to help land the barge back in the city, the trash ending up at its own garbage city settled in Staten Island—Fresh Kills.

My years of walking the mountains showed me that unlikely as the stories that emerged from Deonar's township of trash felt, many were real. Parts of them unfolded in one way or another in most cities around the world. Waste masses even float in the sea, making islands. I came to see these mountains as an outpouring of our modern lives—of the endless chase for our desires to fill us. Our pursuit only grew the mountains, providing the raw material on which the wastepickers built their lives and left us unsated, searching for more, unseeing the world our castaway possessions made. The story that follows is of Deonar's mountainous township of trash and the lives lived in its long shadow, but also, of elsewhere.

ONE

FARZANA ALI SHAIKH RUMMAGED on a mountain clearing on a hot April afternoon. The sun warmed her head and made lurid colors swim in her eyes. The smell of rotting prawns wafted up from the mountain. She jabbed her long garbage fork to push aside translucent fish scales, crackling prawn shells, entrails, and animal dung, and scooped up the broken glass jars that had just poured out on the clearing.

Smoke and heat rose up as forklifts shoveled glass away. It blurred Farzana's view of the trash strewn around her and brought up burning smells that mingled with the stench of decaying flesh. Scavenging birds swooped low beside her, searching for entrails. Farzana kept her eye on the glass and hacked her fork into the mess, keen to retrieve it. She didn't usually work on the *jhinga*, or prawn loop, as this mountain was known. It was made mostly of animal remains from the city's municipal slaughter-house, its vast port lands, and elsewhere. But that afternoon they had waited long for trucks before she and her younger sister, Farha, who was fifteen, had chased one winding up the unsteady slope of the *jhinga* loop, also known as the *gobar*, or cow dung loop.

Farzana worked quickly, shoveling glass jars, shards, and saline bags that had fallen out of the truck into the large plastic bag she dragged along. The truck had probably come from a hospital, and its contents would fetch good money. A straggly crowd of ragpickers grew around her, also eager for the glass. But at seventeen, Farzana was tall, athletic, and fearless. Her eyes were trained to spot plastic bottles, wire, glass, German silver, a metal alloy used to make appliances and machinery, and cloth scraps. She snapped up her pickings before others could get to them.

Farzana looked up to make sure Farha was picking close by. It must nearly be time for their father to arrive with lunch, she thought. She clanked her fork into the glass heap again and, this time, brought out a heavy blue plastic bag. Farzana thought it must be filled with smaller glass bottles, which usually fetched a good price. She squatted on the warm slope, with flies hanging close, untied the string, and gently upturned the bag, expecting delicate glass vials to fall out, clinking and glinting in the sun. Instead, a single large glass jar plopped onto the clearing. As she bent low to see what was inside the jar, she could see arms, legs, toes, and tiny, bald heads swimming inside it. She squinted, looked again, and screamed. A few friends gathered to examine the jar crammed with floating limbs.

Farzana opened the lid and nearly brought out a baby girl, a little bigger than her large bony palm. The city sent a steady supply of dead babies, often girls, to the mountains, along with its other expendables. Mothers who couldn't bear to tell their families they had delivered a girl sometimes threw the baby in the trash instead. Farzana had occasionally unearthed them while rifling through rubbish. But as she tugged the baby girl out of the jar, two baby boys came up too; their stomachs were fused to hers. The three had probably died because they were unable to survive with or without each other, she thought. Farha said she had heard lunar eclipses caused unborn babies to split or deform within wombs. A baby must have been born as three, bringing it here, she told the group that had gathered.

Farzana stretched her arms out, to cradle the lifeless babies. She began to make her way carefully down the wobbly slope, holding them gently. Behind her, the mountain rose like a teetering hulk, made up of Mumbai's detritus held in place with a topping of mud.

She waited for her friends to catch up. From high up on the next peak, they could see the vertiginous trash mountains curve around them and stretch out into the distance. Together, the hills curled like a long sliver of crescent moon. Across a broken wall, and dug into the mountains, were shrunken homes made of cloth scraps, plastic sheets, torn sarees, soggy bamboo poles, and metal sheets full of holes. On the outer edge, a shimmering creek arched around the mountains. The creek ran into the Arabian Sea, which rimmed the island city of Mumbai. Ragpickers such as Farzana called the garbage mountains *khaadi*, the Hindi word for creek. Nobody quite knew where the name came from, but standing high on a mountain clearing, you did feel as if you were floating in an undulating and smelly sea of garbage that faded into an unending expanse of glimmering blue sea in the distance. Farzana continued her walk through the rising and ebbing trash.

When they neared the creek, Farzana's friends dug their garbage forks into soft sand where trash slopes petered into a rivulet. A few pickers came out of houses built on stilts, which lifted them above the trash at low tide and nearly immersed them in waves at high tide. They walked over to see the babies and helped Farzana's friends shovel sand. The tide was rising and gentle waves inched closer to them. Torn clothes and plastic bags bobbed in the water and dripped from the branches of mangrove trees that edged the creek. Farzana felt a gentle breeze approach through the water. It rustled through the old trees, through the leaves and plastic that filled their branches, and shivered through her.

She lowered the babies into their shallow grave. Her friends covered them with sand and whispered prayers. They usually came this way later in the afternoons, to wade and swim in the rising tide. Farzana liked to stay until the setting sun almost faded behind the fetid hills, giving them a dusty, pink glow, and the waves turned metallic. That was when she thought the mountains looked their best.

After the makeshift burial, they walked hurriedly back across the hills to find their father, waiting and hungry. Hyder Ali was standing, tall, gangly, and gaunt, on a quiet slope, his face lit up in a tobacco-stained grin. They sat down to eat. Both sisters wore salwar kameezes with cotton jackets to keep mud and trash away from their clothes, and errant strands spilled out of the scarves they wrapped around their long, loosely bundled hair. While Farzana was prickly and quiet with teenage awkwardness, Farha had stayed smiling and baby faced. Over the lunch he brought from home, she told their father about their morning adventure. Uncharacteristically terse, he asked them not to venture near the graves again. *"Ye sab cheez chhodta nahi hai,"* he remarked. *These things have a way of not leaving you.*

HYDER ALI HAD moved to live in the shade of the mountains just months before Farzana was born. He had come to Mumbai in his teens, from his village in Bihar, nearly two thousand kilometers away. For years, he had worked as an embroiderer's assistant. He enjoyed the long, quiet hours of filling fabric, tightly stretched out on the frame, with lacelike patterns. Half made flowers, rising vines, and wingless birds made shadows on his face and limbs when he curled up to sleep under the frame. Then a wife, Shakimun, and five children followed, forcing Hyder Ali to seek a life outside the embroidery room that formed his world.

He had heard of the mountains that never ran out of work, vast dumping grounds at the edge of the city, where the remnants of everything Mumbai consumed came to die. Nothing had ever been composted, incinerated, or recycled. Instead, it lingered on at Deonar, adding to fetid and ever-growing mountains of garbage. Hyder Ali had heard from his friends that the mountains were older than the oldest pickers who worked on them and larger than the largest trash hills in the country. They stretched over 326 acres and some rose more than 120 feet, monuments to the increasingly ephemeral desires of the city's more official residents.

Hyder Ali's friends trawled the slopes all day, selling the trash they collected to traders who would sell it on to be remade anew. They foraged for mangled plastic that could be pressed into sheets or pulled into filament. They traded glass bottles to be refilled with new drinks, metal to be melted into new parts for gadgets, and cloth scraps to be stuffed into toys and quilts or sewn into clothes. Hyder Ali had heard you could earn good money on these slopes, and their edges could yield space to make a home for his growing family. He had also heard they sustained pickers, fed them, threw up treasures that had made fortunes, and fueled rivalries and ambitions.

So, in 1998, he moved his family to a spot where a drain that ran down the mountains met a lane that curved around them. Their lane was called Banjara Galli, or Gypsy Lane, for the itinerant inhabitants who had left before city drifters replaced them. Farzana was born months later. Two more daughters and a son would follow, filling the house they would build on the edge of these shape-shifting foothills.

At first Hyder Ali looked for embroidery commissions, while Shakimun strapped Farzana onto her back with a dupatta and waded into the township of trash hills. But finding embroidery commissions on his own was hard work and soon he followed her into the rolling landscape of garbage. At first, the mountains' rising stench made Hyder Ali throw up. His bony hands stank and when he ate; he felt they transported the smell of garbage through his mouth into his stomach, making him nauseous. Mountain trash swam in his eyes. He could not eat or sleep for days, whittling down his already skeletal frame. Hunger made him dizzy.

Hyder Ali developed a technique to protect his hands and appetite, clenching his toes tightly around cloth scraps while balancing himself precariously, on the wobbly slope, with his other foot. He would bend his knee and lift his leg, clinging to the cloth, depositing it into the bag that Shakimun held open for him. He often lost his balance in this acrobatic act and fell flat on his face into muddy trash amid a swarm of pickers. If he didn't get to something fast enough, someone else would. Eventually, he had to discard his leg curling technique and use his hands to work quicker. As his hands and feet filled up with cuts and bruises from stumbling on glass and metal, he also learned to dodge the stray dogs and birds that chased them for trash. Determined, Hyder Ali, Shakimun, and the children hung close to the khaki and orange trucks that relentlessly emptied the city's moth-eaten possessions onto the rising mountain clearings.

Hyder Ali liked to tell Farzana and her siblings that there was nothing he had not seen while trawling through this sprawling necropolis. Everything that gave meaning to Mumbaikar's lives, from broken cell phones, to high-heeled shoes and gangrenous and dismembered human limbs, ended up here. He, like most pickers, believed that the spirits of people and possessions that had been sent here for unceremonious burials hung around the windswept slopes. Delivering the Urdu books that he found in the trash to clerics, he had heard from them that God, who made people, also made spirits and that the evil ones among them were called Shaitans. Unseen and unheard but nevertheless tangibly present, they were said to be a manifestation of people's baser nature, of their rising, unending desires. They gripped people, only to lead them astray.

Shaitans lived in filthy recesses and rose from smokeless fires, the clerics had warned Hyder Ali. Indeed, fires simmered, furtively and constantly, within the mountains' layers of decaying trash. He had seen smoke that rose from fires burning deep within the mountains and flames that danced without smoke. At other times, flames erupted and moved like lightning across the hills, letting off swirling smoke, the two dancing together. Hyder Ali had nearly been encircled and trapped in these traveling fires. The Shaitans were bound to appear on the mountains, a dizzying accumulation of partly sated desires wreathed in fires and smoke, pickers believed. Shaitans arose from them and lay in wait for new homes and younger people to inhabit, they believed.

Hyder Ali had heard of friends who had been tripped on mountain slopes when they crossed the path of lurking Shaitans. Others warned him to stay away from certain hill slopes or claimed they had encountered the tall, floating spirits, known as Khabees in Islamic mythology, in their shrunken, plastic-and-cloth-scrap homes on the edges of trash foothills, where they demanded rent. Hyder Ali's friend Moharram Ali had told him he heard a woman call out to him every time he neared the pile of white cloth scraps he had collected on a slope, asking him to return her shroud from his neatly folded stack.

Hyder Ali knew, of all his nine children, Farzana loved being on the mountains the most. She was the first of them to be born at their feet, and had learned to walk on the gentle incline of trash foothills. As soon as she could make the short walk from their home, Farzana had come wobbling over to them and it had been a losing battle to keep her away from them, ever since. At first, Shakimun sent him to get Farzana back, worrying she would get buried under the garbage showers that erupted from emptying trucks. She had heard of children getting mauled by dogs, falling off garbage cliffs, or tumbling down mountain slopes. Hyder Ali often found Farzana swinging from abandoned car fenders or digging for toys buried in trash. He delivered Farzana home, crying, and returned to work on the slopes. Soon enough, Farzana escaped again and followed him.

FOR MONTHS, FARHA and Farzana would remember the day they buried the babies as the day they got thrashed. When they arrived home, their oldest brother Jehangir was waiting for them, his face filled with rage. "*Mardaani ho gayi hai? Bache gaad rahi hai?*" he asked, his voice rising. *You think you've turned into men? Burying other people's babies?* Without waiting for their answer, Jehangir, who was eight years older than Farzana, slapped her and then Farha. He asked why they hadn't called him. He was at a clearing nearby that afternoon, he said. He would have taken care of it, or asked the municipal officials to. Don't get into these messes, he shouted. Nothing good ever comes out of them.

Farzana couldn't answer. Tears choked her. Besides, fighting with Jehangir was never a good idea. Everyone at home knew of their wiry and intense brother's explosive anger.

In that long hot summer that stretched between her and adulthood, Farzana worked through the smoke that drifted over the slopes, the constantly burning fires, their sharp smell, the heat that turned humid as rain clouds approached, and even the new security guards that arrived to patrol the hilly township's hazy rim.

It would all end soon, she told Hyder Ali, coolly. The baking sun would give way to Mumbai's long season of torrential rains that would soak their burning township and quench the fires. That year, the summer would also end in the holy month of Ramzan (known elsewhere as Ramadan), filled with daylong fasts and feasts that would occupy much of the night. And three days before the first fast, on June 2, 2016, Farzana would turn eighteen.

Hyder Ali later came to believe that it was in this long and boiling summer of waiting, when Farzana found the glass jar filled with lifeless babies, that the mountain spirits entered his daughter—though they did not know it at the time.

TWO

HYDER ALI HAD MADE a living from mountain finds but the shadow of the Deonar mountains was longer than he knew and breaking out of it had proved to be harder than he had thought. He had often asked Vitabai Kamble, who lived a few houses down the lane, for help in escaping it. He had first seen her as a rolling cloud of gray on the hills, draped in jewel-colored sarees, chasing arriving trash. Pickers said that she was among the oldest on the slopes, that she had seen the mountains before they were mountains. She spoke of the legends that floated in their halo, which said that the mountains were older than the oldest pickers. Like most legends, some were true and others were not.

"On the morning of July 6, 1896 there was a strong smell, as if sulfureted hydrogen was generated over the north of the island and especially from the salt channels across Matunga and the vacant ground to the north. The smell seemed strongest furthest to the north," Dr. T. S. Weir, Bombay's health officer, wrote in the assiduously compiled administration report the municipal commissioner sent to London every year. "At this time, a migration of rats had been observed across Sewree [a neighborhood along the island city's eastern sea board], and I believe the smell was due to the decomposition of dead rats, for a number of bodies of rats were afterward found in the suburbs. The Commissioner of Police and I happened to go over the north of the island on this morning in connection with arrangements being made for the inspection of traffic by the roadways into Bombay and we tried to ascertain the cause. The smell was most offensive, tainting the air, far and wide.

"A blue haze was often observed in the evenings of September and October and rainbows which I had not observed in Bombay for a long period," Weir continued. "At this season boils were very prevalent. On September 9, a gale blew and the sky looked like a monsoon storm. In the evening, rain fell. A little time afterwards dead rats were found on the west foreshore."

Days later, Dr. Acacio Viegas, a physician who practiced in the Indian quarter of the city, was called to attend to patients stricken with fever. During his visits, Viegas found nothing to explain their raging temperature and listlessness other than a small red welt. The following day, before he could diagnose their illness, their fevers spiked and they died. Using fluid extracted from their welts, he identified the disease as bubonic plague. He began reading of more plague deaths in the newspapers.

By the 1800s, opium and the cotton trade had transformed Bombay from the rocky fishing islands the British had received from the Portuguese in the seventeenth century into one of the Empire's most majestic and important trading ports. The British built a fort, reclaimed land from the sea to join the islands, and, on the sliver that emerged, they built stately European-style buildings with Indian flourishes. While the British lived in the breezy, tropical London growing within the fort's walls, the lanes outside got packed with Indian migrants, drawn from around the country by the promise of work. Garbage and infectious diseases followed. Soon, Weir began getting reports of hundreds of plague deaths a day. France imposed restrictions on Indian passengers and trade.

Officials believed the disease had arrived in the city with pilgrims returning from a religious fair in North India. Later colonial reports would conclude that it emanated in Yunnan, China, arrived on trading ships from Hong Kong and was carried through the lanes outside the fort by rats moving through the overflowing filth. Over time, the garbage dumping grounds at Mahalakshmi, where Mumbaikars had sent garbage for years, had nearly swollen into the homes around it, emitting smells, rats, and diseases that sickened residents and threatened trade. But the campaign that Dr. Weir planned to control the epidemic would grow, thorn-like, between the colonial administration and Bombay's residents. "There is only one measure from which any effect can be expected and that is quarantine," he wrote.

With plague cases rising, British troops began keeping travelers arriving into the city in camps. They entered the slim Indian lanes around the fort, where they dismantled tile roofs to let light into dark homes, emptied granaries piled with months of supplies, and cleaned drains and sewers by flooding them with seawater that gushed back into homes. The returning waters brought dead rats, trash, and all that the drains were supposed to purge. Soldiers searched homes for the sick and lined up residents outside, so they could examine them for buboes. They burned patients' possessions, lime washed and quarantined their homes, and kept their families in the hospital for weeks. Even the graves of plague victims were to be layered with quicklime or charcoal to contain plague fleas within.

Fear and rumors gripped the city. Many Indians hid the ailing inside cupboards and protected them, with knives, from being taken away to the hospital, afraid that they were being taken there only to die, alone. A plague patient had jumped out of a moving ambulance taking him to the hospital and was later found dead, having walked a long way. "They had some idea that the ambulance would give them a shock that would kill them," Weir wrote in the municipal report. "Men have said to me, 'You think we are like mad dogs, and you want to kill us as if we were.'"

Late one night, Bombay's municipal commissioner, P. C. H. Snow, walked across this widening rift, into the Indian lanes. He discovered a town, growing unnoticed, so tightly packed that the plague was bound to travel fast. Snow found nineteen men, twenty-one women, and seventeen children sleeping in the same room. "In fact, the room is a passage with a door in front between closed walls. . . . What can anything done outside this room, do for the people in their misery inside?" he wrote. As the city's budget surplus was wiped out by the fight against the plague, it was only spreading further, beginning to touch the edges of the constricted, island city. Snow wrote of seeing patients walking city streets in delirium and lying beside the road. Some could be revived but others were long dead. More than 1,900 people died of the plague every week for the rest of the year, according to newspaper reports. The recently built Victoria Terminus was packed with residents leaving Bombay.

On October 14, with plague control measures tightening, a group of Indians wrote to Snow asking to ease the regulations. Enforcing them would only accelerate the surge of leaving residents, they wrote. Fleeing patients had already taken the plague to the historic neighboring city of Pune and beyond. In both cities, those who remained protested, often violently, as the Empire and its soldiers inspected their homes, bodies, and rituals.

Late on the night of October 30, 1896, Snow and Weir met the police commissioner, H. G. Vincent, at his imposing stone office, across from the city's busy, electric-lit market. Shops had closed early and angry crowds swelled in the dark lanes nearby. Inside, Vincent pled for a retreat from the plague measures or, he feared, there would be riots. He and Weir worried the Halalkhores, or waste cleaners, would join the crowds leaving Bombay. This could precipitate "a vast panic and exodus" from the city, Snow wrote. "Bombay in a few days would have become uninhabitable, left to reek in a mass of sewage, sweepings and pollution, with no one at hand to conduct the daily routine of sanitation, much less adopt a single preventive measure against the plague." The three officers withdrew their patient isolation measures that night.

Instead, they let the city's mosaic of communities pour into their own plague camps, hospitals, and burial grounds and turned to pushing out the city's mounting refuse. With it, they hoped to edge out both the discontent and the diseases they had battled for years, including malaria, measles, mumps, chicken pox, smallpox, cholera, and tuberculosis.

EARLY IN 1897, the British governors identified an 823-acre marsh in the distant seaside village of Deonar, where they planned to send Bombay's waste from then on, replacing the overflowing, rat-filled grounds at Coorla and then Mahalakshmi. The government acquired the land from its owner, Ardeshir Cursetji Cama, that May.

Cuchra, or trash, trains, filled with the city's refuse, began arriving at the Deonar grounds on June 7, 1899, its construction having been delayed by concerns that passenger trains passed close by. The smell of garbage, it was thought, would make them gag. The municipality hired workers to empty wagons and fill the vast grounds, which were partly submerged in the sea, and dotted with shrubs and an endless expanse of weeds. "As the refuse contains large quantities of broken glass and old iron, frequent injuries occurred to the feet and legs of men emptying the wagons," a municipal report recounted. "The wounds were often very serious," delaying the clearing of wagons and the return journeys to the city. Workers developed fevers, eye infections—and as the new loads of garbage had to be deposited farther away from the end of the track, the work only got harder. Slowly, the workers learned to live with the trash and injuries and two trains of twenty-five garbage filled wagons each began arriving every day.

A bund was built along the edges of the Deonar grounds to keep the sea from seeping into the site, and garbage from flowing into the creek. That year's municipal commissioner's report said that officials expected the marshy bog to fill with trash in twenty-three years. It would become "a valuable Municipal estate," yielding more than a lakh of rupees as rent from farmers, who would cultivate the grounds, enriched with rotting garbage, and form the new edge of the extending city. "It was thought that, by this method, a large area of waste, an unhealthy swamp, could be converted into fruitful agricultural ground," the report concluded.

And, as Bombay kept growing, its remains and its ghosts had indeed slowly filled the distant bog at Deonar, draining trash from the city. The plague receded too. Officials dug streets in the city's Mandvi area outside the British fort, to fix drains, extend sewers, widen streets, open passages for the sea breezes, and build homes for the growing migrant population. Beneath the streets they found older trash, deposited perhaps forty years before the city was built over it. *Cuchra* trains ferried it away and continued to deposit the city's detritus at Deonar for nearly nine decades, where it remained both in plain sight and out of sight. This arrangement had kept an uneasy calm between the city and its waste until it erupted again, more than a century later.

In 1960, Bombay had become the capital of the newly formed state of Maharashtra. New buildings for the state legislature, stock exchange, a planetarium, and condominiums began to emerge from cleared slums, the city's hastily extending edges rising from the sea and farms perching on their trash foundations. The grounds had fulfilled British administrators' plans, more than a decade after they left the country. Rains sometimes washed the garbage along the ground's ends into the sea, drifting it back toward the city, but the shrunken grounds refilled fast.

IT WAS AROUND this time, in the mid-sixties, that Vitabai Kamble arrived in Bombay as a new mother. She and her husband had set up their home, made of plastic sheets and sarees, on a pavement in central Bombay, across the street from the state-run television channel's newly built studio and its cloud grazing antenna. When the breeze opened their billowy ceiling, the spindly antenna nearly became a part of their house, bringing in Bombay's stardust. It helped Vitabai find her way back from wealthy homes where she washed dishes while her husband did odd jobs. It was in the home in the television tower's shadow that her children were born and where Vitabai believed she had lived the Bombay dream.

Migrant settlements like Vitabai's swelled and spilled out of the tenements that Snow had written about decades earlier, onto the city's railway tracks, along its stretching water pipelines, across its pavements and roads. But the city bulged with an aspiration that edged them out.

One day, Vitabai got papers saying the municipality had given her a plot of land, instantly elevating her to the status of landowner. The papers became her most prized possession. She bundled her two toddlers, husband, home, and the land allotment papers into a municipal truck, and they drove through the city until it petered out into salt pans and mangroves. When she saw the fetid dumping grounds and the chalk marked section of rubble that was hers, Vitabai's dream of home ownership crumbled before her eyes.

Unlike Vitabai, other slum dwellers had fought the municipality's attempts to move them to Deonar. The rambling cloth and plastic settlements in the city were often consumed by blazes in those years, and while their residents tried to reassemble their homes amid the dying embers, the municipality took the opportunity to resettle them at Deonar. Many had filed court cases, alleging that the fires were deliberately set, meant to hand their settlements over to developers so they could build apartments and office towers. Expelled by Bombay's expanding concrete dreams, trucks filled with extraneous people and their disappointments arrived at the dumping grounds with almost the same regularity as the trains arrived with abandoned things, while the city stretched and rose over their homes.

The municipality could hardly remove the slum dwellers fast enough. Newspaper reports from those years say that Bombay's streets and pavements still overflowed with trash, people and their makeshift homes, known for flying with the city's fierce monsoon winds and then dying with it, only to fly again. Garbage piled higher and higher on city streets throughout the day, breeding flies and mosquitoes, stinking and sickening residents. *Cuchra* trains went once in the morning and then at night, when residents along its tracks knew to close their windows to block the traveling smell. Over time, the municipality created a *cuchra* fleet, with trailers, donkeys, and tractors to supplement the aging trains. Together, they filled Deonar's swamp with trash, all day and all night.

For the holdouts, the city positioned the edges of the dumping grounds as planned communities for the poor. Newspaper reporters wrote about the wide roads and concrete houses. There were numbered blocks, tarred roads, a toilet for every ten people, and large workshops to house their small businesses.

But Vitabai, like most others, didn't get a home like the one in the newspapers. She got a patch of rubble edged with chalk, to ensure she did not spill into her neighbor's plot, causing a fight. It was filled only with the smell of the distant city's refuse, which she remembered as being much worse than it was in later years. The truth could also be that she got used to it: that the smell had settled in her, along with the many wounds she sustained from being too tightly packed in with the ghosts of the things Bombay had thrown away to make space for its dreams.

The slum dwellers' new settlements turned the flower-filled swamps on opposite ends of the dumping grounds into Lotus Colony and Padma Nagar, or "the town of lotuses." A string of small hamlets grew between them, digging into the dumping grounds, making a crescent curve. As you arrived from the city, you first came to Lotus Colony, which was followed by Baba Nagar, named for the mystics that once roamed its desolate marsh. No one was sure where along the curve Rafiq Nagar, also known as Rafi Nagar, ran into Nirankari Nagar and then Sanjay Nagar, situated in the deepest bend of the mountains' moon. It was named for the politician from the seventies, known for demolishing Delhi's slums to make way for a modern city. Banjara Galli, where Farzana and her family lived, was part of Sanjay Nagar and had indeed been demolished several times. No one knew where the name of Shanti Nagar, or "the town of peace," came from, for behind it was the wall across which trucks endlessly rattled and returned after emptying on hills. It was followed by Padma Nagar, which ended the township. Around there was Bain-ganwadi, the hamlet of eggplants, Bandra Plot, named for the posh suburb the residents there had been resettled from and others named for the area's rustic past or the glamour of the incoming city.

As they filled and grew, the dumping grounds began to emanate a toxic halo. Nothing made it out; things only arrived and stayed to slowly rot and decay. As Bombay came to be known as the city of dreams, Deonar became the sprawling necropolis of those dreams' remains, a noxious and wondrous world. Only its putrid air and water mingled, unseen, with the city's.

The fastest way for Vitabai to return to the city for work would have been to sit atop the stinking, open-topped rakes of *cuchra* trains. Instead, she and others began to empty the mangy wealth from their wagons, hoard it, and sell it. Vitabai waded through the ground's shrinking marshy tracts in search of treasures, stumbling on animal carcasses or glass shards sticking out of the mud. *"Panyat mele lekra bhetayche,"* she would say. *We found dead babies in the water.* Often, she turned back to find Nagesh, her oldest son, and then her daughter following her. Forgotten by the city, they made lives on all it spat out.

IN 1992, AS the cool winter winds lashed the mountains, riots had broken out in the city over the demolition of the Babri Masjid, a mosque in North India, where Hindus believed Lord Rama was born. Vitabai, a Hindu surrounded by neighbors she had not noticed until then were Muslims, had stayed inside her house for days. She heard of rioters dressing as police, neighbors gone missing, the dead being flung into trash slopes and the living hiding with them. When she finally came out, some of her neighbors were returning home, battered, while others had begun unending searches for missing relatives.

Hindus had begun to leave, aware of the ruptured air in their lanes. Some had moved across the creek, to the newly formed municipality of New Bombay or other distant but gentrifying fringes of the city. After the riots, Bombay's lanes—where everything had lived on something else, where languages ran into each other to make "Bambaiya" and cooking styles melded together—became segregated. Muslims were moving to flinty, far-flung enclaves and those who could not afford to settle even there arrived to fill the lanes around the mountains.

"Naapaki mein rehna to Shaitan ko neota dena hai," a cleric Hyder Ali delivered books he found in trash had told him. *Living in impurity and dirt is an invitation to the Shaitan.* When people settled, bringing light and cleanliness to the ruins, mountains, filthy recesses at the outer edge of society that Shaitans, or evil spirits, inhabited, the Shaitans

left, the cleric had said. But with nowhere else to go, migrants and the city's slum dwellers constantly arrived to live in the shadow of the mountains and in the lanes that had stayed unsettled even as they filled. Consumed with the hunt for overlooked or discarded treasures, Vitabai had stayed too, her days only getting more frenzied with the growing trucks.

She began by calling garbage truck drivers to ask what they filled up on in their rounds of the city. If trash from hotels, hospitals, marriage halls filled their bellies, and they weren't booked by the big garbage traders already, Vitabai asked them to empty only for her. She got her sons to corral these trucks as they entered the township and direct them to quiet mountain clearings, then ran to them so quickly she turned to a blur. She pulled out notes from the fanny pack she made with torn sarees and tied around her stomach to pay guards to look the other way while she picked through the trucks' contents and to pay bulldozer drivers so they would not shovel it away before she was done. Then she filled it into the pickup van her younger son Santosh, born at the mountains' rim, drove and took it to her daughter Babita's *kata* shop, where trash was sorted and sold by weight to traders who would sell it ahead to be remade.

IT WAS SOON after Hyder Ali arrived, in the early 2000s, that Deonar probably became the world's largest trash township of the kind where nothing had ever left or been treated. The mountains had risen as high as twenty-floor apartment blocks. Mumbai had already stretched over the smaller dumping grounds in Gorai and Malad. The Malad grounds were handed back to a developer who quickly topped them with glass and chrome buildings that housed call centers and entertainment company offices, where executives got headaches and computers rusted too quickly. This was known as "sick building syndrome": scientists had discovered that the gases from hastily closed dumping grounds didn't settle for years. Instead, they permeated the buildings that rose over them and sickened the people and devices within them.

Mumbai was at a growing impasse. The trash that used to be deposited at the now closed Malad grounds came to the Deonar mountains instead, increasingly ringed by the growing band of the city's castaway people, who only waded deeper and brought out more of the trash they built their lives on. The dumping grounds spewed foul air and smoke that the municipality countered by spraying herbal disinfectant and deodorant. It had to clear garbage from city streets and pavements or it would lead to the same infectious diseases that British reports had recorded, at an unimaginable scale. But the mountains were beginning to intrude into the city that had ignored them for so long. If they got any taller, officials worried, sections could tumble down in dangerous landslides of garbage. Flights coming into Mumbai might crash into the trash peaks. The mountains inched above 120 feet, the city's lengthening garbage caravans emptying constantly on the rising hilltops, making it harder to shrink them.

THREE

FARZANA'S EARLIEST MEMORIES ARE of watching her house collapsing into the muddy trash and rising from it again every few days. Hyder Ali had taught her older brothers and sisters to spot municipal officers on eviction drives while he was away at work. Farzana helped empty the house, then the older children untied the bamboo sticks that they had brought back from the hills to make its bones. Finally, the siblings stood aside and watched, giggling, as the plastic and tin sheets they had collected to make their home fell noisily in a heap.

In 1995, Bombay had become Mumbai. Its boxy, socialist-era apartments, best known for squeezing a lot into very little space, were giving way to gated communities that brought first-world amenities, complete with garbage chutes. In this world, stretching far into suburbia, buildings were named after trees—such as Cedar, Oakwood, and Birch— that were never seen in the city's muggy weather. Malls, gyms, and multiplexes arrived, turning Mumbai aglow with India's growing wealth.

They were all filled with new things whose remnants came to the mountains, to be reborn only through the ministrations of ragpickers.

Growing desire brought plastic bottles that had contained purified water, takeaway boxes half filled with unseen foods, soiled diapers, and wires from new devices. From giving many lives to things, Indians embraced sachets for shampoo, hair dye, and ketchup. Their expendability provided a new thrill even in families that had taken pride in passing things down through the generations. Glass and metal containers were replaced with plastic pouches and boxes made of tightly packed layers of foil, paper, and plastic that left homes when their contents emptied but lingered forever, at the dumping grounds. Emptiness, sadness, longing, and aspiration: it could all be doused with purchases and possessions.

At the township at Deonar, in the growing gush that erupted from trucks, trash could be trash or it could be gold. While Hyder Ali, with his laid-back style, found only broken bits of cement flooring, his friend Moharram Ali, whom he had taken a loan with, found long marble slabs that had recently come to fill Mumbai homes. The city's growing wealth poured out onto the mountains and Hyder Ali and Moharram Ali floated in its rising tide.

In September 2000, three months after Farzana turned two, India's environment ministry had framed rules, for the first time, to manage waste. Moved by the growing mountains of garbage around the country, the Supreme Court had asked the ministry to take control of its trash, which was hardly mounting as dizzily anywhere as it did at Deonar. Among the many rules, encroachers such as Farzana's family were to be kept out of the township of trash so officials could secure and manage it. The municipality, tasked with meeting the rules, stepped up eviction drives in their lanes, which had been happening, on and off, for years.

But as soon as officers turned their back, the pickers' shacks rose again. Chasing the city's constantly arriving discards had become an illicit but unwavering addiction, a forgotten treasure always seeming close. Squashed plastic bottles bundled together in a load that almost matched the pickers in size could be sold to traders to get them through the day. A palm-sized emerald, which Hyder Ali heard someone had found, could lift their lives entirely. He watched *houdhi*, or pond pickers, make bunds on slopes, encircling trash, fill these enclosures with water, and sift through wet sand for gold dust mingled in city dust. *"Kisi ka kachra kisi ka bhangaar hota hai,"* Hyder Ali said, explaining his work and his township. *One person's trash is another person's scrap.* And it all arrived ceaselessly, growing the mountains. Pickers hoarded it, sold it, slept on it, ate it, and inhaled it.

AS A TODDLER, Farzana wobbled and crawled around the jewel-colored cloth scrap hills that filled their home. Shakimun, Hyder Ali, and the older children collected these scraps on the slopes, filling them into outsized bundles they slung over their heads and that dangled in their eyes as they carried them downhill. Made of odd-shaped scraps from city tailors' workshops, the cloth hills in their house would soon get sold to stuff pillows, quilts, and toys. Then hills in new colors would rise afresh on their floor. Farzana took her first steps on this terrain at home, practicing for the trash hills that rose behind them.

When he could not spot the older children on the slopes, Hyder Ali topped Farzana's head, since she was little more than a toddler, with useful finds. She brought down mud to fill the drain that flowed down from the mountains, along Banjara Galli. She carried chunks of cement slabs flecked with fading green, orange, or silvery glass or the dark stone blocks that were laid as flooring in Mumbai apartments from the seventies and eighties. Municipal guards sometimes chased her. As she ran down the unsteady slopes to stay ahead, Farzana often fell or dropped her floor slab. The mountain fragments that made it home were sold or thrown down to fill the watery bog beneath their home.

When she was five, Hyder Ali enrolled Farzana at the municipality's Urdu primary school for girls nearby. Every morning, Farzana walked to school with her sisters, Afsana and Jannat. Every afternoon, the breeze began blowing inward from the creek, bringing a whiff of the mountains into their home, and drew her up the slopes. Standing on trash peaks, Farzana breathed in the sea and its unconstricted gusts as she looked out for her other sisters, Sahani, Jehana, and Farha, who worked there. Soon the balance fell in favor of the mountains, drawing her increasingly toward them. She and her sisters spent afternoons swimming in the creek and collecting cloth scraps to swell the pile their father made on a mountain edge.

Even amid the frenzied scrambles around emptying garbage trucks, Hyder Ali walked as if he moved to mellow music playing in his ears through invisible earphones. *"Khaadi mein koi bhooka nahi jaata,"* he had heard older pickers say. *No one ever goes hungry here.* This reassurance intensified his laid-back air. When Hyder Ali came to deliver his day's pickings on the pile he was accumulating on slopes, it always looked bigger than he had left it. The children helped keep their household afloat. He could not keep them away from the slopes.

It was Jehangir, his oldest son, who had never been to school, who fought with Hyder Ali to keep his sisters away from the mountains and at school. Jehangir hungrily chased the forgotten fortunes that had eluded his father. The deeper he sank into this giddy mountain addiction, the more he wanted to keep his sisters away from it. He turned them back home from the slopes, or to the school whose four-floor building faced the mountains, a fading foil to their sickening allure. They were back the next afternoon, trailing trucks.

Farzana was growing to be all arms and legs and what her sisters called *aadha dimaag,* or only half a brain. The rising mountains had leaked into it, they thought. As the peaks rose higher, rains gushed down harder every monsoon, bringing the trash into their home. Farzana fell asleep to the clatter of rain and woke up to see her slippers floating close to her, amid unknown objects that had flowed down the slopes. Blearily, she folded her salwar over her knees and waded through the water to retrieve her books and shoes drifting through neighboring homes.

Then she walked up the squelching slopes, away from school. She and her sisters dragged reeking wooden planks that Jehangir and their brother Alamgir, the third of the nine children, nailed to the walls at home and piled their soaking household on. At night, they clambered on to sleep amid their belongings while trash-filled waters sloshed below. When the rains paused, Farzana helped Shakimun throw out the garbage and bring their damp provisions and trash they had stored, and that had turned to mush, out to catch the sun peeking in their slim lane. She brought out her water-stained notebooks. Everything she learned had blurred.

Trying to catch up was futile. *"Vaise bhi uske man mein gobar bhara tha,"* her friend Yasmeen, who was a few years older and lived down the lane, would say. *Her mind was filled with cow dung!* Fragile looking and out-spoken, Yasmeen, who would later marry Alamgir, was home only for the holidays. Her parents had enrolled her at a Madarsa in the neighboring state of Gujarat, to keep her away from the mountains and at school. Later, Hyder Ali enlisted her to teach Farzana to read the Koran, which had sunk without a trace in Farzana's mind. The mountains filled her head, and her friend's too. Their school was emptying out onto the hilltops.

MOHARRAM ALI'S DAUGHTER, Hera, was imperious, beautiful, and one of the few girls from Banjara Galli who had made it to middle school, farther into the city. She was just two years older than Farzana and hardly ever picked trash. When Farzana walked to work, in the afternoons, she saw Hera leave for the Arabic, computer, or tailoring classes her mother had enrolled her for. *"Unke ghar mein safai kitni thi,"* Farzana would recall. *Their house was so clean.*

Mountain air had elevated the tall and rakish Moharram Ali more than most others in their community. Farzana had heard how the mountains had delivered their fortunes in his hands. Her father called Moharram Ali Shaitan Singh, or Mr. Troublemaker, for his gift for amassing high-quality trash. He was a part of the small band of nocturnal pickers, among the mountains' most relentless treasure hunters. Garbage trucks arrived through the night but only the most fearless picked through their bounty, the slopes lit dimly, only with a few lights fixed on high masts. Jagged bits of glass and metal cut pickers as they walked up, and garbage rained on them in dark clumps from emptying trucks. Moharram Ali fixed a torch into the baseball cap that he wore backward and took his pick of the trash under the moonlight, freed of the scrambles that erupted during the day.

On moonlit nights, the creek, the rivulet, and salt pans formed a glassy rim around the mountains. When he got to the trash peaks, Moharram Ali felt like he was floating in the creek, along with the fishing boats he saw in the distance. The boats stayed out, all night, trawling through the creek, in good weather. He thought they gave him company. He moved his head slowly from side to side, baring treasures in torchlight. In the quiet and dark of the night, he had found a silver idol of a Hindu goddess and a pillowcase stuffed with banknotes, buried in the trash.

When he left the mountains, he often ran into morning shift pickers, coming in to work. Hyder Ali and the others ribbed him, asking him to leave something for them. As the sun rose overhead, Moharram Ali often returned to chase the endlessly arriving trucks. That's how the mountains grew on him, he would say. *"Ek insaan ke jaisa lagaav tha. Khaadi hum logon ko bulati thi."* *I became attached to them like you would to a person. They called out to me.*

He had told Hyder Ali that his father was the Mujawar, or caretaker, of a saint's mausoleum in their village in North India. Their house was filled with musty books, bound in deep but fading colors. Moharram Ali and his father could not read anything in them except their faint prices, a few pennies. His father practiced rituals passed down from his own father and, probably, the books in their house. He chanted prayers that rose to fill up rooms with heady smells and wafting smoke that took supplicants into a trance. When it all ebbed, the devotees, who came long distances to pray for miracles, often found their ailments cured. Moharram Ali had learned his father's courtly manners and enduring rituals. He told Hyder Ali that the prayers kept spirits away from him and brought mountain treasures in his hands. It fueled the legend of Shaitan Singh in their lanes.

Jehangir had tried working night shifts too, in search of Moharram Ali's luck. He was ten years old at the time, and, instead of mountain treasures, Jehangir had encountered only a *chudail*, a female spirit, who had died unfulfilled. He saw her floating a little above the dark and mostly empty slopes, draped in white clothes with her feet turned back. He had retreated to working in the day and begun to hang around with older boys, bullies, instead. He learned to smoke and hurl the abuses he had heard them spout.

He began ferreting out the currency notes that Hyder Ali never seemed to have quite enough of to run the house. Their father found ways not to ask how he got them. Farzana heard, around the hills, that Jehangir had been drawn into the gangs' fierce fights for territory and the trash that came with it. At home, Jehangir thought his money gave him a voice in household decisions. Hyder Ali did not.

The two clashed over nearly everything, but most of all, over Farzana. After her older sister Sahani dropped out of school to work on the mountains, Farzana, nine, and Afsana, who was two years older, became the two oldest children at school. The boys had never been to one. While Afsana wanted to stay, Jehangir fought with Hyder Ali, to keep Farzana at school though she didn't want to, to give her a life away from the mountains. "*Paak saaf rahein,*" he told Hyder Ali, repeating what he had heard from clerics. *They should stay pure and clean.* And yet, Farzana was on the slopes, after school, every afternoon.

MOHARRAM ALI'S WIFE, Yasmin, and their children hardly ever worked on the mountains. Yasmin spent afternoons at home, watching cooking shows on the used television set they had bought at a *kata* shop. She got friends to pass on batter mixes that came in the trash, post expiry, to try the recipes she saw. She tossed frozen peas into rice to make pulaos. Hera and Yasmin practiced dropping spoons full of rice and lentil batter mixed with yogurt into a pan and spreading it in slow, circular motions to make dosas, crisp like paper. They borrowed molds to steam it into fluffy idlis.

For dessert, Hera got her friends to collect packets of semolina mix for Gulab Jamun, when they saw it fall out of garbage trucks. Over long, slow afternoons, they rolled the moistened batter into dough balls that they fried and then dipped in warm sugar syrup they made. They plopped the golden, hot Gulab Jamuns into their mouths, spurting sugar syrup amid giggling and gossip. She saved leftovers for the elaborate dinners she helped Yasmin cook sometimes and that Moharram Ali barely made it home for.

One morning, Farzana was leaving for school when a friend dropped in to say that Moharram Ali had found a gold necklace in the trash. Hyder Ali looked surprised. He hadn't seen Moharram Ali in days. Hyder Ali walked over to his house to ask if he really had dug gold out from the mountains.

Moharram Ali said he had been home, sick for a week. His fever had ebbed only the previous evening. The soft, sweet smell of steaming rice filled the house but Yasmin would not serve dinner unless he brought home trash to sell. She had cooked with the last of her supplies.

"Gaali de ke gaya to kuch to lana hi tha," Moharram Ali said with a grin. *I'd left the house with an insult, I had to bring something back!* He had walked up the slopes, hoping to find something easily, a bag stuffed with cloth scraps perhaps, and return home to eat. He switched on his flashlight, swung his garbage fork lazily into the slope, and hit something soft and creamy. He dug around it and pulled out a tawny leather ladies' handbag.

He unzipped the pockets, rummaging inside to discover worlds so secret that women sometimes forgot to clear them out even while throwing bags away. Moharram Ali had found letters written in curly handwriting, delicate miniature bottles of perfume, monogrammed handkerchiefs that could be washed and sold as white scraps, and sometimes even crumpled currency notes, saved too safely from tight household budgets.

As Moharram Ali felt for zippers and opened inner pockets, that night, something flashed in the light. A gold necklace, with flowery patterns engraved on it. It was strung with black beads, the sign of a married Hindu woman. He stuffed it into his pocket and looked up to check if anyone had seen his glowing find. Pickers' lights moved around him. They were immersed in their own search for overlooked treasures. He left, hand in his pocket.

When Moharram Ali got home, Yasmin and their five children were wilting with hunger. He pushed aside their cold dinner and brought his hand out of his pocket, asking Yasmin to see if his necklace really was gold or the cheap metal women wore in their lanes. Since she had no way to tell, excitement and imagination sustained them through the night.

Weeks later, Hyder Ali heard Moharram Ali had opened his own *kata* shop, striking gold in the pickers' constant ambition: of becoming a small trader or, with some luck, even setting themselves up in work away from the trash business. Others took loans to open overfull *kata* shops, while some pickers made tin-sheet attics over their homes. Vertical, metal staircases climbed into these sun-filled lofts that they hoped would be the starting point of their journey out of garbage. These rooms hung over the hills and offered panoramic views of the city's refuse. Sun-dried paper and plastic wafted on the breezy slopes outside. They were filled with half-manned rows of tailoring machines pickers bought to stitch stacks of precut shirts or jeans, while others were piled with shoe soles to be sewn onto glittery uppers. These were mostly sold in Mumbai's dizzyingly busy street markets. Piles of gauzy, brightly colored fabric lined Hyder Ali's windowless and often unmanned loft. The fabric would get covered with sequins soon, he would say.

Unlike the unending garbage that rose behind him, and filled his home, embroidery commissions were hard to get and harder to deliver. Embroiderers would often leave Hyder Ali's workshop for better paying ones. They'll be back right after the next festival, he would say, for months, as the festivals passed by, one by one. He had struggled to teach Jehangir and his second son, Alamgir, the patient art of embroidery and make them his only assistants.

In those years, Alamgir kept Hyder Ali's embroidery business stuttering along, while Jehangir rose with the mountains' gangs. "*Naak ka baal to bachpan mein hi jal gaya tha*"—*The mountains' stink had burned the hair in my nostrils right in childhood*—he would say. There was nowhere else he could be. Farzana spent long afternoons walking the slopes. The municipality, with its guards and police, hung lightly over their township of trash, leaving pickers to their forgotten world and their unremitting chase. The year she turned ten and graduated from fourth grade, Farzana spent every day of the long summer on the mountains.

"*Padhne mein man nahi hai. Ghar mein reh ke kya karegi?*" Hyder Ali mumbled to Shakimun, one afternoon, when they were alone, in their dark, crammed home. *What's she going to do at home? She doesn't want to study!* Shakimun grunted to say she was listening to him even as she carefully piled the slim edges of the gleaming steel dishes she had just finished washing on top of each other, in the cooking area.

"*Apni galli koi theek hai kya?*" Hyder Ali said, his voice rising. *You think our lanes are safe? Nahi,* Shakimun said, so softly, he could barely hear it over the din of falling dishes. *No.* The dishes flashed reflections in the room as she began stacking them up carefully again, until they rose high against the wall. "*Kharche mein madad kar sakti hai,*" Hyder Ali went on. *There are expenses she could help with.* His workshop was fumbling, he said. Jehangir walked in to collect something. Seeing him made Hyder Ali's mercurial temper boil over, shouting that if he didn't want Farzana to work, he'd have to make up the money himself. At eighteen, Jehangir retreated from the fight with his father. Soon to be ten, Farzana joined the illicit army that hoarded the slopes all day.

FOUR

IN THE SUMMER OF 2008, when Farzana dropped out of school and came to work on the mountains through the day, a simmering battle to shrink the mountains and their halo reached a boiling point. Dr. Sandip Rane, a doctor who lived in a genteel neighborhood near the township's edge, had filed for contempt against the municipality for failing to shrivel the Deonar township. It came more than a decade after residents of a neighboring building filed a case to shrink the mountains, their smoke and stink. But the mountains had only grown in the face of court orders to fix them, he said, submitting photographs "which show a film of gas over the waste," later court observations said.

A decade and a half before, when Rane had set up his cardiology practice in the mountains' shadow, he had expected to see older patients with coronary disease. His waiting room had filled with asthmatic children instead. He suspected their lungs were filled with the smoke he woke up to see rising from the trash hills nearby. Rane knew, the residents of a neighboring building had filed a petition in the Bombay High Court asking to fix the trash hills and their toxic smoke, in August 1996.

They watched the mountains light up with fires at nightfall, the residents had said, in their plea to the court. Dark smoke clouds drifted through the night, into their homes, constricting their breath. Fires rose and smoke traveled until sunrise. They had heard garbage traders got ragpickers to light these fires so lighter trash—plastic, paper, cloth—would melt away, leaving copper, silver, lead, and other metals, the most expensive of mountain finds, for them to sell. Fine particles of toxic chemicals, or "suspended particulate matter," left over from these fires hung thick in the mountain air, the level up to seven times more than the rules allowed. They entered the lungs and bloodstreams of pickers and residents nearby, making it hard to breathe and rooting themselves deep in their internal organs. The fires left more than twice the amount of lead allowed in mountain air, and could cause brain damage in the children who breathed it in.

The municipality's response at the time declared the mountains lit up in "spontaneous combustion." The slowly decomposing garbage let off methane, which erupted in flames when it met the burning mountain sun. These self-ignited fires burned even on mountains where no new garbage had been dumped, officials wrote, suggesting fires were bound to erupt from the dizzying accumulation of things packed together, and were not their fault. The nightly smoke and smog in the petitioners' homes came also from fires pickers lit for metal, officials said, and the growing traffic from the highway that ran by their homes.

Since the 1996 petition, successive judges had asked the municipality to settle a modern trash township elsewhere. Until it could, the judges had tried to make Deonar's aging and sprawling township follow the waste rules. They had asked for its mess to get topped and pressed down with mud to hold it all in place and make evenly spaced hills. They had set timelines to tar the dirt tracks that wound through hills, fix streetlights, and tighten security along their faint edges so pickers could not get in and light fires. They had asked for fire engines and water tankers to patrol, curbing these nearly continually burning fires and their rising smoke. They pushed for the trash township to change, to mirror the modern city whose desires fed it and whose dark reflection it was.

APPOINTED TO A court committee around then, the tall and unbending Rane sat, every Wednesday, in a portable cabin at the dumping grounds, watching over the project to bring the mountains in line with the rules—for years. He watched the illicit army that Hyder Ali and his family belonged to filling the slopes.

Hills got more carefully formed, beginning near the municipal office, where *cuchra* trains had once ended, delivering the city's shed possessions. The first one, closest to the office, was mostly reserved for offal waste. Others rose along the creek's curve, filling up with everything else the city discarded, layered with mud, ending in the eighth mountain, whose steep cliff dropped into the water.

Rane watched electric poles and wires arrive at the township to install streetlights. But the lights had not come on. He heard pickers stole them to buy drugs or that cables snapped from the weight of trash or from coming under its trucks. Later, a few lights came, installed on high masts, casting a distant light on night pickers.

The municipality fitfully began measuring the chemicals that hung in the mountain air, as the waste rules asked it to, making its halo that irritated lungs, eyes, and caused respiratory diseases around the mountains.

Doctors around the mountains said that more than half their patients came with respiratory ailments. They had asthma, bronchitis, persistent coughs. Pickers' weakened chests made them an easy home for tuberculosis and drug-resistant tuberculosis. An airborne infection, it ran deep in the cramped homes in the lanes around the mountains. Pickers also arrived with interstitial lung disease, which would thicken the tissue around their lungs, consuming them within five years of breathlessness and coughing. The patients who came with chronic obstructive pulmonary disease, the air sacs in their lungs weakened and their airways badly inflamed, would live longer, but doctors knew that in both cases there was no cure, only deterioration. The doctors prescribed oxygen pumps they knew their patients could not afford.

"The problem is, you can't tell if a person is sick because of living near waste. You need an expert," Marco Armiero, an environmental historian from Naples, explained. The Mafia in his own region, called the Camorra, had brought toxic industrial waste from northern Italy and strewn it at landfills, as well as deserted country roads and on Neapolitan farms, known for their produce, ripened by the balmy Tyrrhenian Sea air. From long distances, drivers could see the flames from bonfires made of heaps of wires to extract the copper within, just as Farzana had done with her slim pickings, making the region known as the Land of Fires. Rates for some cancers had risen to twice the national rate around then, giving the region another name: the Triangle of Death.

FOR YEARS, AS the court hearings in Mumbai wore on, municipal lawyers described how the municipality had tried to keep the township out of city limits, to prevent toxins from leaking into the city air and water. But the mountains crept in. There were nearly 13 million metric tons of garbage at the Deonar Dumping Grounds, officials estimated. How could it place a floor under it, as the rules asked it to? The hills stretched over 326 acres. How could it make a ceiling to contain the air that blew into the city? A boundary wall built on layers of trash would be unstable, bound to fall, they said. The lawyers pled for more time.

Rane sometimes heard of the tests the municipality ran to incinerate garbage and produce electricity, as cities elsewhere in the world did, as the court had asked. But Mumbai's garbage was too soggy from the rains, too gloopy from rotting food for the incinerator to work. The trash township spilled out of the municipality's attempts to shrink it.

Meanwhile, the slim island city's open spaces had filled up. The relentless sprawl of suburbia had brought even distant places that could have formed possible dumping grounds in proximity with homes whose residents would be nauseated by the stink. They did not want open spaces around the apartments they had saved for years to buy to fill up with the city's mess. Farmers did not want the waste to pollute their fields. Any open space the municipality found, came with rival claimants.

In the years after the 1996 petition, deadlines to meet the waste rules and court orders came and went, but the mountains had hardly moved. The waste rules had outlawed them, mountain smoke sickened them, and yet Hyder Ali and his ilk, the desperados of Deonar, still filled them, carrying away all that had value. Clouds of flies obscured them and guards' eyes glazed over when they looked at them, turning pickers invisible as they continued to hunt for the dregs of Mumbai's fortunes. As the city, hemmed in by the sea, inched up, its garbage mountains and their halo followed in step.

Early in 2006, under pressure from the court, the municipality had appointed a private consultant, who delivered a report on resolving the problems at the Deonar township, the smaller mountains at Mulund and closing the trash hills at Gorai. Deonar's aging waste could make for rich compost, the report said: a waste-to-compost plant could shrink the township. To get there, the municipality would spend more than ₹10,500 crore (1.47 billion USD) on its three dumping grounds, nearly half of which would go into shrinking the Deonar township, building the waste plant and cleansing the murky air and water it spewed. It was the

Mumbai municipality's most ambitious attempt to manage the city's waste since the Deonar grounds were settled more than a century before.

Consultants and officials invited bids for the projects. Officials worried whether a private company could really manage the Deonar township, where ragpickers fanned out on slopes, their homes inched into hills, and gangs fought for trash. None of the companies that bid for the chance to remake Deonar met the technical terms, and the contract was not given out. Trash arrival and its surreptitious removal went on relentlessly. More came than pickers could take away. Garbage inched up on the mountains and spilled into the creek, stealthily swelling the township.

HAVING WAITED FOR more than a decade for the mountains to move or shrink, Dr. Rane had tired. In the summer of 2008, he filed his contempt petition. In these twelve years, the toxic cloud of Mumbai's festering possessions had only grown, he said. It hung heavily over the municipal ward around the mountains, where a quarter of all deaths came from respiratory diseases, Rane showed. In a ward further away, by comparison, it was less than 1 percent. He presented medical studies that showed the haze was thick with the carcinogenic chemical formaldehyde. Another study showed that benzene, another carcinogen, also festered in mountain air, many times higher than at any of the landfills the authors looked at elsewhere in the world. While it fell within permissible limits set in some other countries, Dipanjali Majumdar, the study's author, said those limits were set for short exposure, not a lifetime of inhaling it, as pickers at Deonar did. Their exposure was chronic, she said, the health risks considerable. Those who lived in the mountains' halo had a life expectancy of thirty-nine, living little more than half the lives that other Indians did.

The mountains' thickening halo sickened the city too. "The gases emitted from the landfill and other pollutants in air cooks a range of other hazardous dust and gases using sunlight in the atmospheric kitchen," Majumdar said. "These pollutants cooked in the atmosphere, called secondary pollutants, can cause severe air pollution and can even lead to climate change."

In search of answers, Rane began walking the sprawling, colonial-era court's angular corridors as hearings on his petition to fix the mountains restarted. "I am the kind of person, if I train my guns on something, I don't give up," he said later. The municipality pled for more time. Justice Dhananjaya Chandrachud's patience wore thin, a testiness seeping into his orders: "The rampant and unregulated dumping of garbage continues and despite orders passed by this court, no serious attempt has been made to alleviate the problem."

When asked what it was like being trapped in the mountains' deadly aura, Hyder Ali pushed his bony chest out. "*Hamko kya hua hai?*" he would retort. *Is there anything wrong with me?* He was healthier than anyone he knew, he liked to say, even after two decades of working on the rising tides of trash. He had seen friends silently replaced by their young children at the mountains while they retreated to waste away in the lanes, consumed by tuberculosis. Others had left to take in the village air, to help them recover, and never returned. While walking up the slopes, to work, he often passed by pickers vomiting. Their ailing chests could not take the gentle, uphill climb anymore. Others had faded into the haze, their disappearance unnoticed in the unrelenting chase for the city's moth-eaten treasures. But Hyder Ali, and his friends, didn't think their treasure-yielding township and the livelihood it provided for them, had anything to do with it.

FIVE

I T WAS JUNE 2008 and the school year had just begun, along with Mumbai's months-long rainy season. But Farzana had come to work on the mountains all day. Most mornings, when she arrived at the trash peaks, she started by collecting the overripe tomatoes and eggplants that arrived with the discarded food, or sprouted from it with the rains. She waited for her friends' hazy figures to emerge on the rugged slopes, and threw her pickings at them, making dark, wet splotches on their clothes. They swiveled in pain and confusion. When they spotted Farzana, her friends scrambled to look for their own tomatoes. They scoured through the trash that had arrived overnight for bits of watermelon or eggs and hurled them at her. Giggly tomato fights ensued as they chased each other around the unsteady, sun-filled slopes, rotting fruit in hand. Laughter and light refracted in the halo of the forgotten mountains.

As the fights ebbed, drying pulp mingled with sweat and clung to them in the humid heat that hung heavily between rain showers. Farzana bathed under the leaky taps of water tankers posted at their hilly township. The rest of her family, whom she joined at work, had asked to be spared from her messy welcomes and perfect aim. Farzana and her daring spirit grew up together in the mountains' thickening fog and extending shadow. "*Main pehle se hi aisi thi,*" she would say breezily, when asked where she got her fearless spirit, her sense of adventure from. *I've always been like this.*

As she turned ten, dark monsoon clouds grazed and then cocooned trash peaks. She watched trucks approach through the outer slopes. Filled with older trash and topped with rich mud, the mountainsides glowed emerald with grass.

Drenched in wind and rain, Farzana walked among clouds, which also floated in the pools that filled mountain troughs. At first, the water looked clear, like the thick and empty plastic of the milk pouches that fetched the highest prices. Farzana collected the squashed plastic bottles that drifted in the pools, like bubbles, amid lotuses.

As the rain continued to lash their township, the overgrown green slopes became muddy, hilltops turned molten brown. Farzana turned brown too from wading thigh deep into the mud. Dodging herds of cattle that their minders had brought to bathe in the water and graze on the grass, she slipped into the pools to bring out bottles, gloves, or glass floating within. She came up for air, coated in muddy water and saw friends emerge, dripping slush too. She dipped back in for more.

Bags filled, Farzana walked downhill, collecting spinach, cucumbers, and other vegetables for dinner. She looked for pumpkins growing under rain-soaked trash and watched papayas cling to tall, spindly trees that sprouted from it. Farzana had heard that not everyone ate vegetables grown in trash. Some rubbed overgrown leaves, from plants she did not recognize, onto wounds to heal them or chewed them to get intoxicated and work longer on slopes.

When the rains receded, Farzana and her sisters began their wait for Diwali. They were Muslims, like most others in the mountain communities. But on the slopes, Diwali brought breezy winters and creamy, candy-colored sweets, sprinkled with saffron strands, crushed cardamom, sliced pistachios, or silver slivers that tumbled out of garbage trucks, for days. City confectioners made hundreds of kilos of sweets, with disclaimers to consume them within a day or the fresh cream they were made with would sour. What didn't sell at stores made it to Deonar for hilltop Diwali parties. *"Hamara har shauk poora hua khaadi mein,"* Hera, who came only to collect treats, would later recall. *The mountains fulfilled our every desire.*

Balmy, fleeting winters gave way to unending summers. The township turned gold under the blazing sun, and Farzana watched trash shine or fade on the sun-baked slopes that rippled around her, edged by the glimmering creek. Plants withered quickly, leaving an expanse of dried mud and trash. Long, hot days were redeemed only by extended swims or discovering puffy, white boxes stuffed with ice cream cups, long past expiry, in the trash.

Farzana knew the end of summer was near when thick bunches of blotchy, red lychees began falling out of emptying trucks. She bit through their scaly skin and pulled it away with her teeth. The juice within dribbled down her chin. She spun the fruit in her mouth, spat out the long black seed, and swallowed the translucent white pulp that cooled her as it went down, swirling the sweaty last dregs of summer with sweetness.

FARZANA WAS SUDDENLY growing to be tall, like both her parents, and athletic, like her mother. She poured her coltish energy into chasing the city's unending trash caravans. She watched garbage trucks lurch slowly up the rubble- and trash-filled slopes. As they got to hill clearings, she raced other pickers to get to them, clambering onto their side rails before they halted and began emptying. She leaned onto the truck's edge so she didn't fall off, dipped both her hands in, and skimmed the cream of junk before anyone else could. She held on to the railing, turning and twisting aside when burning trash fell out of trucks, ignited when thin plastic bags were jammed too tightly with still simmering cigarette butts. She brought out hard-boiled eggs or bags of crisps. She sat in a circle with her sisters and snacked on them. What they could not eat, Farzana enveloped in her outstretched arms and carried downhill for her younger sisters and brother.

Unlike his daughter, Hyder Ali worried about the remains of city people—their melted desires, the spirits that arose from them and were marooned on the mountains. To him, they were an ever-present danger, hanging around the slopes, unobserved, only to ensnare his daughters. He told Farzana how he had seen unclaimed dead bodies tipped out of dump trucks at the edge of the grounds, where trash hills ran into the creek. He had watched burned ashes from Mumbai's cremation grounds emptied on hilltops.

Passing on the rules he had accumulated during the years he spent on the mountains, Hyder Ali reminded Farzana to stay away from the path of the Shaitans. Once, Farzana and Farha had waited for the trucks all day as the rain soaked their township, the city, and them. As day turned to dusk, they finally heard that the trucks had been delayed in the city and would arrive soon. Night fell and the day shift pickers began to leave, but Farzana heard the trucks were now on their way and she decided to wait on. Around 10:30 P.M., she watched as the trucks' lights appeared through the darkened paths of the township. She and Farha got their pick of the cloth scraps that fell out of the trucks, unhindered and raced quickly down the muddy slope, thinking they would deposit the scraps on Hyder Ali's pile. That's when they saw a woman, in white, floating above the scrap pile, just like the *chudail* Jehangir had told them about. Farzana and Farha held on to their bags and went straight home, returning to deposit them and chase more trucks the following morning. "*Usko bolenge nahi karna hai, to Farzana ko karna hi hai,*" Sahani, her older sister, recalled, with a grin lighting up her almond shaped, kohl rimmed eyes. *If you asked her not to do something, Farzana had to do it.*

Some mornings, her friends stopped by her home while everyone was still asleep. Farzana left with them, and whichever sister she could wake up. They ran up to clearings where trucks had delivered trash from Mumbai's luxury hotels or the airport, sat on hilltops and ate hotel breakfasts. Pointing to Arif, their fourteen-year-old friend, shriveled by tuberculosis, Hera would later say that the bread they had eaten was as long as he was. They sliced breakfast rolls with cutlery that came in crisp airline packaging and slathered them with butter, jam, or ketchup from single-serve packets thrown away at breakfast buffets. After breakfast, Hera left to go to school while Farzana and her sisters went to chase the arriving garbage trucks.

As Mumbaikars moved to wearing ready-made clothes, buying from shops rather than wearing tailor-made, cloth scraps had faded from the slopes, and Farzana had begun to collect plastic, copper wire, and German silver, rather than the bright offcuts that Hyder Ali had taught her to chase. Farzana emptied her bag in her lane, accumulating long loops of electric wires and retrieving tight coils from within the gadgets that crammed Mumbai homes, but had to be discarded because they rotted in its salty, coastal air and felt outdated as soon as they were bought. She burned the wire to recover copper and stuffed broken television sets, rusted ceiling fans, and video players into her burlap bag. She bashed stones on them, quickly covering her ears to muffle the sound of cracking. Sifting through the broken shards, she pulled out the metal frames of television sets to sell.

Collecting up to ten kilos of plastic and trembling copper wire or German silver, which took a few days, could earn her up to ₹300. Farzana sold her haul and handed her money to Hyder Ali, who earned a few rupees for a kilo of cloth scraps, his earnings shrinking with the waning supply of cloth scraps, his languid air and long breaks to chat with friends he ran into at work. They told him how the scraps now went straight from textile factories to traders in their lanes.

THE TALLER THE mountains grew, the harder it got to move them. At court hearings around April 2009, Justice Chandrachud had asked Mumbai's compact and erudite municipal commissioner, Jairaj Phatak, to go to the Deonar township to see the forgotten world with his own eyes.

Trailed by his entourage of civic officials, Phatak, who was an engineer and had recently also completed his doctorate in economics, saw the halo of gas that ringed the mountains that Rane had photographed, and in which Hyder Ali and Farzana had worked. "I was told this smoke was not due to fire set by ragpickers but due to methane gas in the garbage, which starts burning, letting off smoke, without anybody being near the spot," Phatak wrote in his report for Chandrachud.

With contempt proceedings looming, Phatak returned to his office and rifled through the inspirational quotes he assiduously accumulated. He settled on one from Theodore Roosevelt, which he wrote out in his pocket diary: "In any moment of decision, the best thing you can do is the right thing, the next best thing is the wrong thing and the worst thing you can do is nothing."

Months after his visit, the municipality's lawyers announced that it had agreed on a plan. A few weeks later, they gave a presentation in the courtroom, which had been darkened for the occasion. The first air conditioners were just being installed in a few of the lofty, high-ceilinged court rooms, and the long-handled ceiling fans, which had whirred noisily and drowned out court proceedings, finally fell silent. Creaky slatted wooden windows closed, after years of standing open to catch a breeze.

On a screen installed in the courtroom, a new Deonar township appeared. Officials showed tarred roads winding through mountains, vents jutting out of trash peaks to release the fires trapped within and a plant that would reduce their trash to compost. Half the hills would be shoveled to the side, freeing space for the compost plant that would feed Mumbai's fading gardens, officials said. Dried trash would also burn to fuel machines at factories nearby. The plant would create municipal card-carrying jobs for pickers on the trash hills, allowing them an official employment, a pension, and some security. If it all worked, Mumbai's waste would leave the mountains legally, as compost, for the first time in more than a century.

Contempt proceedings circling closer, Phatak and his colleagues had relooked at the bids that the two short-listed companies had made more than two years before.

In October 2009, the municipality gave United Phosphorus, one of the world's largest seed and fertilizer companies and which had come close to meeting the terms, the Deonar contract. It quickly convened a company with two partners: they called it Tatva.

AT FIRST, THE municipality's plans had not worried Hyder Ali. The pickers didn't sell the food that rotted slowly on hills. Besides, he had only ever seen the mountains growing higher, stretching further into the creek. The city sent enough trash both for pickers and the municipality's plans, he thought.

He and the children chose from more than a thousand trucks that streamed in every day. Long, lurching garbage caravans, filled with the remains of desires that had flickered and been sated in the city, emptied on hilltops, so more could be accumulated in the apartment blocks and suburbs where they had begun their lives. Farzana and her sisters bent low on hilltops to read the alphabets stuck on the front windows of the khaki and orange trucks that passed below, indicating the city wards they came from. They raced to trucks that came from wealthy neighborhoods, loaded with saleable trash, gliding deep into whirls of muddy pickers that surrounded them.

After she brought out everything she needed to sell, Farzana often emerged from the receding scrambles, dragging felled branches or cracked bamboo poles that came from tree-lined neighborhoods. She, and her sisters, dug them in to stand upright on quiet hilltops. They threw burlap, plastic, or long, dried-out palm leaves over them to make shelters from the beating sun, competing with the boys in making larger, better cabins.

Teetering at teenage, Farzana had acquired a sudden taste for gossiping in the interiors of these cabins in the lull between truck arrivals. She and her friends chatted over rice or instant noodles, ferreted out of trucks and cooked painstakingly over small fires they lit. City trash yielded slender, long grains of rice that were never seen in markets around the mountains. Sometimes, they pooled their money to buy spices and minced meat and cooked it to go with the city rice and invited friends over. Younger security guards often joined them for parties or for shade from the scorching mountain sun. They told Farzana and her friends that they would leave soon and then new guards would replace them.

In December 2009, Farzana did begin to see new officers, guards, and machinery settling on the mountains, while municipal staff retreated to their office at the entrance to Deonar's trash township, from where they supervised the weighing of trash trucks that drove away deep into the township. Waste was shoveled into piles at the edge of the creek, clearing space for the plant. Rumors floated around the hills; it was hard to know which ones were true and which were not. Hyder Ali's deep-set eyes lit up in surprise when he saw that their lives, which had stretched out in the fog of delays and snags in contracting their township, would change. But even as he watched, the hills started to shrink.

A slim, empty strip opened between pickers' homes and the trash. Then a wall began to rise on it. It would form the township's boundary, marking the hills within as Tatva's territory, no longer the pickers'. Tatva officials set up booths in the lanes around, offering jobs at the soon-to-be-built plant. Jehangir, and most other boys, signed up for them, hoping to have municipal employment that would make them legitimate on the mountains. Jehangir had gotten married to their cousin, Rakila, and had a baby girl soon after. Dreams of a card-carrying job settled in his eyes.

BUT ONCE TATVA staffers discovered the fetid and secret world that Farzana lived in, they knew it would be hard to manage. They wrote to municipal officials and asked for help. The mountains burned constantly, throwing up smoke, they wrote. Slopes were filled with the illicit army of pickers, overrun by cattle and their handlers, and their far edges were carved out between violent gangs. More than two hundred garbage trucks arrived every hour, during peak hours, delivering twice the amount of garbage Tatva had been asked to handle every day. Pickers and traders believed it belonged to them. How could they even begin to deal with a situation like this, they asked?

Outside the mountains, a storm was gathering. Almost since its creation, Tatva had been embroiled in a controversy surrounding the circumstances of its winning bid. The uproar had made it to the state assembly. The chief minister ordered an inquiry.

At Deonar, Tatva worked on, stretching the wall further, stranding the pickers outside. To begin with, Farzana walked along it and slipped through its cracks to get to work. Soon, the wall seemed unending and she could not make it in. Work stalled in their communities. Court orders and waste rules had finally arrived at the township.

Stuck, Farzana hung outside the wall for weeks. She paced restlessly along the wall until she began seeing ropes fixed around the craggy stone edges. She pulled herself up and over, just as she had seen other pickers do, and got to work. Amid the shrinking mountains, she found a pair of blue jeans, lying stiffly against the unfiltered mountain sun, late one afternoon. She picked them up and held them against herself. She had seen actresses wear them in movie posters, while she sat in buses or rickshaws that inched slowly through the Lotus market. Filled over time with stores, handcarts, and stalls, it was the tunnel that delivered their township to the city and new things from the city to them. Like her sisters, Farzana mostly wore salwar kameezes, with long dupattas to cover her hair. But she brought the jeans home, washed them repeatedly and saved them for the occasional family trips Hyder Ali took them on. In the meantime, she kept scaling the wall to get in and work, watching the hills contract inside.

Dr. Rane too had watched the wall stretch and the hills shrink. "Everything I had asked for was happening," he would recall. "I saw sections of the ground getting closed for dumping." In January 2011, he withdrew his court case.

The inquiry report on awarding the contract to Tatva came out that September. It said the tender process had material flaws. Report in hand, municipal officials wrote to the commissioner to ask if the Tatva contract was now to be rethought or scrapped. No response came. Instead, a cloud settled over the mountain shrinking project, the recycling plant, and the municipal card-carrying jobs.

SIX

EARLY IN THE MONSOON of 2011, Jehangir was working on the mountains when someone came over to tell him that his plump boss, the garbage trader Javed Ansari, better known as Shanoo Bhai, was walking to his house with a sword in his hand. Jehangir ran home, followed by Farzana, Sahani, and their other siblings. They watched as Shanoo slashed the plastic sheets that made up the walls of their house. When the roof collapsed, Shanoo walked into the heap of ruined plastic that was once their home, pulled out stones they had brought back from the mountains and laid down as flooring, and threw them out into the lane.

Shanoo and other garbage traders had always fought to amass trash at the township. But as Tatva struggled to make the plant at Deonar, the traders hacked cracks in the boundary wall, moved deeper in, coralled trash hills and clearings, accumulated all that trucks emptied, and then resold it. Where pickers worked on their stretch of the mountain, the traders' lackeys also claimed the contents of their bags, paying them little or nothing, and reselling from their *katas* for a profit. Their presence was inescapable in the lanes around the mountains, where they offered illegal connections to the electricity, cable TV, and water supply—and charged a fee for it. Traders' battles for control over the mountains, township, and the lanes around it grew increasingly vicious.

Legend in Farzana's lane had it that some years before, Shanoo had taken on a murder charge for a rival trader in exchange for rights over garbage that was left on the hills closest to them. When charges could not be proven against Shanoo in court, he returned and inducted Jehangir into his gang and claimed the mountain territory promised to him. Through a mixture of beatings and abuse, Shanoo had trained Jehangir to intimidate other pickers, and to fight other gangs with swords he provided. "*Shanoo ne hamare liye kya kiya? Hamne uske liye kiya,*" Jehangir would later say. *What did Shanoo do for us? We made him.*

Most of all Jehangir and his skinny friend, Miya Khan, who was better known as Babu and had been in Shanoo's gang nearly as long as him, clashed over trucks filled with hotel remnants. In the city, weddings, banquets, and conferences at hotels had begun stretching for days, bringing their growing remains to the mountains. Pickers resold bent forks, plastic packaging and kept the food and alcohol. The clashes to direct these trucks to their own clearings got so fierce, the municipality had tried diverting trucks arriving from hotels to the dumping grounds at Mulund from Deonar. On nights when Jehangir and Babu brought back a large stash, Shanoo sat with them on the dark trash peaks, passing the liquor bottles around and telling them stories of all he had seen on the mountains.

For months, Shanoo had suspected that Jehangir was filling garbage trucks for his rival, Javed Qureshi, who was a rising man on the mountains. Shanoo had seen Qureshi's hills inching closer to his own territory, and began to suspect that Farzana, Sahani, and Farha sold their trash to him too. That evening, Shanoo had slashed their house as punishment. After Shanoo left, the rain had fallen harder against the darkening light, turning their house into a muddy puddle. They ventured in, wading knee deep to find fresh plastic sheets from the trash they had saved up, strung them close around themselves, and slept within its fragile protection.

Farzana's sisters stayed away from Shanoo, picking surreptitiously. But she often stayed ahead of them, getting the boys who hung around the wall to push her over it on days it was freshly repaired and had no cracks to slip through. Inside, she chased trucks with them. If Jehangir found her playing marbles with boys, she would grin and show them her hand, tell them she'd be right back, and follow him home where Jehangir would lash her with his belt. She hung out with boys too much, was how she would explain his beatings later. "*Mujhe to vo bahut chahta hai,*" she would beam. *He loves me a lot.* It was a kind of love he had learned from Shanoo.

The two years Tatva had been given to build the plant had expired in the winter of 2011 and the municipality had still not received permission from the state government to lease the grounds so construction could start. Payment was now due for the plant, which had not been built. Tatva officials said, payments were delayed. Negotiations continued. In May and July 2012, Tatva wrote to the municipality, reminding it to lease the vast township, so it could begin making the plant. The municipality in turn wrote again to the state government for permission to lease the Deonar township to Tatva. The state government did not reply to the municipality, which in turn, did not reply to Tatva.

IN NOVEMBER 2012, Shanoo, who had recently been exiled, and lived in Navi, or new, Mumbai, after a trader he had beaten brought a court case, died in a road accident. His family and gang members brought him back to be buried in the Deonar cemetery. The graveyard, which was not far from the mountains, had filled up with the poor Muslims who had moved into the area in the wake of the religious riots of 1992, looking for makeshift homes and endless work on the rising slopes of trash. "*Chori ka paani, chori ki bijli, aur ek gareeb ko chahiye kya?*" a gang boss, who had arrived in an earlier wave of migrants, once said. *Stolen water, stolen power, what more does a poor man want?* It was somewhere to live, and somewhere to die.

The new arrivals at Deonar filled the thicket of lanes in the mountains' growing shadow and ended their days in the graveyard at its edge. Gravediggers looked for empty slivers of earth to inter the dead who streamed in every day. They brought up half-consumed arms, legs, and long hair still growing from bodies, melded into the earth. The gravediggers quickly refilled the graves with mud sprinkled with salt or potassium and dug elsewhere, hoping that bodies that should have turned to dust in four months would disappear in two. Illness and violence, the twins that stalked the mountain slopes, meant the gravediggers filled not yet old graves with young, new bodies. "*Yahaan boodha ho ke to koi marta hi nahi,*" a cleric from the area once mused, thinking of the funerals he conducted. *No one dies of old age here.*

For Shanoo's funeral, gang bosses from around the mountains' rim set their rivalry aside for a day and streamed into the unkempt Deonar graveyard. They watched his teenaged underlings make their way around the overgrown shrubs, tombstones, and broken benches, organizing proceedings. While leaving, several of the gang bosses asked Jehangir to stay in touch. "*Collar upar,*" Babu remembered hearing, as he wilted in the sultry, midafternoon heat and the uncertainty that lay ahead. *Keep your shirt collars*—spirits—*up,* one of them told Babu, who was a year younger than Jehangir. He had worked on the mountains in his school uniform, escaping class, until he dropped out and began working with Shanoo all day and late into the night. That afternoon, the hair Babu had carefully piled into shiny *seeng*, or spikey horns, to elongate his frame, flopped limply on his face. Sweat soaked his shirt, sticking it to his back.

In the wake of Shanoo's death, Jehangir needed a new job: he became a father, on December 9, for the second time. As the legitimate job he had signed up for at the plant hovered forever on the horizon, delayed by Tatva's negotiations with the municipality, his expenses were growing. The gang, already sputtering out in Shanoo's exile, had dissolved completely after his death. So, Jehangir struck out on his own. He bought glass from pickers on slopes, bribing or befriending guards to let him take heaps of glass out through the walls' widening gaps. Farzana and his other sisters washed and cleaned broken shards so he could get a better price for them. Jehangir had watched Javed, and his bosses Atique and Rafique Khan, take over more territory on the mountains. He sold his findings at Javed Qureshi's *kata*, for more than Shanoo had ever paid him.

THE BROTHERS RAFIQUE and Atique Khan had arrived at the mountains, in 1975 as children, when it was still a watery forest between the dumping grounds and the creek. Atique, younger of the brothers, remembered worrying about falling into the swamp, when he first moved as a ten-year-old. "*Log daldal mein gir ke mar jaate the,*" he recalled. *People fell into the swamp and died.* Regardless, his father and others had put down rubber tires, plastic sheets, cardboard, and settled Rafiq Nagar on Deonar's marsh and the edges of trash slopes. Police and municipal officials demolished their homes, but they kept resettling them until the municipality finally acknowledged the settlement, making skinny roads and building a nursery school, tilting on the slopes.

The Khan brothers' father had opened a restaurant in the Lotus market where the brothers had started out waiting tables. They had filled mangroves with mountain mud and made plastic sheet homes over them that they rented or sold. But they knew, any fortune around here would have to come from trash. Around 2005, Atique cajoled their father into opening a *kata* shop in the mountain-facing stretch of road, which was already filling up with them. Shop owners competed for pickers as they descended the slopes, carrying back bits of the mountains on their heads. The traders stopped at nothing to beat out rivals and redirect their trash, but Atique and Rafique had brought a fierceness that had never been seen before.

In October 2009, Kadeer Shaikh, a rival of the Khan brothers, had died from stab wounds on the slim dirt strip between the mountains and their *kata* shop, even as a small crowd watched, immobilized. His mother had refused to collect the body until Atique and Rafique were charged with her son's murder, Atique recalled. But when police looked for witnesses to build their case, Kadeer's murder became unseen and unheard. Atique was kept in custody for a month, while investigations went on and then let off, burnishing the Khan brothers' image as one of the mountains' bosses. More accusations of threats and violence piled up, but remained mostly unproven and the two brothers unconvicted.

Soon after Kadeer's death, Javed Qureshi, the Khans' acolyte, began appearing on their mountain clearings, while the brothers worked from their offices at the mountains' edge. The Khans' name and their writ controlled life in the lanes of Rafiq Nagar and the mountains around them. Rooms in the skinny lanes opened out to damp, sunless alleys or rambling, sun-soaked trash slopes that petered into waves. Walking through the lanes could yield roosters collected for prize fights, retrieved couches spilling foam, and aging gangsters crouched against shrunken doorframes that blocked the sun. Cable television, water, trash, jobs:

everything that made up life in the lanes was ultimately said to be controlled by the Khans and other gangs, as their cavernous sheds at the mountains' edge expanded.

WITH EVERY DELAY in the plant's construction, the mountains were receding back into invisibility, while the gangs' grip on them, and the lanes around them, extended. The brothers' men began patrolling their territory, which was strung with cameras that beamed footage of any intruders back to their headquarters. Jehangir's fortunes rose with Javed, who lent him money for his sister Afsana's wedding. Jehangir took glass into the city to sell it to traders, who would in turn sell it to be melted into new shapes or refilled with new drinks. *"Vo ek number ka aadmi hai,"* Jehangir would gush about Javed later. *He is a first-class person.*

Jehangir had named his baby daughter Shifa, meaning "healing." He came to believe she had mended his luck. Business with Javed grew fast: the following year, Jehangir replaced the family's plastic sheet walls, the ones that Shanoo had slashed, with a few feet of bricks, topped with long layers of tin sheet. He made a loft, where he and his wife, Rakila, lived, with their girls. *"Iske aane se na unki kismet badal gayee,"* Rakila would say about Shifa. *She brought luck in his life.* As business grew, Jehangir hired teenage pickers to clean his glass heaps. Every few weeks, he packed them into the drivers' cabin with his sisters, broken shards jangling in the back to sell to city traders. He dropped them at Chowpatty beach, for an outing, after he sold his mountain treasures to traders.

Away from the mountains, Farzana wore sunglasses, a sun hat, and long tunics with her jeans. She splashed in the sea, ringed by buildings nearly as tall as the mountains. While her sisters made castles out of the windblown sand, Farzana walked far ahead, along the gently curving shore, pressing her feet into the sand to leave footprints. She walked through the world she had known only through its detritus and turned back against the sun, every little while, to see how far she had come.

When they got to the beach, in the midmornings, Farzana watched college students arrive, with their overfilled backpacks, to escape class or shield gently forming relationships from prying eyes. As the afternoon wore on, groups of women, in flowery burqa-like Ridaas or sarees and dangling handbags, came for a respite between the unbending mealtimes they labored to meet, in their claustrophobic kitchens. Farzana watched shifting, lacy shadows from the trees that lined the beach fall on bejeweled honey-mooners and couples through the day. They all sought the busy beach, and its inadequate shadows, to escape Mumbai's cramped family homes.

Farzana felt, fleetingly, like she belonged in this world of people whose lives were filled with things and who discarded trash, not hoarded it. When Jehangir came to take them home, she inevitably begged him to stay a little longer. They watched a deepening pink sky frame the rising skyline, the sea turn molten, and the bronzed sun melt slowly into it, extinguishing its glow. Then they got back into his truck and drove through snaking traffic, almost following the same route the city's trash took to reach them.

GARBAGE TRUCKS WERE often packed with the debris of stumpy old buildings, getting increasingly torn down to make place for shiny new skyscrapers. The detritus created by Mumbai's never-ceasing construction industry was mostly supposed to be buried in far-flung quarries. The cement, asbestos, rusted metal, and chemicals they gave off could hang in the city air and settle in residents' lungs, making them sick.

But soon after Kadeer died, in 2009, Rafique, the older of the Khan brothers, was said to have begun offering a way around these long and expensive quarry trips, which delayed new construction, as rebuilding was usually permitted after the torn-down buildings were disposed of. Municipal officials working nights had seen trucks arrive in the dark at

Deonar from the city, slipping through holes in the wall at the far end of the township's official entrance. They saw a secret suburb of gray concrete hills rise above the wall. When the debris hills got too high and wobbly, fires burned on them, water tankers doused them, bulldozers flattened the burned remains. The debris hills rose again. It allowed the city's instant reinvention, and was said to have lifted Atique and Rafique's fortunes too.

Further along the mountains' broken boundary wall was a rambling estate where waste came from some of Mumbai's largest hospitals and was said to be Atique and his partner Javed's turf. Pickers the lackeys let in collected the thick plastic gloves, saline bags, and bottles that their landlord resold. Across both Atique and Rafique's territories, thin plastic sheets, shopping bags, and the garbage bags that did not fetch much money, were collected and piled into trucks. Pickers had heard they went to factories in distant towns where they were pressed into little plastic pellets and sold across the country and abroad.

Jehangir's business was growing with the traders' gangs on the mountains. He and Babu had appropriated a mountain clearing where trucks emptied only for them. He, Alamgir, and Farzana, the oldest of the sisters still at home, kept their house going while Hyder Ali's workshop sputtered as he made repayments for the loans he had taken to build it. Hyder Ali had thought the loans and the workshop would get him out of the hold of trash, but its grip on his children was only growing. Farzana often went along when he went to apply for loans, wanting to accompany her father for the trip into the city, then nudging him to say it was time to get back. She could not stay away from the mountains for too long.

BETWEEN THE ESTATES of debris and medical waste was an empty space where the municipality planned to make a new graveyard. It had stayed vacant for years, officials worrying rains and trash could come gushing down mountain slopes, bringing up newly buried bodies. They began seeing it fill with debris from dead buildings instead, the gangs said to be inching their way across it at night.

In July 2013, Tatva wrote to the municipality again, asking for the lease to the township so it could mortgage it and begin making the plant, which would lead to the mountains' closure. The chief minister of Maharashtra, Prithviraj Chavan, announced the formation of another committee to probe the terms of the municipality's contract with Tatva. While it investigated whether permission could be given to lease out municipal trash townships to private companies, the township stayed in limbo.

In September 2013, Tatva wrote to the municipality asking it to form a dispute resolution committee, to hand over the township's lease and pay its dues. Copies of the letter began arriving at a range of municipal offices. The following month, the municipality wrote back saying it would form a committee. More letters from Tatva arrived at municipal offices, attempting to set it up. No responses came. In December, Tatva filed a court case to get the municipality to pay its dues for their work clearing the site, as well as their failure to provide the lease to make the plant that still hung unmade over the mountain air.

Late one afternoon that winter, Jehangir was buying trash on the hills when another picker called him to the creek. He ran down the burning slopes to find a small crowd collecting near the mangroves. As he got closer, he saw Farzana and Farha already standing around a boat that had run ashore in the sand. He craned through the crowd and saw the fading, yellow sunlight glowing on gold. A middle-aged woman was sprawled across the boat, dressed as a bride. She was dead.

He asked Farzana to turn away but she remembered staring, transfixed, at the gold bracelets that lined the woman's arms. They shone against her lifeless skin. They could hear police sirens in the distance, and finally the policemen arrived, walking the final stretch over the garbage-strewn tracks. Jehangir saw them cover the luminous woman with a white sheet and take her away.

For weeks, Farzana asked him if he had heard anything about the woman who had floated into the city's graveyard of possessions. How did she get there? she asked Jehangir, most evenings. Who sent her? All the woman's prized belongings had not been enough to fill the emptiness in her life, Farzana thought. Someone must have killed the woman and put her into the boat that had drifted into their town, Jehangir had said. Like everything else on the mountains, he told her, the dead woman in her bridal jewelry had probably floated into their lives in the hopes that she would be forgotten—even in plain sight.

SEVEN

LEGEND AMONG PICKERS HAD it that expensive belongings could only have arrived at the mountains because they brought their owners ill luck. Surely, they could not have forgotten about such things, or thrown them away, pickers figured. This misfortune would follow pickers if they kept any of these thrown-away treasures, they believed. Instead, pawn brokers walked their lanes to rid pickers of their fortune-draining finds.

It was only in its infancy, but 2015 was turning out to be the year of dwindling fortunes at Deonar. The sparring between the municipality and Tatva dragged on in court, and outside. In late January 2015, a state government inquiry concluded, predictably, that the contract with Tatva should not have been signed before permission was obtained to lease the township from the state government, and that there had been irregularities with the tender process. Soon after the report was submitted, the recently reelected state government denied permission to lease out the sprawling trash township, drying up the plans to fund the compost plant and shrivel the mountains. The pickers would have to look elsewhere for better work and the elusive municipal identity cards. Hardly anyone fell, in these attempts, faster than Moharram Ali, once the luckiest of mountain denizens. Somewhere in the middle of Tatva's slow fade away from the mountains, he disappeared too.

Municipal officials had already been planning for a new waste-to-power plant, replacing Tatva and its plans for a plant that had stayed grounded. They were staring at court orders that had said the township was to be closed that year. As the municipality began looking for funds, and a new company to build a waste processing plant, warm winds blew over the mountains, aggravating the season of fires. The monsoon, which usually calmed the fires for a few months, wouldn't arrive until June.

Fires burned for over a week in February while municipal officials helplessly looked on. Official correspondence also showed that around then the municipal commissioner had said there were several complications and risks involved in making a waste-to-energy plant, especially one the municipality would own only jointly with a private company. It took back the plans for the plant.

The garbage caravans continued to arrive and Tatva shoveled their contents onto hills, as it had for more than five years. Meanwhile, in court, the company pushed for the appointment of an arbitrator to award its unpaid bills and damages for being unable to make the plant. Municipal lawyers countered by saying Tatva had worked for years, awaiting permissions: it was content, they suggested, with piling trash on hilltops rather than making the plant. The municipality had paid Tatva for the work it did do, its lawyers said. Mediation was not written into their contract. At the township, broken fragments of the wall stood stranded, a reminder of the future that had so nearly arrived before it sank into the trash that the pickers had waded through their whole lives. On March 19, 2015, Justice Shahrukh Kathawalla granted

Tatva's plea for mediation with the municipality. That winter, arbitration proceedings would begin.

WITH PROSPECTS OF the job he had signed up for at the plant fading, Moharram Ali decided to take more loans for new businesses to supplement his trash-picking. As well as the *kata* shop he had started after finding the necklace on the slopes, he rented out rooms for a commission, and took masonry jobs. It was the best time to be a masonry artisan, or *karigar*, he claimed.

Just as the mountains were said to add a few feet of trash every day, the straggling communities at their rim were always growing too. Mosque towers were rising above tin sheet dwellings; corner shops in the Lotus market were turning into internet cafés, cake shops, and clinics. Farzana raved about a new sweet shop that made a dessert that melted in the mouth like soft cotton, soaked in sweet milk.

But years of treasures falling in Moharram Ali's hands had made him unused to the slow grind of masonry. Struggling to deliver commissions in time, he returned to his village often, bought a small plot of land there, took loans and spent months building a house on it. Stretched too thin, his glow began to fade. When he returned to Deonar, the pickers who had sold him trash for his *kata* now sold it to others instead. His fragile fortune was slipping out of his hands, replaced by growing debt. He took larger loans, repaying them unfailingly by secretly taking fresh loans to repay overdue ones, always coming up with a new plan to earn back enough to repay them all.

Yasmin, his wife, struggled to run the house while he was away and ran up her own debts. The necklace Moharram Ali had found often floated in her eyes. She thought about the night she held it in her hands and thought her life was about to get better. She now came to believe the necklace had brought ill luck to its original owners and had followed her family too.

Hera, who had inherited her father's long nose and good looks, dropped out of high school. Months after she turned eighteen, she took a loan to buy a used sewing machine and began to stitch curtains. Sharib, their oldest son, whom Moharram Ali had wanted to learn to drive so he could work at the plant, picked trash all day. At fifteen, he was still baby-faced but seemed suddenly taller, his eyes blurred under his floppy hair. For years, Yasmin had berated him for picking at the slopes and dispatched him to school. But with Moharram Ali away, she began keeping his money, settling Sharib in the grip of the mountains she had wanted to keep her children away from.

She tried enrolling him at night school instead. He returned home, soaked in mountain mud, only after class had already begun, fell on the food Yasmin could rustle up and then stretched on the floor, hardly ever making it to class. Later, Yasmin would say that with Moharram Ali away and creditors at her door, she had become addicted to Sharib's earnings. She watched his smile turn scarce and brown. She turned away when she saw him chew the tobacco that stained his teeth. She knew it kept him working through long, hungry days.

When she came to drop garbage bags or refill water bottles, Farzana began seeing Yasmin in her house, collecting the fabric strips that Jehangir's wife, Rakila, gave women to stick beads on, in pencil-marked flower patterns. They would get stitched on and shimmer on the edges of kurtas, burqas, and sarees in the city. Neighbors streamed in after the mountain pickers left for work, collected these pieces, and exchanged gossip, children in tow. Farzana wondered why Yasmin took work that fetched just a few rupees for pieces longer than herself: her family had always floated a little above the others in their lanes. And yet, here she was on most afternoons, telling them she needed to stay busy while Moharram Ali was away.

By the time he got back, Yasmin was desperate. Moharram Ali returned to stalk the mountains' overlooked riches and waited restlessly for his luck to turn again, bringing treasures back in his hands. Then his father called to say he had fixed his youngest daughter's wedding, Moharram Ali's favorite sister. He left to sell the village house in order to fund it, returning to struggle with his dwindling fortune and growing debt. He took loans to repay previous ones, to run his string of failing businesses and moved secretly to avoid creditors. Yasmin struggled to send him to work as she once had struggled to send her sons to school.

She decided to step in, taking a loan herself, to start a Vada Pav stall at the market on 90 Feet Road, which was named for its width and followed the mountains' curve. Yasmin, Hera, and Mehrun, her middle daughter, fried potato patties and green chilies that sputtered in the pan and brought tears in their eyes, through the afternoons. She handed them to Moharram Ali, in oil-stained newspaper, to slice into fluffy buns and sell as the market came to life at dusk. Reluctantly, he set up the kind of stall he had kept in business for years. Then friends dropped by. Yasmin heard he gave them free food. The stall folded, adding to their string of failed businesses and swirling loans.

Yasmin faltered on repayments, making new loans unavailable and handed her nose pin to Rakila asking her to pawn it to start a new business. She bought groceries for a meal service for the artisans who made shoes or clothes or filled them with embroidery at the many workshops sprouting in the lanes. An embroiderer began taking a lunch box, eating dinner at home with Moharram Ali and retreating into the dark lane with him to giggle over their glowing phones. His payments got sucked into buying the family's food supplies, Yasmin could not add new clients, the business shut down and Rakila wore the nose pin for months, while she looked for loans to retrieve it.

At home, Moharram Ali raged at Yasmin for his stained clothes, for not pressing his feet until he fell asleep and for her steadily growing quagmire of debt. Amid it all, Hera had turned nineteen, a year over the sanctioned age for girls in their lane to marry. At Rakila's house, the women told Yasmin to find the striking and fiery Hera a match before she got too old.

One of the neighbors told her about a relative in the upscale Mumbai suburb of Bandra who had a son with decent job prospects. Yasmin borrowed jewelry for herself and Hera and took Moharram Ali, who she said was a successful trader, to meet the family. He smiled and looked the part, helping settle the wedding. Hera would finally slip out of the mountains' grasp, as Yasmin had always wanted. And yet, pulling it off needed more money than they had.

Yasmin went to Rakila's house and enrolled her and Hyder Ali to start a Bishi. An underground Mumbai system for raising larger sums for desperate times, the Bishi's members contribute fixed installments into a shared pot every month. Each month, one of the subscribers is able to withdraw the pooled sum, minus a commission for the organizer, the payout rotating until everyone has been able to withdraw from the pot. Yasmin's offer was even better. She would collect the installments and return double the amount, including interest, every month, she told them. Hyder Ali joined so he could grow his embroidery workshop when he got the increased amount and Rakila planned to take on more bead work. Moharram Ali often asked for these installments, to make his own repayments. Yasmin resisted. They argued.

IN SEPTEMBER 2015, soon before arbitration proceedings between Tatva and the municipality were to begin, the municipality sent a pertermination notice to Tatva. It would later send a termination notice on January 22, 2016, asking Tatva to leave the Deonar township on January 31, only six years into its twenty-five-year tenancy. Until the municipality could begin fixing it afresh, the township would continue to take in more of the city's reeking secrets, employing only the illicit army of pickers.

One night, when Yasmin brought installments, Moharram Ali asked for them again. He would replace it soon, he said. Yasmin refused. Hearing their parents' voices raging within their home, glowing in the dark lane, the children decided to stay out. Later, they slipped in and slept on the floor before the voices quieted. In the morning, Yasmin was sleeping next to the children. Moharram Ali was not. When Yasmin sent Sharib and her younger son Sameer to look for him on the mountains, he was not there. She asked Hyder Ali to go to the 90 Feet Road market, but it was deserted; shops had not yet opened.

Around noon, the Bishi organizer made his way through the small crowd at home. He asked Yasmin for the installments. But when she opened her wooden cupboard and looked under the clothes where she had hidden the money, it wasn't there. She upturned clothes and the broken dolls Moharram Ali had picked from the mountains for Mehrun and Ashra, their younger daughters. He had left with the money.

Days later, when Hyder Ali walked to Yasmin's house to ask for his money that had vanished instead of doubling, he saw her beaten-up television set, washing machine, and Hera's sewing machine being carried out of their home. Creditors would sell them to retrieve what they could. Yasmin's room was filled with others, pressing for their money. Farzana began seeing Yasmin lock her house from the outside and leave through a back door, before creditors arrived.

A tired disappointment replaced the dreams of gold in the lanes around the Deonar mountains that winter. The failed compost plant had become one of the mountains' ghosts, even before it materialized. Tatva's staff was leaving to work elsewhere. The latest court deadline to stop dumping garbage at the Deonar township, to fix it or settle a modern trash township, had passed months ago. Garbage caravans came unabated, letting Sharib and Sameer work and keep the house going.

Hera's wedding had got called off, Yasmin had pulled twelve-year-old Mehrun out of the free municipal-run school to manage their home and enrolled eight-year-old Ashra, her youngest daughter, who was at a private English school, in it. Ashra returned with disheveled hair that Yasmin tried to tame and empty notebooks she did not notice. As their household suddenly curled at its edges, Ashra's words began to get stuck inside her. They came out fitfully and sometimes only in her intense, green-eyed stare.

Ashra was hardly ever in class, her third-grade teacher at her new school, Shireen Mohammed Siraj, told Yasmin, and doodled when she was. Days later, Yasmin walked slowly through the school corridor, looking down at the floor, which was wet and slippery from the children's water fights, and watching the mountains seeping in through classroom windows. In the principal's office, a couple of burqa-clad teachers were speaking to a burly consultant who had been assigned to supervise area schools. "*Pen se nahi likhte par whitener jeb mein rakhte hain,*" a teacher said. *They have not started writing with pens yet but they carry white-out.* The consultant nodded, knowingly: he had seen students inhaling it in stairwells around mountain schools. Yasmin and Siraj decided Ashra needed remedial classes.

Every morning, Lallu, Ashra's cousin and classmate, came over to walk to school with her. He tucked his blue-and-white-striped school shirt into navy blue shorts that bunched up under his school belt and hung below his knees. His socks rolled under them and over his knee-caps. He wore a clip-on tie, pressed his hair down with oil, and slung the schoolbag that seemed to outweigh him over his shoulders. He waited at the door while Ashra searched for a bit of her uniform, or nursed an upset stomach, inside. She often emerged only after he gave up and left, singing made-up ditties of lines she heard Yasmin say to creditors and dancing, with the flies, on the loose stones that covered the drains.

Lallu picked trash on the mountains or through their lanes' overflowing trash cans, after school, to supplement his father's earnings from selling medicinal herbs. He pushed his mother, who was Moharram Ali's sister, to apply for a bank account or an identity card when teachers asked him to. In their walks to school, he reminded Ashra that the municipality would deposit a rupee in her bank account for every day she attended. She just stared ahead.

Yasmin began to notice that, on some afternoons, Lallu returned home without Ashra. Siraj said she was not at class. When questioned, Lallu said that Ashra had left with a tall, slim man. Worried a creditor was trying to kidnap Ashra, Yasmin handed him some of her borrowed notes and asked him to check who it was. Moharram Ali, Lallu reported back: he had hung outside her school until Ashra spotted him, ran up, and hugged him. They walked nearby, getting a snack, Moharram Ali asking her to keep their meetings secret. After this discovery, and on Hera's instructions, Ashra made Moharram Ali walk her through Rafiq Nagar's skinny lanes so she could report back on it to Hera and her mother, without the risk of their father getting caught by his creditors.

The two entered a lane just wide enough to fit a person, with a slim, open drain, flattening against the wall to let others pass. At the passage end, not far from them, Ashra saw a leafy, old tree, rising from the watery swamp. Moharram Ali turned and unlocked a room, and a small, childlike woman followed him in, from a neighbor's house. This was Shabana, his new wife, he said. He had left with her, to escape the unending wait for jobs at the plant, money to repay mounting loans and treasures to tell friends about. The following morning, Hera, her friends, and Yasmin followed Ashra through Rafiq Nagar's lanes and rained blows on Shabana, who Hera had heard was a year younger than she was. They returned home with no one to wait for.

For weeks, Ashra came home to find Yasmin curled up on their thin, single mattress or speaking to Hera through tears. *"Mere karze ki vajah se gaya,"* Yasmin said. *He left because of my loans.* She should not have collected Bishi installments and tempted him, she said. She wished he hadn't found the gold necklace that had upturned his luck, her marriage, and their lives. The two had piled on debt and new business plans thinking mountain luck would turn their way again. Instead, loans had grown, teetered, tumbled, and consumed them while, Yasmin believed, the necklace had turned mountain luck away. Only the debt had stayed, piling up.

ONE AFTERNOON, LATE in January 2016, when Yasmin returned home from one of her money-seeking trips, Hera pulled out a marriage certificate with her photo stuck next to Wasim, from the lane next to theirs. Mountains rose from his doorstep, and their rubble formed its floor. Wasim had liked Hera since they were at school, but she had seemed out of his reach. He had dropped out in middle school while she went to high school. He picked trash; she wanted to be a teacher. He seemed destined for a life on the mountains and she for one away from them. Then, the mountains had tugged her back. He heard she lived inside a padlocked house, flashing her anger to keep creditors away while her friends had married. During one of Yasmin's long absences, they had gone to the municipal ward office close by and got the marriage certificate.

Both mothers feared the scandal the clandestine marriage would evoke and hastily planned a small wedding party. When Moharram Ali heard, he called Yasmin and said he wanted to attend—although he had no money to give. Hera refused. She could not bear to have him watch her finally bind herself to the mountains she had nearly left.

She wore the simple red dress that made up her whole trousseau. Wasim's family walked over to Yasmin's house, as the early winter dusk fell over the mountains and their lanes. A priest came for the ceremony, followed by a small party. The women chatted inside the house and Sharib served snacks to the small group of men spilling into the dimly lit lane outside. As he turned back, Sharib thought he saw Moharram Ali's hazy figure at the edge of the group. Sharib went in and asked Yasmin what he was doing there. Hera heard them and kept up her smile. When Sharib came out to serve soft drinks, his father had vanished.

As night fell, Hera walked over to Wasim's house, taking a disappointment that would settle within her. Her plans had joined the many dashed dreams that filled the mountains' shadow that winter: shaking off the curse, both the city's trash and their fortunes had proven too hard.

EIGHT

THREE NIGHTS AFTER HERA'S wedding, in the early hours of January 28, 2016, Hyder Ali awoke in his bed before dawn. His chest burned. He rubbed his eyes, opening them sleepily, seeing a haze. He shut them and tried again. A pale mist floated in the dark.

He slung a shirt over his favorite blue check lungi and woke up the children. He walked carefully into the small passage outside, letting out his goats and chickens, hoping it would quell their racket. Hyder Ali and Alamgir stepped out into their slim lane, filling with smoke, swelling and floating ahead, taking their long-forgotten township into the city.

Hyder Ali cursed the new migrants who filled Banjara Galli these days. One of their workshops must have exploded, he mumbled. They stumbled through their lane, bumping into hazy figures of neighbors, to reach the mountains' edge, filled with light. Flares lit up the night sky. Fires raged on the mountains as far as they could see, smoke spiraling above. There was not an inch of the mountains that was not burning, Alamgir remembered thinking.

Jehangir, who was already there, told them he had seen the fires simmering since the afternoon. Watching them grow into the night, he, Alamgir, and the others were not sure who to call. Tatva was in the middle of its long departure from the mountains. Its contract was to end in three days. The pickers couldn't find the guards.

From the crowds gathered at the edges of the mountains, Alamgir heard the fires had started at the far edge of the township, on the eighth mountain, which was mostly in the Khans' control. The creek curved around it, but winds were howling in from the sea that night, and the fires traveled with them. By 3 A.M., when Alamgir and Hyder Ali arrived, the fires blazed through much of the township.

Alerted, municipal officials spoke to Tatva officials, who told them their staff was working to douse the fires with the bulldozers and earth-movers they had on hand. But as the night stretched on, they could only watch as the fires grew and traveled deeper into the hills. Hoping to take decisive action, the municipal officials on night duty wrote a memo to their counterparts at Tatva, asking for fire engines. But with smoke filling the cloudless sky, cell phones became unreachable, officials were not sure where Tatva's staffers were on the grounds and the memo was never delivered, they would later tell their superiors.

Ahead of the watching pickers, an impenetrable wall of smoke built and rose. As the sky turned flame and then blush, officers began calling their bosses in the municipal corporation's solid waste management department and asked for water tankers and fire engines. The fire engines entered the township's fog around 7:10 A.M., winding slowly through flaming trash hills. Garbage trucks, blinded by smoke and stuck in trash strewn on the dirt tracks, blocked their way. Firemen saw pickers work amid the wafting mist and heard dogs whining within it.

The firemen stepped out, uncoiled their hoses, and pointed them at the flames, but even before they turned on water sprays, the fires extinguished themselves. Others calmed under the hose rain, only to travel through secret passageways within hills, erupt magically on distant hilltops and travel farther through hills. The water they sprayed ran off slopes without cooling the blazing innards of the more than 120 feet high mountains. The firemen sprayed on, amid the rising flames and smoke, not knowing what else to do. High winds and smoke rising with it, firemen could barely see ahead, so that some of them became so ill they had to be taken to the hospital.

Through the windows of her fourth-floor classroom, Ashra watched the mountains blur to smoke that morning. Coughing fits had woken Yasmin before light, and she had tried to wake up Ashra. Half awake, Ashra said she was coming down with something. Her throat and eyes felt scratchy. She could not go to school. But Yasmin was irritable too, and Ashra caved in and went, tripping over garbage and goats in the foggy walk to school.

She walked up the stairs to her classroom, where the sea breeze was blowing the smoke in, clouding the shrunken communities below and filling the room with a sharp burning smell. Coughing and teary-eyed, the children were edgy from the screeching of fire engines below. Teachers wrapped up early, thinking they would make up the next day, when the fires quieted. Ashra was home again soon.

But smoke clouds were only traveling farther. Firemen had not found water storage tanks or water hydrants at the township. Instead, smoke and the nearly magical dance of flames that Prabhat Rahang-dale, Mumbai's fire chief, said landfill fires were known for the world over, were only swelling. Residents in the high-rise buildings that had edged closer to the mountains and nearly ringed them had felt the smoke burn in their chests, coughed through the night, and woken to see a gauzy veil floating around them. In their vertiginously high homes and offices, they felt dizzy for reasons that had nothing to do with height.

As the mountains drifted farther into the city, they arrived in places worlds away from Banjara Galli. From high up in their glass offices, Mumbaikars took pictures that captured the faint outlines of monolithic office towers suspended in woolly smoke. They posted the pictures on social media, adding captions wondering if they had woken up to a dystopian nightmare.

Television news headlines about the strange fog settling in the city were accompanied by NASA satellite pictures that showed a trail of dense, white smoke rising from the mountains, gusts from the creek carrying it deep into the slim, finger-shaped city, hiding it. After eleven decades hidden in plain sight, the Deonar mountains had returned to Mumbai, carrying glowing embers of every resident's life and memories.

The municipality had invested in new khaki and orange garbage pickup trucks, a few years before, to take away the trash that piled up outside the apartments Mumbaikars spent their lives working to buy, the cavernous offices they spent their workweeks looking out of, and the malls, multiplexes, and gyms they retreated to on weekends. Every day, the city was renewed, shedding its debris into the overfull, black plastic bags that lined street corners, and filled garbage trucks that ferried it quickly away to the Deonar mountains, where it accumulated silently. As dusk fell, city residents watched flames glow at Mumbai's far edge; the stench and smoke itched in their chests, running down their eyes as tears.

The next day, police filed a case against three young boys for lighting the fires. A woman had seen them running away from the blazes in the dark. The case was against Tatva too, for negligence. It would be rescinded, later, as mistakenly filed: the figures the woman had seen had been obscured by dark smoke, and she could not identify them.

The fires continued for days, unrelenting, turning into an embarrassment for the state government. On the streets and in the media, residents and opposition politicians protested its failure to douse them. The water that it was spraying on the undiminished fires took away from the city's drinking supply, they said, but the fires were only growing.

As the mountains' toxic cloud inflated over Mumbai, the city's air pollution measured 341 on India's newly launched Air Quality Index (AQI): the acceptable limit was 200. Around the mountains, it was higher. On the mountains, particles of burned garbage hung in the air, keeping the respiratory suspended particulate matter, the most harmful form of air pollution, at 192 micrograms, nearly twice the permissible level. Nitrogen oxide was 97 micrograms; it should have stayed below 80 micrograms. The smoke mingled with the sun's heat to create the growing smog, making breathing around the mountains hard and sapping already weak lungs. Mumbaikars should stay inside to avoid inhaling its air, they were advised, although that would hardly protect those in the lanes around the mountains. Doctors all over the city reported seeing patients with smoke-induced breathlessness, scratchy chests, coughing, giddiness, nausea, fever, and watery eyes.

THE CLOUD HUNG over the global investor conference, to begin two weeks later, from February 13, 2016, and was designed to be Mumbai's glittering showcase. City and state administrators had spent months cleaning and prettying the usually gritty city. Driving through Mumbai's gridlocked traffic, the slim road dividers had been filled with newly planted petunias, purple, pink, and white. They filled baskets that were strung from streetlights, and hung over the passing cars, swaying wildly in the same sea breeze that fanned the flames on the mountains. Oversized, electric versions of traditional Indian oil lamps appeared on traffic islands—they would light up to greet investors into the city.

Other slivers of open space filled up with larger-than-life lion cutouts. One was filled with colorful Lego blocks, another with rusty nuts and bolts, a third with twirly machine parts. Looking for lions became a pastime for commuters waiting for Mumbai's perpetually stationary traffic to move. A red one on a billboard perched high over one of the city's busiest intersections. They were all mid-stride: a lion on the move was the symbol of the Indian government's newly launched "Make in India" campaign. The national government, elected a little over a year earlier, hoped it would attract foreign investment in its struggling manufacturing sector.

Prime ministers and presidents of several countries and a galaxy of global corporate bosses were due to arrive in weeks. In the city's new business district, metallic screens in the style of Mughal-era *jaali*, or stone latticework, were welded together to make conference pavilions that would fill up with stalls showcasing how cutting-edge products could be made in the state. Traditionally, these lacy patterns were hand-carved into stone to let light and air pass through long, winding passages in medieval fortresses, letting sunlight stream in and casting filigreed shadows.

The prime minister, Narendra Modi, was to inaugurate the event. At the opening, a lion would appear on the giant television screen, and then leap to life onstage, like the country it represented. The hologram would stride through the auditorium, filled with international investors, a symbol of the global economic powerhouse awakening.

Instead, the garbage mountains and their smoke seeped in through the metallic screens, casting their fetid shadow in the half-made pavilions, just weeks before the conference. It was as if a primitive and discarded city drifted through the new, dogging the steps of the striding lion. The organizers worried about how they would sell the promise of new things amid the burning detritus of the old, and whether guests would pull out because of the toxic air quality.

AS THE DAYS went by, the smoke cloud seemed to cover much of the city except the mountains' shadow. Hyder Ali sat at his doorstep, chatting with friends. He had seen fires since he started working on the mountains, nearly two decades ago. This was not new, he said. He had even sprinkled silver powder to quell them.

Farzana was at a friend's place, he told them, airily. It's what she did these days, he added, going on about the fires he had seen. At that moment Farzana came walking home, a bag full of garbage in hand. Farha trailed behind. She must have made it to the mountains he said, looking unsurprised, lurching up to see what she had. She opened her bag to show him the still-warm, mangled metal she had collected.

He and his friends went back to looking at the pictures of fires in the papers. "*Ye to kahin bhi liya rahega,*" Hyder Ali said. *These photographs could have been taken anywhere.* Another picker who had dropped in to chat pointed out that fires burned on the mountains all the time, that these had only made it to the news because sea breezes carried the smoke into wealthy homes. Some of it was true. Some of it, Hyder Ali and his friends told themselves so they could keep working, or taking their children's earnings, collected from the burning mountains.

Farzana, Sahani, and the other children walked the mountains all day. "*Hawa jahaan daudti thi, vahaan dhuaan daudta tha, aur uske peeche peeche ham,*" Sahani said. *Where the wind blew, smoke followed, and we followed behind.* As Farzana walked up slopes, they sent heat shocks through her slippers. They crumbled under her feet. The smoke that rose from them burned in her eyes, throat, and chest. She took to wearing black lace-up shoes she found. She waved burlap to clear the air, so she could see the unrelenting garbage caravans that continued to arrive. She followed their approaching headlights, searching for a way through the growing fog. She trailed them as they got to the far end of the township, to empty on hills where fires had not yet reached.

Tatva's guards had left and policemen had come to support the firemen. They tried keeping pickers away from the burning slopes and unloading trucks, but the pickers, long-practiced, evaded them. When trucks emptied tightly packed plastic bags on warm slopes, dead fires erupted again on the hilltops.

Phugawalas, or Plastic People, such as Farzana, sifted through slopes with forks, trawling slowly for bits of the remaining plastic that had escaped the fire's heat. *"Itne tarah ka tha ki kuch na kuch to mil hi jata tha. Safed, kala, neela, paani,"* Farzana said, speaking of how she became one, years ago. *There were so many kinds that you always found something. White, black, blue, and water colored,* or transparent. But now it was all melting away, and instead the fires brought up metal, the most elusive and expensive of mountain finds.

She watched the Chumbakwalas, Magnet People, trace the slopes with magnets tied to sticks. This was their time and Farzana decided to join the Chumbakwalas. She bought magnets from the 90 Feet Road market, tied them on to long sticks that she waved over burning trash slopes. Bits of nails, coins, wire, and dismembered gadgets flew up through smoke and ash and stuck to her homemade metal detector. She prized the hot metal away with a thick, old scarf and stuffed it into her bag. Farzana bought water and vada pav from vendors who walked the slopes so she could stay out longer, tracing the mountains with her magnets all day. Did the flames and smoke scare her? No, she said. Did they make her sick? Why would it? she replied, not remembering how she coughed. She earned more than she had before the fires, she said.

The Chindiwalas, or Cloth Scrap People, whom Hyder Ali belonged to, were mostly out of work on the slopes. Instead, they collected scrap bundles from tailors in the city and sifted through them at home. Like them, Hyder Ali stayed home. Unlike them, he hardly worked, worry debilitating him.

From the mountaintops, Farzana watched the municipal and police convoys stream in. Tatva's contract had ended while the fires raged, and it had left the township, sending the municipality ₹36.19 crore in unpaid bills, the day the fires began. Municipal staff were returning to manage the mountains. From up high Farzana watched bulldozers demolish the homes and shops that crowded the mountain's entrance, so fire engines could enter more easily. She turned back down to wave her homemade metal detector over the mountains and fill bags with metal to sell.

The municipality had called experts and scientists who suggested a range of chemicals to be thrown over the burning township. But trash burned in layers buried far below the chemicals' reach. The fire department fielded frantic calls from residents of distant and varying neighborhoods every day, as the breezes blew the smoke in their direction, making them sick. Fire engines splashed water from new angles to change the direction of the smoke clouds that Farzana felt rose in shapes like people floating in the air.

Yasmin had not seen the smoke that rose on hills behind her house. She didn't think Ashra's wracking cough had anything to do with it. When he was home, Sharib sprawled facedown on the floor, turning just when he seemed to be asleep. The soles of his feet turned red, purple, and then puffy black from the burns accumulated on the slopes. Fluid oozed out of these blisters. Yasmin knew he could barely stand or walk. But when she nagged, he would lift himself up and limp out of the door to work, blister fluid sticking on his slippers. In the last few months, Yasmin had become caught in a tangled mess of debt and despair. Sharib provided their only steady income, even if it was meager. She could not let a fire disrupt it. So, Yasmin warmed castor oil and rubbed it on his soles or applied potions whose recipes were passed around their lanes, at night. It was all he needed, she said.

"*Uparwale ne mere bachon ko bahut taakat di hai,*" she said, when asked if the fires had caused the wracking coughs in her home. *God made my children very strong.* At first, she had procured for Ashra cough syrup that doctors prescribed. But when Ashra began running through bottles without getting better, Yasmin stopped buying them. It only drained her household budget. She didn't see the fires. She didn't feel them. Others in their lane, too, worked so hard through the fog, they didn't see it at all. They did not feel it burn in them.

Desperate, municipal and fire officials hitched water hoses onto the forklifts, which usually shoveled mud and garbage, to extend their reach deeper through the fog, to the burning hills. Alamgir and other pickers sat atop the swinging forklifts as they drove into blinding smoke, directing drivers deeper into glowing mountain recesses. They would jump off just as the forklifts dived in, shoveling aside trash to unearth blazes, burning deep within. Water tankers moved in to spray water and coolant to douse these fires. Then the forklifts blanketed the uncovered fires with gravel and debris from unburned hills. Alamgir said that the forklifts he was on were a little above the toxic smoke clouds, rather than within them.

AVIATION AUTHORITIES WORRIED that the smoke would prevent planes coming into land at Mumbai Airport. Then, on February 5, little over a week before the Make in India conference, the fires were doused and the smoke began retreating from the city. After Prime Minister Narendra Modi inaugurated the conference, Maharashtra's chief minister, Devendra Fadnavis, made a pitch for the state as the most developed, industrialized, and investor-friendly one in the country.

Thousands of foreign investors and Indian business heads drove through the lacy pavilions in golf carts, exploring investment opportunities. India was one of the world's greatest consumer markets, officials told them. Months before the conference, $5 billion had been committed to making iPhones in the state, as India was soon to have the world's second-largest number of cell phone users. Cool February evenings were filled with Bollywood galas on Mumbai's beaches, walks through its colonial-era naval dockyard, lit with fairy lights, and fashion shows that showcased the state's handwoven textiles.

Hyder Ali spent his days after the fires sitting outside his house, chatting with the friends still left in the lane. Some pickers had moved out to the homes of friends or relatives outside the city, to exorcise the smoke that itched in them, fogged their minds, and trickled down from their eyes as tears. Others ran through expensive medicines that did not soothe their burning chests.

Although Hyder Ali would not admit it, the fires were unlike any he had seen before. The city's discarded desires had burned like the fires in hell that clerics had told him about. Jinns and Shaitans arose from them, they had told him. In the evenings, he waited for Farzana, and the other children, to return with warm trash and new stories that swirled about the mountains.

He heard that they would be shut down forever now, that cameras, like blinking, black eyes, would hover over their peaks and that the garbage would be dumped outside the city. Some of the stories he heard were true and others were hazy as the smoke that floated above him in those days. Within weeks, he turned bonier, his eyes sank deeper into his face, and his hair turned gray and then startlingly orange. He had applied cheap, chemical-infused henna to hide his sudden crop of grays.

NINE

T**HE FIRES HAD RELENTED** just enough for the conference to get underway, but within days, the distant, simmering hills erupted again. Flames spread across five acres near the creek, which the fire engines struggled to reach. Engineers at Deonar's municipal office looked up with dread as the night sky glowed amber. Then, surprisingly for a February night, it rained, spoiling outdoor events at the conference that evening and soaking into submission the fires that could have raged for days.

Weeks before the fires first broke out, and officials, politicians, television, and camera crews came to swarm the mountains, the diminutive and graying Raj Kumar Sharma had walked around the township's broken wall in his puffy, high-waist pants, with a camera slung around his neck. He had slipped through its gaps to photograph the mountains, filled with wastepickers and nearly emptied of security guards. He took pictures of the municipality's security cameras that did not work and was captured on the gangs' cameras that did. He photographed the empty guard posts taken over by drug addicts, assiduously cataloging the township's brokenness. He had gotten a lawyer to present his photographs with a petition in court to show that its orders to mend the mountains had not reached them and to ask that the court to reopen the case to fix them.

Sharma had lived in an airy, terraced apartment, minutes from Deonar's trash township, since his childhood, in the 1950s. It was in a leafy lane in Chembur, a neighborhood with a gentle, fraying charm. Down the street was RK Studios, where some of the Hindi film industry's greatest dreams had been made. Sharma's home had once belonged to Lalita Pawar, one of RK's favorite vamps. She was best known for having a glass eye and tough demeanor that occasionally yielded to reveal a golden heart.

Sharma's family had rented the house and when her movie career waned, the trips to RK Studios fading away, they had bought it from her. The Chembur, in Sharma's childhood memories, was full of fruit orchards and picnics sprinkled with the stars. He had heard and smelled the open-topped *cuchra* trains pass by, at night, to reach the Deonar township. He had watched the mountains grow precipitously, and now, graying, was full of ingenious ideas to mend them, to address the municipality's disregard for them. He walked the mountains and traveled the country in search of solutions and returned to push them with the municipality and in court.

His photographs and petition to restart the closed case on fixing the mountains and processing the city's waste arrived at the desks of Justices Abhay Oka and C. V. Bhadang, of the Bombay High Court. Along with fires and the news headlines that followed, it had forced them to reopen the case. In Justice Oka's outsized, wood beamed courtroom, along the court's angular and winding ground floor corridor, Sharma asked to set a new date to close the mountains. The municipality's lawyer argued to keep the Deonar township going for a little longer. Restricting garbage flows, as Sharma had asked for, would mean trash hills being built in the city, sickening residents, he said.

Oka was the fourth most senior of the court's seventy judges. He had shiny black hair, neatly pressed down in a side parting, a toothbrush mustache, and a commanding presence in his stately and always-packed courtroom. He often heard more than sixty cases a day, with a break for lunch, a rate of work that meant he could cut through the obfuscation lawyers indulged in to buy time and avoid commitment. An impish smile often played under his mustache, as he perched his face on his palm and asked lawyers to turn to page numbers and paragraph numbers, in their written petitions, that contradicted their own arguments. That afternoon, Oka bore down on the municipality's lawyer.

He pointed out that the municipality could not start redirecting its garbage caravans, across the creek, to the village of Karvale in Navi Mumbai that had been selected nearly a decade ago for a modern landfill to replace the Deonar township. It turned out the land was dotted with private homes and tribal settlements. Their owners had resisted selling and moving out. They had attacked municipal officers when they went to measure the land to settle a purchase price. Even when officers returned with police protection, they had not been able to survey the sprawling plot. The municipality had to keep the Deonar township going a little longer, its lawyer said.

In the busy courtroom, Oka's impatience was palpable. He confronted the municipality's lawyer with the more than a decade-and-a-half-long failure to meet regulations and previous court orders. Oka reminded him that the municipality had a legal obligation to manage its waste responsibly. In the orders he later passed, Oka noted caustically that the rules "are being observed only in breach." It all made the dumping of garbage at Deonar illegal, Oka said.

From Sharma's petition, Oka drew out the lawless bubble that had grown on the mountains for display in the courtroom. When the fires erupted, there were too few cameras installed and none of them worked.

The boundary wall was broken, the township carved up by gangs. Security guards were nowhere to be found on the site. The mountains burned even as lawyers argued, Oka pointed out. He seemed incredulous when the municipality's lawyer suggested that the city's waste could fill Deonar's rising hills for longer. How could the city's shadow have space when Mumbai was sprawling out and growing upward, Oka's look suggested.

On February 29, 2016, Oka passed orders saying the municipality had allowed reckless construction and development in Mumbai, without thinking of its mounting flow of trash and the reeking township it emptied into. In fueling the growth of the city and its township of trash, the municipality had violated its residents' right to life, protected by the constitution, which included the right to live in a pollution-free environment, Oka wrote. He stopped fresh construction until the municipality came up with a plan to manage its waste and shut the Deonar mountains down, although the tearing down and rebuilding of old buildings, which made for most construction in the space-starved city anyway, could continue.

Oka set a deadline of June 30, 2017, a year and a half later, to stop dumping garbage at Deonar. He set up a committee, made up of a former administrator, a police officer, two environmental scientists, and Sharma, to ensure his orders reached the mountains. A new committee to oversee the municipality of castaway belongings.

ON THE MOUNTAINS, pickers had heard there was a court case to stop growing the constantly filling trash mountains. But they had only seen the mountains grow, their lives and work stretching on in the face of delays. In a city where wealth and aspiration were reflected in dizzying real estate growth and its greatest fortunes were made through its skyscrapers, stopping fresh construction would send tremors. The court order had finally brought the mountains into the city, connecting residents and their detritus with the distant mountains that had exploded in flames and smoke.

On March 20, 2016, the mountains were bathed in the glow of fires that belched dense smoke into the city once again. Flames traveled across hills and the city woke up to the now familiar smoke and sharp smell of burning from Deonar. A television news channel's headline described it as a "smog shroud" that had fallen over the city again. In the mountains' shadow, doctors struggled to cope with snaking lines of breathless patients, to find ventilators for their sickest patients. They tried to revive a breathless baby who, newspapers later reported, died.

While fire engines tried to subdue the fires, schools around the mountains, which had remained closed for more than a week in January, closed again. At others, farther away, students were not allowed to play in the playground or were asked to wear face masks, flimsy shields between them and Mumbai's deadly air.

This time, tired authorities were full of conspiracy theories. Such raging and uncontrolled fires could not possibly be accidental, they said. Maharashtra's environment minister blamed his alliance partner in the government and thought it suspicious that the fires had first erupted days before Tatva's waste processing contract had ended prematurely. Much of what Justice Oka's judgment identified as the municipality's failings, its officials thought should have been laid at Tatva's doorstep. After all, it had managed the mountains when the fires broke out.

WITH THE FIRES still continuing, Vitabai Kamble heard Prakash Javadekar, India's environment minister was coming to their township. She took Nagesh, her oldest son, and walked toward the municipal office to meet him, following Nagesh's large gray curls to the front of the waiting crowd.

The midday sun warming her head, her life on the forgotten mountains played in Vitabai's mind. She wanted to tell Javadekar about it.

She thought of her fading scars, of how, at first, mountain smells had made her stomach churn even after eating four vada pavs. She thought of how Nagesh, the skinny ten-year-old who began trailing behind her on the slopes, had turned shapeless and gray on them. Her friend Salma Shaikh had brought her son, Aslam, to the mountains as a toddler and her younger son, Rafique, as a hundred-day-old baby, strapped to her back with a saree, after her husband died. Salma kept them in a shelter she made with dried leaves that fell from trucks. While she worked, Aslam had wobbled out of the shed, picked trash, and grown to middle age on the slopes too.

Vitabai wanted to tell Javadekar that the pickers had made a life on the mountains. They could not have burned them, as the news swirling around them suggested. She knew traders' lackeys burned nightly fires on the mountains to unearth metal. *"Ani amcha maran"*—*and we are to die*—she said, speaking of the blame that fell on hapless pickers. She wanted to tell him that as one of the mountains' oldest inhabitants, she had picked up after the city for decades. She dreamed of having an official job doing it, a municipal identity card that would turn their secret army into legitimate workers. The card would make officials leave wastepickers such as herself alone, instead of threatening them, asking for bribes or detaining them for being trespassers.

The long convoy arrived and Nagesh nudged his mother to stay close to it. The crowd jostled restlessly outside. The strong burning smell and fear of new eruptions hung thick in the air. Vitabai and Nagesh waited in the hot sun until the official cars drove away. No one stepped out of the vehicles. The pickers returned home dispirited. In Delhi, Javadekar told reporters the fires revealed the contractors' carelessness; a team of environment ministry officials had visited Deonar and would investigate what had happened.

Weeks later, Farzana was bent over her metal detector when the police lined the mountains again. She heard Rahul Gandhi, an opposition politician, was coming. She and Sahani followed the pickers to the municipal office. Gandhi, dressed in white, looking pink and flushed amid pickers' tanned bodies and muddy clothes, walked the trash hills. Farzana did not know that the photos would be printed on posters that were later plastered all over the city to showcase the opposition run state government and municipality's failings.

At the same time, pickers from their lanes were getting picked up for questioning, and some were arrested. There were no cameras on the mountains. To penetrate the mountains' fog, police relied on rounding up pickers to interrogate them about the fires and the dark world of the mountains. They asked about suspicious happenings in the days leading up to the fires. The mountains and their inhabitants, which had grown for so long in a bubble of secrecy, were suddenly visible, their bubble stretching thin, threatening to pop.

TEN

OGETHER, OKA'S ORDER AND the endless fires had diverted most garbage caravans, after February 2016, to the grounds at Mulund and the new hills at Kanjurmarg, where trash hills were to be dehydrated until they turned to compost. Farzana and her sisters did what they had always done when trucks dwindled: they walked to what they heard was Atique Khan's estate. They reminded the lackeys who guarded the estate they were Jehangir's sisters and slipped in to fill up on what they called *ganda maal*. Dirty stuff.

They tied handkerchiefs around their faces to keep away the rising smell of boiled flesh and sifted aside disembodied limbs and gangrenous fingers. They collected freshly steamed syringes, their backs cut off, so they could not be refilled; saline bags; water bottles; and long bloodied swabs of gauze and cotton. For every three filled bags they handed over to the lackeys, they could keep the fourth for themselves. Farzana filled frantically, hardly feeling unknown blood stain her, syringes poke her, and broken glass bottles cut her. Syringes jabbed them a lot, Sahani later

explained, but they tied something around their wounds and kept working, not feeling the pain. It was the only thing better than picking from
the municipality's garbage caravans.

Bags filled, the sisters walked back home, the smell of people's steamed
remains clinging to them. The smell stayed stubbornly on them, even after
they washed. "*Koi hadsa dekha to man mein reh jaata hai*," Sahani would
say. *All we see lingers in us.* They would never return, the sisters decided,
as they had for years. But in a few weeks, they would be back, as they
always had. Garbage trucks were dwindling.

I'LL ACT LIKE *I beat you and you act like you cried*: the old Marathi idiom
explained the official shadow play that had let the city's detritus acquire
its dark afterlife at Deonar, one official had said. Its contract reportedly
said Tatva was to make the boundary wall and fix the breaks in it that
had created an estate within the township, where nightly convoys brought
the remains of buildings to make debris hills, said to be Rafique Khan's.
A municipal letter to Tatva said it would fix the break in the wall itself,
while police settled a booth across it. For years, the booth had stayed
unmanned, the wall broken, convoys streaming in while the Khan brothers and their rivals were said to have amassed dead buildings, dead people,
leftover hotel food. As the city's water lines, power lines, and sewers
stopped before their stretching lanes, pickers had little choice but to cling
to the gangs' largesse. It nearly strangled them. But now, as the fires lit up
the forgotten trash township and the shadowy, private estates within it,
the municipality and police had to reel it in. The mountains began moving
from under the feet of its illicit and invisible residents.

Manoj Lohiya, a police officer who had been tasked with bringing
this secret world out into the open by the police commissioner, gave an
interim and then final report saying the failure of the plant meant
methane stayed trapped within the mountains and seeped through them,

hanging in mountain air. That night in January 2016, fires had begun at the far edge (in what was said to be Khans' territory), sea winds had howled, swelling the flames, taking them deeper within trash hills and into the sky until they were out of control, Lohiya said. The delay in the fire engines' arrival had taken the fires farther into the city.

As they started building a case against the Khans, police began walking the slopes, discovering the world Farzana had always lived in. They saw cameras and lights surround hills staked out by gangs, as Sharma the petitioner in court had. Getting caught in their gaze brought out lackeys to defend their turf, unlike the municipal cameras that once installed, did not work.

The sprawling, private estate of medical waste within the township was settled not long after the municipality had cut out a far corner of the township to make its medical waste incinerator in 2007. While municipal trucks made the rounds of city hospitals, bringing their waste to the incinerator, Atique Khan bought a small pickup truck. It was said to make trips to the city's largest private hospitals, unofficially redirecting it to this estate, where pickers sorted it and lackeys resold it. Farzana had learned the names of some of the city's best hospitals from the drivers of trucks that veered away from her on hill clearings to this estate. It was not trash meant to be strewn on hills for pickers. And yet, for Farzana, it was too good to leave: thick plastic from saline bags, medicine bags, and glass containers that sold well. She had followed these trucks to the edge of this territory, pleading for entry. But that summer, as police began walking the slopes, fewer trucks came to this estate. What made it to the incinerator blew toxic clouds into the air that the pickers barely noticed.

Police discovered that the clashes for dead possessions had led to gangs lighting fires in rivals' territories at night, burning away other traders' fortunes. A rival gang boss had written letters to the state's chief minister, police commissioner, and others referring to the Khans as Matti

Mafia, or Mud Mafia. The Khans accused him of grabbing a part of the township. Farzana's Banjara Galli formed the overlap between two of the area's fiercest gangs. Life on the mountains was controlled by the Khan brothers and life at home by their namesakes, Atique and Rafique Shaikh, also brothers.

The Khans provided satellite television in Baba Nagar, and minions who claimed to work for the Shaikhs collected power bills in Banjara Galli. Atique Shaikh's face was featured on police posters around their lanes, with a headline saying, "Wanted." Farzana's family, like most others, only used legal power to accumulate bills that made them exist in official records, which they hoped would help them show they were legal residents, eventually. They bought illegal power to keep costs low and the army that patrolled their lanes placated: any payment delays could lead to disconnection, threats, and abuse. Through Farzana's childhood, their lanes had been lit through pickers' ingenuity. But later these foot soldiers had come to patrol the lanes collecting payments, even though police busted their illegal network several times.

The Shaikhs, who had started out picking trash and grabbing pickers' garbage-made homes, had later retreated to build flourishing careers in business and politics. They were also charged with many crimes. Rafique's third wife, Noorjehan, was the area's corporator, an elected representative in the municipal corporation, allowing her to raise the area's concerns with officials. It was her responsibility to ask why trash in the lanes around the mountains was not cleared, speaking on behalf of the lanes near where the city dumped its own garbage, endlessly. At one of her campaign events, Rafique had brought a bottle of muddy tap water and emptied it to show area representatives and municipal officers that they were failing to provide drinkable water. It was through these shows of largesse from mountain bosses, trickles of sustenance from the municipality, and leftovers from gang wars that life came to Farzana's lanes. And it was in their tangles that it stayed stuck.

On the edges of the Shaikhs' territory, along 90 Feet Road, which Farzana's lanes nearly opened onto, the Khans' lackeys were said to collect fees for parking the pickup trucks, auto rickshaws, and taxis that pickers had saved up to buy, so they could build lives away from trash. Owners of these vehicles told officers they had been threatened, intimidated, beaten, or their vehicles impounded if they did not pay.

The police and municipality set out to reclaim this forgotten world, which had grown so tangled while they looked away. Mumbai's municipal commissioner had announced that the township of trash would become a prohibited zone: anyone, other than municipal staff, seen on the trash slopes could be a fire hazard and would be detained or fined. It threatened the fragile gray economy that had grown around the mountains and their bounty. New guards had replaced the ones Farzana knew, and there were more patrols on the mountains than she had ever seen before. Construction workers dotted the edges of foothills. Once again, they began fixing the mostly broken boundary wall and brought barbed wire rolls to top it.

Farzana heard of pickers being turned away from the mountains. She heard of friends getting into work before dawn to evade the guards and cameras that were to begin watching the hills. With the city's glare glinting through the mountains' halo, their world was beginning to spoil at the edges, crinkling their lives and shaking their futures. Farha waited for unguarded moments to get in and work. Hyder Ali perched himself on the ledge that jutted out from their wall, as he often spent his afternoons. He walked over to the mountains' edge sometimes, not picking trash but hoarding the stories that pickers carried with them when they returned, inhaling their worry, growing gaunt before his children's eyes.

ONE EVENING, WHEN Farzana returned home, she saw the wispy Salma Shaikh sitting outside the house, filling Hyder Ali in on the events of the day. Salma had draped her flowery orange saree around her shoulders, drooping as if weighed down by the mountains. As she got closer, Farzana saw Salma run her fingers around a plastic necklace, which she later heard was retrieved from a trash bag. It gave her an elegant, worn air. She heard Salma softly hurl the insults she had accumulated over four decades on the mountains at the new guards. Hyder Ali listened, looking bemused.

Arif, her fourteen-year-old grandson, had taken to working predawn to avoid the guards, she told them. He kept picking trash, one morning, as the sky turned from ink to rose to gold. Guards had come in to work and spotted him, half-filled bag of plastic bottles in hand. They chased him, waving their sticks frantically, Salma told them. Arif ran down as fast as he could, stumbling over the wobbly slopes, drained by the persistent cough and fever he had caught from his father, Aslam, who had tuberculosis. He struggled to stay ahead of the guards and their flailing sticks.

Then Arif felt a sharp and piercing pain in his foot. His knees buckled and he fell into the sun-dried trash. He turned his foot to see a rusting nail had pierced through his thin slippers and made a deep cut in his foot. Blood gushed onto warm, torn plastic bags and glinting tablet strips. Guards closed in on Arif as he slumped on the slope, in pain.

The guards let him go, with a warning never to set foot on the mountains again. Salma had taken Arif to get an anti-tetanus injection and get his foot wrapped in a gauze bandage to keep him limping. "*Beta kabr mein ek pair hila ke aaya,*" she told Hyder Ali, talking about Aslam. *My son already dangled one foot in the grave.* She had only Arif for help, now she was alone.

When her softly delivered invective abated, Hyder Ali suggested she get the nonprofit that gave them identity cards to complain about the guards who had chased Arif. What could they do if pickers kept sending their children to the slopes, Salma replied. The volunteers would ask if they had given birth to children only to send them here, she said. She knew she had to help Arif build a life away from the mountains but they were all she knew, the only thing she had passed on to her son and grandson.

The best mountain views shone in the elegant, bristling Salma's eyes. When the mountains' weight had pressed her down, put the grit in her soft voice, they had forgotten to take away the whispery softness, the lingering mischievousness that clung to her like the paper scraps that she sometimes picked.

She had tried to get Arif employed as a waiter or dishwasher, she told them. But his sickly face, chipped tooth, and bony frame made him look younger than his fourteen years. He got work only on days there was a big wedding and the caterer was so desperate for staff he could persuade himself that Arif, in his rumpled white shirt and frayed bow tie, looked eighteen. On most days, Salma admitted, Arif tried creeping back to work, before light, on the mountains, often getting beaten, getting warned, getting detained.

Another evening, Farzana found Hyder Ali, at their doorstep, talking to a newly married picker with a thin mustache. Early one morning he had gone to the mountains to relieve himself and looked up to find a black eye buzzing high over him, he told Hyder Ali. He had heard the television news crews that hung around mountain edges these days used small, flying cameras to bypass security and film the seething mountains. Pictures of him relieving himself would reach his newly acquired in-laws, back in his village, he told Hyder Ali. He had told them he worked in an office. They would see where and how he lived in Mumbai, on television news. He would crumble in their eyes, he fretted.

When he left, Hyder Ali went inside the house and put on the television set that he had bought at a *kata* shop, had repaired and perched high up on the wall. Farzana emptied her bag outside and heard Hyder Ali flick through channels, looking for news reports on the mountains, as she sorted through the day's pickings. Most talked of police reports that said pickers had lit the fires at night, at the behest of their bosses, the garbage traders. More *kata* shop owners and pickers were getting arrested. As Farzana emptied the bag she had brought back, sorting through syringes, saline bags, swab, and meal trays, she thought, she had to go back to the medical waste estate again.

ELEVEN

THROUGH APRIL 2016 THE township stayed warm, heat building from the seething fires and rapidly warming summer. Fire engines, forklifts, and the assistants who hung off them dotted the slopes. Municipal officials and assorted consultants worked on the mountains, police filled the lanes around them. Everyone was here to fix the mountains' seething mess, which had suddenly and unexpectedly frozen the endlessly inching-upward city. The pickers' subterranean world had been discovered and they were being evicted.

Salma had been in and out of the hospital through the fires. *Ghabrahat*, or mortal fear, was the only way she could describe the range of symptoms that paralyzed her, none of which were directly related to air quality. Her blood pressure had shot up. She had visited doctors and swallowed medicines secretly, so she didn't alarm the already sick Aslam and Arif. The week she felt better, fires had erupted again. Salma's blood pressure increased so much, a blood vessel had burst in her eye. Everything had blurred. The world looked different. She needed surgery to fix it, a procedure she would later remember as cataract surgery.

As the summer warmed, the mountains began to shrink. Mumbai's sultry, humid heat sucked out any moisture left within, deflating them. Madan Yavalkar, a municipal engineer who had managed the mountains for years, and knew them better than most, had described the mountains' seasonal inhalation and exhalation in the municipality's fire inquiry report, in Marathi. "At the height of the monsoon's fury, when rain waters seep into the mountains, they expand and when the burning summer sun draws out the moisture, they contract." Pickers' luck too was deflating with the mountains.

More and more often the guards turned Farzana back from the slopes. When she sneaked in, she saw the township emptied of garbage trucks as she never had before. She spent boiling, windless afternoons waiting for them at mountain clearings. The relentless flow of trash gushing onto hilltops, tumbling down slopes, tangling into mangroves, and flowing into the creek, the endless torrent of castaway possessions that Farzana had always seen, had slowed to a trickle. In just a few months, the amount of garbage dumped on the mountains had dropped by more than a third. Until Deonar's hills cooled and consultants drew up a plan to fix them, the caravans would move mostly to the municipality's smaller garbage mountains at Mulund and the new ones, rising at Kanjurmarg.

Farzana usually worked with Farah, who chatted and joshed around to fill the unending afternoons, the sun warming their heads and the steaming mountains, their feet. Days stretched thinner when she waited with Jehana, her reedy oldest sister, who lived in a tin-sheet room sprouting from the boundary wall, with her husband and six children. The two watched slopes stir in the smoke tendrils that still rose from the trash. In the midst of long silences, they waited for the breeze, or a glimpse of trucks winding through the bumpy roads below.

Seeing a truck emerge from the hills propelled them to their feet, sprinting to the clearing it would empty at. Other pickers swooped in from the silent hills, falling on the trash with the day's pent-up energy. These short bursts of scrambles for garbage were fierce and desperate. But sometimes Farzana found herself on newly empty and uncontested clearings, once the territory of gangs. The growing police glare had shaken the brothers' grip on the mountains. Trash that had only emptied in their estates began appearing elsewhere in the township.

Shoveling around with her long fork threw up used bloodied hospital gloves, or hands, as Farzana called them. It was the only one of the mountains' handouts she could not bear to see or touch. Looking at the stiff, white, blood-stained fingers made her stomach churn. She turned her face away, glancing back from the corner of her eye to hook them onto her long garbage fork before scooping them into her bag. She picked empty saline bags, tubes, medicine bottles, and packaging. Finding thick, hospital plastic made up for the days when guards turned her away.

IT WAS DURING these burning months that Farzana and Farha chased a truck carrying hospital waste to the prawn loop on a slow afternoon. It was then that Farzana reached into a bag that she thought was full of little glass vials, but brought out the glass jar filled with the three lifeless babies, joined at the stomach, joined in their flickering lives and joined in death. After she had buried them in the soft sand at the edge of the township, in the evening, Jehangir had slapped Farzana when he heard what she had done. "*Padne ka hi nahi yeh sab mach mach mein. Kuch achha nahi hota is sab se.*" *You should not get drawn into such messes. Nothing good comes out of them.* "Why do they give birth to them," Sahani had asked, "if they want to send them here?"

Things were going to get better, Farzana wanted to tell Jehangir. The fires that had raged all that year were receding. Her birthday, on June 2, would bring the rains and keep the mountains soaking and cool. She would turn eighteen, an adult, who Jehangir could not slap, Farzana thought, wiping away tears. Adulthood was close, and Farzana kept slinking through the closing wall to work. She needed to save up, buy herself jeans, and have a party to mark her transition. But as the summer wore on, sometimes guards threw Farzana's carefully filled trash bags under the buzzing bulldozers and sent her home. She watched pickers get beaten if they lingered on.

Wilting under the tightened security, the older pickers tried a new strategy: making themselves visible. In her lane, Farzana saw posters and banners strung up for protest marches in the city. Pickers wanted to work on, they wanted identity cards to make them officially exist. Weeks after the environment ministry team visited but didn't meet Vitabai, it seemed to have heard her. The government brought out new waste rules that said pickers were to be involved in sorting the city's trash. But while Vitabai and Salma were to become legal wastepickers and sorters, they did not know it. The rules did not reach the township, and the guards still shut them out. Increasingly pushed out of the mountains and their livelihoods, they still struggled to emerge from their hilly netherworld, now spoiling under the sudden heat.

Vitabai took several long bus rides into the city for protests. She heard of one where pickers met Maharashtra's youthful chief minister, Devendra Fadnavis. If she had made it with them, Vitabai had wanted to tell him how she had joined thousands of mountain denizens who had moved here to make way for the city's dreams. That if it was not for her invisible army, the mountains would have been even taller. That all she wanted was for the city to employ her to sort through and clean its remains. At the township, more guards swarmed. Vitabai felt the tenuous life she had built on trash slopes, crumbling.

One afternoon, she emptied her bag in the lane, while Salma watched and chatted with her. She separated takeaway food boxes, plastic-coated wires to be scraped away with a knife, and picked out a metal ring, topped with a tortoise. Vitabai knew that wearing mountain finds could bring her ill luck. But she had heard people in the city wore tortoise jewelry, as a prescription for good fortune, and occasionally it found its way into the trash. She fiddled with the ring, unsure of what would work, weighing the luck of the tortoise against the danger of finding it on the slopes. She slipped it on. *"Marna to hai hi ek din,"* Salma said with a shrug. *"Pehen ke marein."* We are going to die someday. Better to die wearing what we like.

Stuck outside the wall, with mountain luck teetering and ebbing, Vitabai made rounds of friends' homes asking for numbers of wealthy people who needed help cleaning their homes. She hoarded them, just as she had once collected the phone numbers of truck drivers who sold first dibs on their garbage. She took more long bus rides into the city, filling in for friends who needed a day off from cleaning jobs, hoping it would lead to more lasting work.

Meanwhile, Salma's blood pressure was still raging. She worked when she could, and at other times, she sat crumpled against the wall in her other son's house, where she had moved so Aslam and Arif didn't have to support her. Mostly, she stayed stuck, waiting, outside the mountain wall.

Grounded by the fires, guards, and everything seeming hazy, she agonized over how she could make a fresh start, away from her century-old benefactor. She thought of taking the four-hour train ride to Surat, buying sarees from its famed wholesale textile market, and selling it door-to-door, in their lanes. But she had seen Vitabai's son Nagesh, and others, bring back bags of sarees that they couldn't sell, because no one in the lanes had enough money to buy them. Nagesh defaulted on loan repayments, as did others. He was not seen around Banjara Galli or the slopes. His phone was switched off. Vitabai told creditors and others, he had moved to the village. But neighbors felt they saw him at night.

"Sabko paisa dena hai to aur kya karega?" Salma snorted about Gypsy Lane's disappearing residents. *When you owe everyone money, what else*

would you do? Years of picking trash meant the delicate skills, of embroidery or tailoring, that some of her newer neighbors practiced had bypassed Salma's bruised hands. Their lives braided into the mountains over four decades, she and Vitabai had nowhere to go, knew nothing other than collecting trash. Edgily, Salma waited for her blood pressure and the security to ease so she could return to them.

SALMA HAD WORKED mostly alone for more than a year since Aslam's cough began wracking their home through the night. After he ran through bottles of cough syrup, Salma had taken him to a free, charitable hospital deep into the city, where she had heard pickers took their persistent coughs. She had returned to work, freeing Aslam to take the hour-long bus rides into the city's crumbling and congested old quarter. He waited irritably for doctors to see him while horns blared from the street outside and the flyover that ran above it.

Bargain hunters filled the streets behind the hospital. Together, the maze of lanes was known as Chor Bazaar, or Thieves Market. When Mumbai's grand, old homes were dismantled, the good stuff came here, and the rest went to Deonar. Frayed family photographs, oversized chandeliers, hand-painted Bollywood posters, rusty airplane models, and broken irons lay under jumbled piles and layers of dust. Wealthier shoppers came in search of hidden gems amid household junk as Salma did at Deonar. New things were added. They were scraped to look old and old things polished to look new. They were laid out together to earn shop owners the small fortunes that Salma and Aslam could only imagine earning on mountain trash. Pickers sometimes washed and patched up pants they found in the trash to sell there.

Salma had returned home after long days on the slopes, to find Aslam slumped against the wall, the bright blue t-shirt he often wore hanging more loosely over his shrunken frame each day. A shadow had come over him. He walked little and shaved infrequently. His cough echoed in the skinny Arif. With Arif, Salma tried dragging back trash-filled bags that nearly outsized them. A bag, filled with plastic bottles, that matched Salma in size would fetch ₹50. She needed several of them to buy Aslam's medicines and keep their family of eight, with Aslam's wife, three more boys and a little girl, going. She kept Arif working, hoping it wasn't too late to treat his cough and worrying that it was. She didn't know that Aslam had stopped taking his medicines or making the trips to the faraway, free hospital.

A flower trader had asked Salma to help with the impending gush in demand during Ramzan, asking her to string the fresh flowers he bought from Mumbai's wholesale flower market, so he could sell them in the city. One afternoon, Salma rested her back against trunks piled up with the family's belongings and sat between heaps of sweet-smelling tuberoses, roses, and jasmines in their long, dimly lit room. She bent forward to catch the sun and thread her needle. Amid jabbed fingers and perfumed hands, she learned to braid the flowers in intricate patterns. She made flower blankets that were laid out in the city's filigreed mausoleums to make wishes come true. She made garlands that brides and grooms hung shyly around each other when they got married and wreaths that were laid at the feet of the dead. Most of all, she made flower braids that adorned women's hair, masking the smells of cooking, or the fish they sold, enveloping them in the heady, aphrodisiacal fragrance of jasmines instead.

Aslam sat next to her, tiny crystals making shining reflections on his gaunt face: he was sticking them onto a peach-colored skirt in long paisley patterns. It would later be stitched into a bridal outfit and hang in Mumbai's markets. Salma and he would each earn ₹30 for their work, just about enough to afford a thinly stretched meal for everyone. They had begun getting Aslam treated for his tuberculosis at the government-run Gokuldas Tejpal hospital in the city. That afternoon, he played outside the house with a Frisbee he had fashioned from an empty medicine carton.

Her little granddaughter flitted over Salma's flowers, asking for two rupees. "*Toffee lena hai,*" she said, blocking the sun as she bent over to catch Salma's attention. *I need to buy toffees.* Salma waved her away, trying to get the slight jasmine stems through her trembling needle.

The girl bent lower so Salma would look up at her. "*Ek jhaad lagaya hai,*" Salma said, pulling the thread out of her half-made flower braid. *I've planted a tree.* "It will grow money along with flowers," she continued. "I'll give you the money as soon as it flowers." Befuddled, the girl went out to play. The sun fell farther into the house, Salma slumped against the piled-up trunks and went back to braiding flowers.

Fridays were unfailingly busy for her. It was the day devotees visited the city's milky, marble mausoleums. Entreaties to the saints buried there rose through the crescendo of music and heaving crowds. Worshippers draped flower blankets over the tombs of the saints to propitiate them. They bent low over the tombs, swathed with brocade and flowers and wreathed in incense, and whispered their petitions, hoping the saints would hear and make them come true.

Salma could not afford bus rides into the city herself. She still believed her blankets could keep diseases away from her family and security guards, drones and cameras away from the mountains. Ramzan was not far and she hoped that through her blankets, her prayers would reach the miracle-inducing saints of Mumbai.

NO ONE WAS sure how Farzana made it to the mountains as often as she did. After the long waits for trucks she brought bags filled with plastic, wire, television sets that fetched the highest prices, squashed bottles that earned a little, and the wispy carrier bags that earned the least. But it was getting harder. Some days, she and Farha returned home with nothing, ate and clambered onto the long wooden planks tacked to the edges of their house and slept early, tired from the endless waiting.

One night, Farha woke up to the sound of Farzana muttering insults, her voice rising to threaten someone. In the dark, she called out to Farzana and asked who she spoke to, but Farzana went on. Farha called louder, waking Farzana, who muttered, confused, that she was not speaking to anyone. Both sisters drifted back to sleep. Farha reasoned that Farzana was seeing guards even in her dreams.

Around the end of April, Farzana and Sahani were walking up toward the seventh mountain after lunch, to collect plastic bottles. After a while, Farzana looked up for air. Tea vendors walked around them with kettles. The late summer sunset was at least an hour away. She looked downhill, where a crowd had gathered around the Khan brothers' warehouse. Policemen were bolting it shut. Others photographed the scene, or fixed barbed wire around the private suburb of hills within the municipality's township of trash.

For a few days, the army from these estates waved down trucks and directed them to different parts of the township. Farzana and Sahani decided they were changing tack to dodge the police. It was nearly a week before they heard that policemen had arrested the Khan brothers that afternoon, charging them under the stringent Maharashtra Control of Organized Crime Act (MCOCA), which allowed for long periods of imprisonment without bail. Later they would also arrest Javed Qureshi.

Jehangir was called for interrogation; others melted into the skinny lanes or returned to their villages to escape attention. Officers had shut all the private hill clearings in the township, including his own. He was in and out of the house, his restless energy turning nearly frenzied, as he met traders, offering his trash to anyone who might take it.

MUMBAI'S SUMMER STRETCHED ahead, moving slowly. Farzana worked with Farha on a mountain peak, on an afternoon suspended in the sun. They waited for the breeze and the garbage trucks to begin drifting their way. Their feet were clammy in the socks and lace-up shoes they wore to keep from the heat shocks the mountains still gave off.

Farzana was looking for glass to give Jehangir. It only made him rage at her. There was never enough to fill a truck and make the trips into the city to sell it, he told her. But, not knowing what else to do, Farzana and Farha tried collecting more. The two walked slowly, alongside each other, up a steep hill, until Farha tripped on a discarded shoe, jutting out of the mud, and fell backward on her bag.

Glass, boiling hot under the sun, cut through the material and made a long, serpentine cut on her back. Blood stained the shards within. She had screamed until Farzana called Alamgir to take their injured sister home. Neighbors had followed her howling progress to Hyder Ali's house. She would need stitches to repair her back, but Hyder Ali didn't even have enough money for the rickshaw trip to the hospital. He spilled the tobacco powder that he and Shakimun chewed, into Farha's cut. It burned in her back, intensifying her screams. "*Ye to door se chilla rahi thi,*" he said. *She's been yelling from miles away.*

As the cut on her back filled slowly, to make a dark, curling, tobacco-filled scar, Farzana and the others had taken to calling Farha "snake woman." They believed mountain luck had carved itself into her. It drew glass and other mountain treasures into Farha's hands, even amid the mountains' diminishing fortunes, tightening security and the city getting nearer. It would stay in her through the mountains' endless cycle of turning fortunes.

TWELVE

THROUGHOUT THE SUMMER OF 2016, Farzana and Farha watched the engineering consultants bore holes and lower tubes into the mountains to measure the fires seething within. They heard that some of the vents would stay within the mountains, to release these secret fires and their smoke. They also heard the consultants were mapping the township in order to pick a section for the waste-to-power plant. The map was carefully made with images from drones that had flown low over Farzana as she worked on the mountains that summer.

On a long, warm afternoon, Shakimun squatted next to Sahani, the second oldest of her daughters, at the mountains' rim. They watched as Farzana arrived with a cloth pile, leaving them to sort through some fashionably, and other irretrievably, ripped jeans while she turned to walk back up the slopes for more. Shakimun, sitting with her arms hanging off her bent knees, waited until Farzana had walked far enough out of earshot, then spoke softly to Sahani, in the lilting dialect she brought from her village, decades ago. *"Raat mein ajeeb harkatein karat hai."* *She says strange things at night.* Shakimun was worried: the mountains, with their chaos and poison, were bubbling out of her daughter in nocturnal mutterings and strange behavior. Farzana was born to the mountains. Their contours had shaped her, body and mind. But now she seemed trapped in them, and they were wedged inside her.

A neighbor had taken Farzana into the city for a trip along with her own children. She returned in the evening, swearing to Shakimun that she would never take her again. Farzana had felt faint and needed chips, but not the sweet ones they got. The salty ones were too salty. Without them, she was so drained of energy, she could not walk to get the bus back, leaving them all stranded for a while. She was always weak in those days, Sahani would remember. She always had a headache, a stomach-ache. Always.

At night, more of the family heard Farzana say things that when woken from sleep, she would insist she had not said. Mohammad Salahudin, who had lived a few houses farther down their lane, had recently moved away and often returned to Banjara Galli to wash away unintended traces of the mountains from within pickers with his prayers and rituals. He asked them to bring Farzana over. But just as Salahudin began chanting, Farzana got up and turned to leave. Sahani tried to hold on to her but Farzana was already out of the house. They looked out but could no longer see her. Hyder Ali pronounced that this was a *shaitani harkat*, the doing of the Shaitans that rose from the discarded desires and had burned on the mountains for months.

Hyder Ali tried taking Farzana back to Salahudin for the prayers, but she never sat through them. Later, he got Salahudin to pray over an amulet and got Shakimun to tie it around Farzana's arm. He hoped these portable prayers and the few fasts she would keep during the holy month of Ramzan would dislodge the Shaitan settled in her, perhaps a remnant of all that lay abandoned on the slopes. He asked Yasmeen, Alamgir's wife, to supplement these protections with her Koran reading lessons. In any case, he thought, as Farzana entered the marriage market, being able to recite a few verses would also improve her prospects of finding a husband.

Yasmeen made Farzana, Farha, and Jannat, the youngest of the sisters, sit in the mezzanine, cover their heads demurely, and face the buttery yellow Mecca mosque she had painted on the pink wall while she read a verse: *Do you not see how God drives the clouds, then joins them together, then piles them into layers and then you see the rain pour from their midst? He sends down from the skies mountainous masses of clouds charged with hail, and he makes it fall on whom He will and turns it away from whom He pleases. The flash of his lightning may well nigh take away the sight. God alternates the night and the day—truly, in this there is a lesson for men of insight.*

Yasmeen's baby son, Faizan, crawled out of Shakimun's arms and tried to get into hers. By the time she settled him, Farzana had slipped away. She just would not hold the Koran in her hands, Yasmeen recalled, frustrated. Teach those who want to be taught, Farzana countered: the class was meant for Farha, not her. Farha enjoyed the class, believing the verses washed over the burning mountains, rinsing away their smoke and the smell that had itched in her. Out in their lane, Farzana followed a trail of colored cloth scraps blowing down the slim passage with the dry summer breeze, taking slow, long steps, stamping them down, walking toward the mountains.

Sometimes she took a winding route so she could poke her head into Mohammad Khalil's cool, dark house. He was one of Sanjay Nagar's oldest residents and collected only cracked coconuts from the mountains. Hindu rituals hardly ever began, and new things were rarely used without breaking a coconut to bring good luck. As Mumbaikars bought more new things, more broken coconuts arrived at the mountains. Khalil often returned to Banjara Galli, in his torn vest, walking his bicycle, piled high with coconuts he had collected from wedding halls, car showrooms, new apartment complexes, and temples. Often, he pulled out his plastic-encased bank book, to show it was swollen with more savings than cracked coconut shells might be expected to yield. He would have a big wedding for his daughters, in his village, with his savings, Khalil would tell them. Relatives and friends there would not know his money had the smell of spent luck.

Khalil had made a makeshift, bamboo stick conveyor belt, curving around the edges of his room, filled with drying shells. He would also sell their velvety husks, to be made into matting. They filled his house with an intense, heady smell. Farzana would stand outside for a while, taking in the scent of drying coconuts, then wind her way to work.

ONE AFTERNOON, AS Farzana sat on a mountain peak with Farha, the beating sun kept her anger boiling. That morning, Hyder Ali had told her he had no money for her to bribe the guards to unsee them as she and her sister climbed over the wall. Farzana had left without breakfast, then waited for the guards on patrol to pass by to get through the wall and walk up the slopes, not eating lunch either.

Farzana and Farha saw two trucks emerge, following the winding, potholed mountain roads. As they turned to chase them, the trucks diverged to move toward different loops, turning the sisters in opposite directions. They argued over which one to follow, each worried they would miss the contents of the dwindling trucks that were gone in a flash these days. Farzana's anger, seething through the day, flashed, the sisters' voices rising as they saw other pickers emerge from hills and move toward the trucks.

But even as Farzana saw Farha wave her fork closer to her, goading her toward the trucks, she slumped on the slope. Farha tried calling out to her, shaking her, but her sister would not stir. The sun warmed her inert face. Not knowing what else to do, Farha looked around for Jehangir or Alamgir. She shook Farzana again but she wouldn't move. Farha saw the emptied trucks make their way back into the city. Farzana stayed motionless among the castaway possessions.

When Farha returned with Ismail, Sahani's husband, and his brother Saddam, they found Farzana lying unconscious on the trash peak, glowing against the sun. A small group had gathered around. Ismail lifted Farzana in his arms and brought her slowly down the slopes. Shakimun mumbled frantic, high-pitched prayers as Ismail brought Farzana into their home and laid her on the floor. He called Salahudin, who prayed over a bowl filled with water that he then splashed on Farzana's face. She woke up to a small crowd around her and slapped Ismail. Why had he brought her home? She needed to get back and fill her garbage bag, which was still on the slope. Shakimun asked her to stay home and help her with her embroidery, filling a red tulle sleeve that wafted in the air, with tiny crystals.

When Jehangir came home that evening, he ignored Shakimum's story of how a Shaitan had tripped his sister on a mountain slope. He took Farzana to a doctor nearby, who examined the pale inner rim of her eyes and told them that she was very weak. Working in the sun must have made her feel dizzy and faint. Jehangir got her the multivitamins the doctor prescribed and asked Farzana to make sure she didn't skip meals. He asked her to stay home, to not work on the mountains anymore, as he so often had. Farzana returned to the slopes the next day.

Shakimun sought treatment for her own diagnosis. She had heard of a healer across 90 Feet Road, so holy that he didn't even let the shadow of a woman fall on him, as she told Hyder Ali. With such discipline, he could make anything happen, she thought. She got Yasmin to write down Farzana's name, explaining that she had been gripped by a Khaadi ka Shaitan, a spirit from the mountains. She dispatched Hyder Ali and his cousin Badre Alam to the room, filled with incense and supplicants, with the slip. They returned with more *taveezes*, talismans, for Farzana to wear.

On some days, Sahani ran into Farzana on the slopes, and they picked together as they always had. On others, she found Farzana home, in the afternoons, as she never had been before. Often, she was muttering to herself, Sahani recalled, or was crying. *"Andar andar tha. Baad mein bahar nikalne laga,"* she said. *At first, the Shaitan flickered within my sister. But then he started pouring out of her.*

It was bound to happen if she worked during the afternoon, Ismail told Sahani when she tried telling him of Farzana's affliction. The thing about Shaitans was, he explained, that they came out in the day from around 7 A.M. to 2 P.M. and then from midnight to around 2:30 A.M. *"Iske liye main uske baad hi kaam pe jata tha. Unka saya pade hi na,"* Ismail said. *I worked only after that, so their shadow could not fall on me.*

But as word began to spread in the lanes of the mountains' spirit that was stuck in Farzana, neighbors dropped in at Hyder Ali's home, often with thoughts and opinions about her ailment. One of them pointed out to the anxious Shakimun that Farzana had spent all winter on the burning mountains, within the toxic halo of smoke. A lot of mishaps happen at the mountains, the neighbor told Shakimun. They were all burned. Farzana must have inhaled something. But to Sahani, the answer was clear: they needed a bigger healer. They decided to take Farzana to the mausoleum of the Sufi saint, Hazrat Shah Jalaludin Shah, known for exorcizing seen and unseen ailments from people, on Thursdays.

A short bus ride dropped them at the far end of the neighboring suburb of Chembur. On their way to the Dargah, or shrine, which they had heard was nearly as old as the city itself, they walked past oil refineries that spewed air noxious as the Deonar mountains' halo. The spirit of Baba Jalaludin, who was buried within the shrine, was said to have ensured that the sprawling British-made refineries that came to ring his mausoleum could never cover it.

When the mountains' rim had grown crowded, and new arrivals continued to build slim, double-storied, bedsheet-made homes that hung over the city's roads and inched onto its train tracks, the municipality had sent them to the Mahul area within Chembur to settle a new tenement town. It grew within the halo of the refineries, close to the halo of the mountains. Baba Jalaludin had come to be known as Shahenshah-E-Chembur, or the Emperor of Chembur, presiding over a kingdom of poisonous chemicals and disease.

That evening, Shakimun, Sahani, and Farzana stood in the courtyard of his shrine. It was lined with old trees, simmering cooking pots and outsized drums. Shakimun and Sahani walked ahead, drawn by the shimmering, green trellises that stretched across the mausoleums' silvery, glass-topped inner walls. They turned back to see that Farzana had stumbled and fallen at the doorstep. Akbar Bhai, the healer they had come to see, came out to help. When Sahani told him that Farzana worked at the trash township, had begun to babble through sleep and had fainted, he said, "*Gande saye ne pakda hai.*" *An unclean spirit has gripped her.*

As the sun slowly began to cool and retreat from the courtyard, Sahani and Shakimun watched it fill with people and their aches and troubles. At six o'clock, Dargah staff began beating drums. Some people came out with their feet chained because they were possessed by spirits, others alone, and sat in the courtyard, to be in the presence of Baba Jalaludin. Shakimun, Sahani, and Farzana stood in the crowd and watched. As the Dargah's healers coaxed out the spirits stuck in them, through the sound of their drums, Sahani watched loose hair and bodies swing and then blur to the quickening beat. Their bodies slammed on the ground and rose again, to the drumbeating. As the sky darkened, lights came on, the drumming ceased and the whirling bodies fell to the floor, drained.

Akbar Bhai told Shakimun to bring Farzana for eleven Thursdays in a row, so Baba could extricate the Shaitan.

At home, Shakimun flopped on the plank they had fixed to the outside wall, so that Hyder Ali could sit and watch Banjara Galli go by. Sahani said she could not go to the Dargah again—the swaying, falling bodies had frightened her. Budhi, a plump old woman who had squeezed onto the bench between Shakimun and Sahani, said she could go instead. Budhi's silvery, candy-floss hair and soft, plump frame had begun appearing with the dark and settling to sleep on the bench soon after it was made. "*Usko dekhne vala koi nahi hai na,*" Shakimun later recalled how they had come to take Budhi into their home, though it was already swollen with people. *She has no one to look after her.*

AS RAMZAN APPROACHED that year, Farzana's trips to Chembur Dargah continued. Pickers from their lane tried running the seasonal businesses that would swell the 90 Feet Road market. The month of day-long fasting and evenings filled with prayers was meant to set followers on a path to abstinence, purity, and God. Pickers set up stalls to sell fruit, juices, and food to break their fasts with. Others set up trinket stalls and clothes and shoe shops on bedsheets. It was the small indulgences that made the long abstinence possible, they figured.

Hyder Ali too planned to restart his zari, or gold thread embroidery, workshop. Eid is when women wore their best clothes and there would be demand for his embroidery, he thought. He took bus rides into the city to take fresh loans while Farzana went to the Dargah. Traveling in opposing directions, father and daughter watched the slim, finger-shaped city turning slowly into a dusty construction site, straining and nearly coming apart as it stretched to house its more than 20 million residents.

Farzana was going to the right place, the aging and voluble Roshan Shaikh, who lived in a tenement building near the shrine and often hung out in its courtyard, explained. She must have been standing on a mountain with her hair loose, Roshan said. She did not believe in such superstition, Roshan said, but a young woman from her own building had recently been cured by Baba Jalaludin of an invisible but toxic spirit that had gripped her this way. The family had quickly got her married to someone outside the city, so the jilted Shaitan couldn't repossess her.

Girls these days! They dab scent on, pin flowers into their hair, and go where the spirits lie in wait, Roshan fretted. It is how Farzana, whom she did not know personally, must have been trapped, she said. "*Shaitan aashiq ho jaate hain,*" Roshan concluded. *Shaitans fall in love with them.*

THIRTEEN

T**HE MORNING OF JUNE** 2, her eighteenth birthday, Farzana emptied the money box she had been filling for months. She walked to the 90 Feet Road market and bought herself a pair of jeans. After all, this was it. She was finally an adult. She watched lights getting strung through the long, chaotic street, in preparation for Ramzan. Pickers carefully piled up hills of prayer caps, shoes, and fruit on the pavement, on the road and on folding tables that straddled the two. The fasts would begin within days. Farzana went to the packed sweet shop where she usually bought cream clouds floating in sweetened milk with her carefully saved money. That day, it was cake, wafers, and chocolate.

Turning back for home, she saw pale gray clouds hanging over the mountains that rose ahead and hung like hulks over their communities. Sisters, nieces, and nephews dropped in to wish her a happy birthday through the afternoon, but Farzana had left her bags at home and gone to work. All of the sisters had been the same since childhood, Sahani would often say. They got fevers if they missed walking the mountains for even a day—their bodies ached. Farzana couldn't stay away.

In the evening, Farzana wore her jeans with a new long black top, decorated with multi-colored patterns. She wore gold hoops in her ears and made up her face. The house filled slowly with all the Shaikh siblings, their spouses and children. Only Jehana, the oldest, stayed away: her husband thought he had seen her with another man at the mountains and when they returned home, he hacked his garbage fork into her head, making a deep, bloody gash. That evening, he sat at their doorstep, while she stayed inside. At Hyder Ali's house, the others huddled around Farzana, as she cut the square cake with her name written in white sugar icing.

Even as she sliced the cake and began serving it, Ismail began teasing her, saying that this was the year she would get married . . . but to whom? *"Tere se achha dikhna chahiye!"* Farzana replied. *It better be someone nicer looking than you!* He threw something at her and they chased each other around the packed room, bumping into the others, trying not to trip on Faizan, Alamgir's nine-month-old son, who crawled around underfoot.

Hyder Ali sat next to Jehangir, who had been in the middle of moving out of the house for months, and looked ahead as he spoke. Jehangir had his own trash business now, his own motorbike. *"Gharwalon ke saath kyun rahega? Kyun paisa dega?"*—*Why would he live with his family or share his money with them?*—Hyder Ali asked, caustically. Jehangir didn't respond. He, Rakila, and their three children ate at home but walked over to sleep in a house he had recently rented nearby. Soon they would be gone, and Alamgir too was hoping to follow his brother out, with a new job driving a garbage truck. If that happened, Farzana would become the oldest of the children who handed money over to their father, to keep the household limping on.

Look for a husband for Farzana, Jehangir said, turning to Afsana, the only one of the sisters whose marriage had taken her out of the mountain's shadow. He didn't want someone from the dumping grounds. What if the Deonar grounds close down? Farzana turned sharply away from Ismail.

"Mujhe karna hi nahi hai bhai." I don't want to be married! *"Main yahin rahoongi, tere saath,"* she protested, tears suddenly running down her powdered face. *I want to stay here, stay with you brother.*

THREE DAYS LATER, the sun stayed behind clouds that had been gathering slowly through the day. Farzana, picking on a trash peak in a gentle breeze, had not noticed the sky darken, until, a little before sunset, she was drenched in the monsoon season's first showers. That night, she slept fitfully, to the sound of thunder. The holy month of Ramzan had begun before dawn. When she stepped out into their lane, it glowed before first light under a canopy of freshly strung, silver bunting, high above. Farzana, fasting, already felt hungry.

As the rains doused the fires, the official plans to evict the pickers intensified. The municipality had asked consultants to plan for a plant that would consume 3,000 metric tons of waste, more than half of what arrived at the township every day. In court committee meetings, some members were skeptical such a big plant would work all at once; it could perhaps be made to work in phases. Oka's deadline to stop dumping at Deonar's hills was only a year away, and the fires that had burned all winter were on everyone's minds. The project that had glimmered and faded on and off for decades gained a sudden sense of urgency.

Farzana worked on, watching the outer slopes turn emerald with grass, just as they had when she first came to work. Lotuses bloomed and melted in the rain that rose in troughs. She forked over old trash, gloopy from rains and charred from the fires. A few weeks earlier, Shakimun and Buddhi had accompanied her to Baba Jalaludin's Dargah. Shakimun had unbraided Farzana's long hair so the spirit would not get tangled in it when Akbar Bhai teased it out of her body with his incantation. Alone amid the crowd of entranced people, Farzana had not moved or swayed to the rising drumbeat. The spirit had retreated from her, the healer had told them. The job that should have taken eleven weeks was done in only a few. Shakimun returned home feeling calmer.

But friends who awoke before dawn and went to relieve themselves at the foothills began seeing Farzana in the dark. Farzana, who had always been with one of her sisters, was walking alone on the dimly lit slopes. They took to calling her Khaadi ka Bhoot, Ghost of the Mountains. She had begun returning to the slopes, before light, before anyone woke up, often with money instead of breakfast. She got to work early to beat the guards, she said. She came home, around dusk, with the day shift pickers. When Shakimun sent her a message to come home for lunch, she heard Farzana would buy food from one of the vendors who roamed the slopes and stay on. Salahudin had told Shakimun that mountain spirits didn't leave easily.

One afternoon, after waiting for hours on a mountain top, Farzana and Farha saw a truck winding its way through the dirt track, toward them. Mud splashed as they ran alongside it, on the hills, chasing it to a clearing. Farzana watched breathlessly as trash emptied out. Farha threw herself at it, jostling with the others who had gathered around. She looked up and found Farzana still staring at the mushy trash fallen around them. Others pushed her aside to get their pickings.

Farha went on collecting squashed bottles. She kept an eye out for Farzana, who continued to stand still, gaping. She called out to her sister, who did not seem to hear. She came closer and prodded her tentatively, with her garbage fork. Aren't you going to lift up your fork? Farha asked, thinking of how long they had waited for the emptying truck. Pickers jabbed around them. Are you starting a fight with your older sister? Farzana retorted angrily. "*Akdi nahi uthaegi to ladna padega,*" Farha replied. *If you don't pick up your fork I will have to.*

Farzana swung her garbage fork, aiming it at Farha, who cowered and stumbled away, surprised. Farzana followed her, fork in hand. "*Badi behen ko maregi?" Are you going to hit your older sister?* Farha heard Farzana repeat as she ran off down the hill. Farha laughed as she ran, thinking they would stop soon, clutch their sides, catch their breath, and collapse on the slopes, laughing as they sometimes did. But when she turned back, she saw Farzana's eyes filled with rage, her fork dangling in front of her. Farha stayed ahead. Farzana tripped clumsily on the loosely packed slopes but kept after her. Farha's chest burned. The air was heavy with unshed rain, making it hard even to draw breath. But Farzana's fork was close behind her, and Farha kept stumbling forward.

She saw pickers around them stop their work to watch. She heard some of them call out, asking Farzana to stop, but Farha felt her getting closer. She heard Alamgir call out to Farzana. But Farzana's footsteps remained close behind her.

Farha heard a scuffle and turned back to see Alamgir grab Farzana tightly from the back until she fell on the slope. Farzana held on to her fork even as her long, curled-up limbs rose and fell with deep breaths. Alamgir wrested it away and lifted her in his arms. He was the tallest of the siblings, sinewy where Jehangir was wiry. Farha heard someone say the humidity was shortening fuses on the slopes these days, as she trailed behind Alamgir, breathless and befuddled. Farzana fell asleep in his arms, heavy with exhaustion. He laid her down on the floor at home and began telling Shakimun about the rage that had gripped Farzana, speaking softly so he wouldn't wake her up.

Just as the city's assault on the mountains had assumed new urgency, Shakimun decided she needed to step up her efforts to exorcise the mountains from her daughter. She asked relatives, neighbors, friends. Many had stories of mountain spirits gripping their own families: Hindus had seen the Khabees, a tall floating Islamic spirit in their homes, while Sahani believed she had been possessed, as a teenager, by a Hindu goddess, dressed as a bride. Some of them asked Shakimun to take Farzana to the shrine of Mira Datar, the patron saint of exorcizing spirits in Mumbai. A fifteenth-century boy saint, buried in Gujarat, Mira Datar's powers to unclench the grasp of spirits stuck inside people were legendary. The green outpost of his distant mausoleum on a busy street in Mumbai close to the city's vast port lands featured the same spirit cleansing rituals as in the original shrine.

Farzana tied green glass bangles to the shrine's walls with a thread, hoping it would elicit the green bangles worn by Marathi brides, and others who came into the city, and a calmer life.

Three days later, Shakimun told Sahani, Farzana cried through the night, tormented by the mountain spirit. Through the weeks, more healers came to visit, more talismans were tied onto her arm and yet Farzana kept returning to work before dawn, with no memory of it all. She only remembered once going to the shrine in Chalisgaon, which was hours away.

IN THEIR ATTEMPTS to fix the township, Tata Consulting's engineers looked at waste-to-compost plants and power plants around the world. They were concerned, as other consultants before them had been, that Mumbai's waste did not contain enough plastic, paper, cloth, or wood scraps to burn well as fuel in an incinerator. Nearly half of what arrived at the township was mushy food waste, saturated by the monsoons, and would not burn easily. The plant could work only seasonally, in fits and starts, the consultants worried.

But that May, a new report the municipality had commissioned arrived from the National Environmental Engineering Research Institute, showing that the calorific value of Mumbai's waste, which allowed it to burn well and produce power, was high, higher than in most other cities the authors studied. The city's habits had changed: Mumbaikars had begun throwing away more coconut husk, rice straw, and good-quality plastic, and paper, all of which would burn well. The plant that seemed at first like it would not work, possibly could.

In the city, the builder's association had appealed against Oka's order to stop new construction. They should not be penalized for the municipality's inability to manage its waste, for its failed plans, they pled. But Oka was immovable. Until the mountains were dealt with, there could be no fresh construction in the city. Soon, they appealed in India's Supreme Court.

AT FARZANA'S HOME, the spirits seemed to recede with each incantation, only to return. More suggestions poured in. Farzana was not to treat the slopes as an open-air bathroom, as pickers usually did. The spirits rising from desire could catch you when you least expect, grip you, trip you, then not leave you, friends had told Shakimun.

Yasmeen's mother told her to take Farzana to the shrine of Makhdoom Shah Baba along the Mahim Bay. Known as the Qutub-E-Kokan, or shining star of the Konkan coast, along which Mumbai lay, the saint had drawn aches and pains from across the city and beyond. The lanes around the shrine were filled with the possessed, dispossessed, disabled, and others the city had stretched to a breaking point.

A scholar and saint, Makhdoom Shah Baba was said to have lived seven centuries ago and held court at the spot that later became Mahim's police station. His annual feast began with a procession led by the station's senior inspector, growing Makhdoom Shah Baba's glow. Musicians were said to have come on barges to play at the feast. The fair that went with it, spilled into the beach that stretched behind the Dargah, illuminating the Mahim Bay and holding up traffic movement in the curving, finger-shaped city every year. Shakimun felt sure it was the Mahim Dargah that would bring out the Shaitan lodged in Farzana.

So far, the Shaitan had left only to return. None of the medicines, the talismans, or the rituals seemed to make any lasting difference. "*Kabhi kabhi usko pata chal jata hai, Hazri ke liye ja rahein hain, to thodi der ke liye, vo bagal mein baith jata hai,*" Roshan Shaikh said, explaining how the Shaitan had eluded Baba Jalaluddin. *Sometimes when it knows you are going to have it extricated, it comes out and sits next to you, for a while to escape. But it comes back.*

FOURTEEN

AS EID APPROACHED IN Banjara Galli, fragrant smells wafted into Moharram Ali's house and filled Yasmin's head. She had nothing to offer in return for the food she smelled. She owed its makers money. She told them fasting gave her a headache and she needed to sleep through the evenings to get over it. But she didn't fast.

Moharram Ali had tried to work near Rafiq Nagar through the fires. Many months later, he dismissed the smoke and changed air around the mountains that was unsettling life in the lanes, in his airy, elegant manner. Mountain air doesn't "suit" everybody, he would say. But he had worked there most of his life, a bit of smoke didn't bother him, he said. He would not admit that things had changed, that mountain air no longer suited his family. As security tightened, Moharram Ali had dropped into the family's house at night to pick up money he said he had left behind in his hasty flight. When Yasmin tried calling him, to ask for Eid expenses, his phone was switched off or went unanswered. Friends stalked their home to retrieve loans they had given him. But they never saw him. The legend of Shaitan Singh, of Moharram Ali's invincible luck, had flamed out untraceably, gutting his family.

The area's markets stayed open all night on Chaand Raat, the first night of the crescent moon that would bring Eid. The settlements glowed against the dark mountains, and pickers spilled into the markets to bask in the moonlight, shop with what little money they did have and eat. Others set up stalls to sell bangles, henna cones, spice bundles to layer into pulaos, and edible silver to set, quivering, on sweets, hoping to earn money away from trash. Hyder Ali claimed that Shaitans, creatures of the dark, stayed away in the glow of that night.

Moharram Ali returned Yasmin's call that night: she had not wanted her boys to be draped in the mountain filth while their friends wore new, white kurtas for Eid prayers. In the months since their debts had mounted and Moharram Ali left, Mehrun and Ashra's clothes had inched up and tightened. He would take the girls out to buy new clothes, he said, and send her a set. Yasmin did not know how to tell Sharib, who was filled with rage against his father, that there was nothing left for him or his brother. She went, instead, to ask friends for a loan.

Mehrun and Ashra met Moharram Ali in the 90 Feet Road market, luminescent with fairy lights and bejeweled shoppers. Mehrun wore a sullen pout, thinking about all that Hera and Sharib said about their father. Ashra held his hand and kept up a chatter he could barely hear as they wove through the crowd. They passed butcher shops without customers, with long, bony carcasses that hung partly carved for days and attracted mostly flies, and avoided piles of fruit on the pavement that had rotted on carts until sellers threw them away. Enchanted, Ashra pointed at dresses with sequins that glittered under the halogen lamps, their stiff taffeta layers making it seem like someone was inside them, as they hung on bamboo poles. Moharram Ali's face fell when he heard their prices.

He tried directing her toward cheaper clothes that lay in dark piles. Ashra shook her head, no. Mehrun saw Moharram Ali's face crumple even as Ashra's lit up like the lights filtering softly through the fairy-like dresses. In the end, she said she could do without new clothes, and Ashra quickly picked a long, creamy lace dress filled with gold sequins that came with a long skirt and trousers. Mehrun and Ashra, holding her outsized bag, walked back to Sanjay Nagar, while Moharram Ali took his empty wallet back to Rafiq Nagar.

Yasmin came home a little later, with ₹2,000 she would not have to return: *Fitra* was charity given on the last night of Ramzan. The following morning, Sharib and Sameer bathed, put on their new, white salwar kurtas, and went out for prayers. Scrubbed of their coating of mountain grit, Yasmin thought her tall, strapping sons looked better than any of the friends whose homes they visited, to collect *Eidi*, or money as blessings, and sample the treats their homes were redolent with. Ashra wore her gold dress with the skirt, got Mehrun to make braids in her hair, and left for a friend's house. Yasmin thought her children looked so nice that no one would notice she had not even lit her stove on Eid.

For years, the mountains and their lanes had emptied out in the wake of the festival, as pickers took trips into the city, stretching the festival to *Baasi*, or stale Eid. They visited far-flung mausoleums, colonial monuments, and rocky beaches. But that year, the mountains darkened as soon as Eid was over, the lanes stayed full, and creditors returned to Yasmin's door, hungrier than before.

Yasmin was often out and when she was away it was twelve-year-old Mehrun who faced them, with no money and little to say. Yasmin thought they would retreat in the face of a child. Then, one afternoon, she ran into the Bishi owner, whose money Moharram Ali had disappeared with, as she entered their lane. Yasmin told him, as she usually did, that she would return the money when Moharram Ali returned. He interrupted: if she didn't have his money, she should send Mehrun to his house, at night, as payment for the debt.

Unlike the other Siddiqui children, who were tall and strong, Mehrun was fragile, almost breakable. She seemed translucent, with her milky complexion, permanent blush, and hazel eyes. Her presence in conversations at home, was gauzy too, conducted mostly through glances. Both Moharram Ali and Yasmin thought she looked just like them. *"Mera bachpan hai ye,"* Yasmin had said. *She is my childhood.* In the moves the family had made since Moharram Ali's disappearance, the dolls he had collected from the mountains for Mehrun and Ashra had disappeared, the sewing machine Mehrun had used to stitch clothes for them taken away by creditors. *"Kabhi socha hi nahi ki vo gudiya hai aur main insaan,"* Mehrun said. *I never thought they were just dolls and I was a person.*

YASMIN MOSTLY KEPT her door locked so people would think she did not live there anymore. She needed money not only to repay loans but also to send Mehrun and Ashra to an orphanage or hostel, away from her creditors and troubles, Yasmin figured. The Bishi owner's words played in her mind. A friend told her about an agency that hired women to carry babies for wealthy but infertile couples in their wombs. She told Yasmin that women from their lanes had been applying to be surrogates, a job that could pay them lakhs of rupees. The mountains closing on them, it was the only way to make good money in their lanes, Yasmin heard. She queued up at their office in Dreams Mall, a shopping center in a suburb nearby. She signed consent forms and went through medical tests but, at thirty-seven, was not selected.

With the rent for their room overdue, Yasmin traveled to a hospital across the creek, where she heard a doctor was looking for a surrogate. The hospital was unlike any she had seen before: there were no sick people or medical smells in its softly lit, beige lobby. She got chatting with the burqa-clad woman sitting next to her. They were unlikely to be chosen unless the younger women failed the tests, she said: she had already moved from surrogacy to medical trials. She got paid several thousand rupees for a few days of popping pills and medical tests, she said. Yasmin begged her to take her along.

A few days later, when she got the call to join a trial in the city of Baroda, more than 400 km north of Mumbai, Yasmin left Mehrun and Ashra with Moharram Ali and asked Sharib and Sameer to sleep at a *kata* shop. Then Yasmin took the five-hour train ride north, and returned, days later, with a few thousand rupees that she used to rent a new room and make some repayments. A week later, she got another call. It was a woman she had met at the test center, asking if she wanted to go for another "study." Yasmin told her she would meet her at the train station. With the putrid grip of the mountains fading away, she slid into the dark underworld of medical trials.

At test facilities, managers ushered her into quiet, air-conditioned rooms. Women who tested anemic or had low blood pressure were sent home, usually in tears. Others were ushered into a room where someone explained long legal contracts saying they willingly participated in the test and would not hold the company responsible if trial drugs made them sick. Yasmin could not read a word of the Hindi script they were written in and relied on the verbal explanation to sign the contract. Mostly, she tried not to listen too hard.

Yasmin tested contraceptives, epilepsy drugs, and pills for heart conditions, among others. She listed Mehrun as the beneficiary if something were to happen to her and money was due to her family. The drugs were usually being tested by an Indian organization on behalf of a large western pharmaceutical company that had developed it for use in international markets where it was illegal to test unapproved drugs on people. But without human testing, companies would not know whether the medicine worked, and what side effects it had. So, it was Yasmin, and the other women like her on whom the future of global drug discovery rested.

For a few days, Yasmin and the other women stayed at the test facility while scientists and doctors kept them under observation for any induced illnesses or side effects. Some women threw up, got headaches, dizzy spells, or fevers. Others sat up on their beds, in dormitory-style rooms, recounting stories of the disappointments and struggles that had filled their lives and brought them there. They wiped away tears in the dark.

As Yasmin waited for sleep in the eerily quiet, air-conditioned test facility, the meeting with the Bishi owner tormented her. She had asked a friend's husband to speak to him before she left. Nearly everyone in their lanes owed him money, he had said. When he asked for it, they said they could hardly work on the mountains anymore, that they would pay when Yasmin did. She told him Moharram Ali had disappeared. The Bishi owner said he was nearly broke himself. He regretted it, but he had to force Yasmin.

Cold and awake, in bed, Yasmin thought of her visits to orphanages. She would have to show she was divorced or widowed to enroll Mehrun and Ashra. But Moharram Ali still dropped in sometimes, and she wanted that more than divorce. In the morning, she awoke to days filled with elaborate meals, laid out to give them strength. Yasmin and her new friends dissected recipes and planned to replicate them for their children when they got home with the money.

In a few days, tests were repeated to ensure the drug hadn't caused any side effects, and Yasmin and the others were paid and sent home, with the instruction that they were supposed to be back in a month or so for a final check on how they had reacted to it.

Yasmin returned to Deonar with money and sometimes even gifts. She bought a tin of ghee for Hera, who was pregnant. Next time, she got a box of peanut brittle that she knew the children liked and had not eaten for a while. Creditors dropped in as Yasmin entered Banjara Galli. She handed over her money, curled up on her mattress, and napped to the hum of the children around her. Sharib and Sameer saved up to get her a boiled egg or beetroots: she had told them they were fed beetroot salad at the trial facility to ward off the anemia that the drugs could induce.

SHARIB BROODED FOR days after Yasmin returned from the medical trials. He was apprenticed with a mason, when he could not get to the mountains: soon, he would find a construction job and earn enough to repay their loans, so she would not need to go to any more trials, he told her. Until then, though, she repaid her undiminishing debts, serviced with a rate of interest about which she had no idea. When her creditors found Yasmin, she just handed over whatever she had.

Every time Moharram Ali called in, Yasmin thought he might be back for good. But it was always the same: he took some money, hung out some hope, and left again. The mountains, which had once yielded gold into his hands, now bore down on him. Winds howled on the slopes and rains lashed them. When he walked through their passes and clearings he slipped and slid. Guards patrolled even at night, and the flashlights they waved in curly sideways patterns to catch pickers in the dark, moved in his mind in the daytime as well.

When he was on the mountains, Moharram Ali felt they smelled gingery. The smell, mingled with the stench of rotting trash, made him nauseous and clung to him. In fact, the municipality had given a ₹1.5 crore contract to spray herbal deodorant and disinfectant on the mountains, to quell their stink. Opposition politicians had asked if it was not somewhat indulgent to spend so much on perfuming trash mountains.

Although she was on the trash slopes more often, Farzana had not noticed the smell. Mumbai's garbage convoys were slowly returning, and she was consumed in chasing them. But they often emptied mud and concrete, rather than trash she could sell. Every year, the municipality fixed roads and bridges before rains lashed the city: Mumbai's pounding rains could wash away homes that were too old or too new, and their crushed debris piled up in heaps around the city and arrived at the mountains for weeks. Farzana saw mud, gravel, bits of concrete, bricks and cement emptying at the mountains all day, burying the old trash and pressing it down. Moharram Ali heard that all the gold had melted with the fires and would not be found again.

FIFTEEN

DAYS AFTER EID, FARZANA had awoken, late one night. *"Mujhe chhod do. Main kuch nahi karoongi,"* she had cried aloud, to a roomful of people submitted to sleep. *Leave me. I won't cause any trouble.* Her painful sobs rose slowly, filling the house until everyone was up.

Neighbors came, expecting to see a fight, only to find Hyder Ali and the others standing around Farzana. They watched bewildered as she sat on the mattress, crying. *"Chhod Do. Main vapas nahi aoongi."* *I won't return. Leave me alone.* It was probably the guards she saw in her sleep, Jehangir thought. He should never have let her go back on the slopes after the doctor told her not to. It was the Shaitan, Shakimun knew, pressing Budhi into service for immediate relief. She chanted and splashed holy water on Farzana. The family waited sleepily for the prayers to work. But Buddhi had exhausted them and retreated outside, before sleep overpowered Farzana.

This would have to be the year that the stubborn spirits left, Shakimun decided, soon after Eid. She restarted the incantations, manifestations, and collection of talismans. Healers waved lemons in slow circles around Farzana, then eggs, and then threw them on the floor so they cracked, releasing the spirits drawn into them. A healer burned a lock of her hair in a weak, rain-dampened fire outside Hyder Ali's house while reciting Koranic verses to draw out the spirit entangled in her.

Shakimun returned to the Dargah at Mahim with Farzana. Outsized cooking pots boiled and steamed around them: Makhdoom Shah Baba was known for feeding the city's hungry. On wheeled wooden boards, limbless people circled around the mother and daughter. Old, bent people stretched their arms out, asking for money, to buy food, in Baba's name. Plates of food arrived, paid for by a wealthy patron, and the gaggle around them drifted away. They saw the Mujawar they had met before, sitting at his shop front. He did not seem surprised to see them and resumed his prayers for Farzana.

Then, a few days later, when Sahani came home, she found Farzana sitting alone, resting her chin on her muddied and drawn-up knees. "*Vo dikhta hai,*" Farzana said. *I can see him.* Sahani followed Farzana's eyes, which stared straight ahead at the kitchen counter. "*Vo baitha hai,*" she continued. *He's sitting there.* But Sahani couldn't see anything, she later recalled, and worried her sister was going crazy.

The following Thursday, the Mujawar at Mahim sat Farzana in the courtyard, filling with others seeking separation from spirits. Shadow flowers streamed in through the grill with the fading sunlight. Woody smoke from the burning bark of the Loban tree rose and mingled with the misty sky. It thickened to clear the fog within, as the drumming began. People sitting in the courtyard stirred. They swayed slowly at first and then faster as the drums picked up. They ached and swirled in pain to the beat. By the time it abated, the sun had set and the courtyard was bathed in the cool, purple light of the Mumbai monsoon. But Farzana had stayed cool too.

She was at the mountain slopes before dawn broke, the next day, telling her friends she had only been away for a trip. The city's attempts to shrink the mountains were picking up too. Did she know, pickers asked her, that Tata company was coming to take over the mountains, to turn the mountain waste to power? They were nearly here. Jehangir had heard that Tata officials had already taken plastic and paper from the slopes and used it to generate some power at their campus across the creek. If it all worked out, mountain plastic would begin going to their facility, he had heard. Prices for plastic would go up. He asked Farzana to start picking the thin plastic carry bags that did not fetch much money at the *kata* shops but that would get fed to their plant. Optimism began to rise in Jehangir again.

At Mahim, though, Farzana's spirit stubbornly remained in place. Shaitans could stay elusive in the glare of a crowd, but cling hard, the aging Mujawar told them, like desire itself. The following week, he would trick the Shaitan into believing there was no one around, that it could reveal itself, and then drive it away, in a *parda hazri*, a manifestation within curtains. No one but the Mujawar and Farzana would be there.

The next Thursday, Sahani and Shakimun had stayed at a distance while the Mujawar took Farzana into a room at the back of the shrine. After a while, the Mujawar came out, triumphant: it was a Shaitan from filth, he said. It's gone now. Sahani interrupted him, to say yes, Farzana was a trashpicker—the Mujawar had got it right this time. *"Ab vo theek ho jayegi. Bas vahaan vapas jaane mat dena, Unka saya rahta hai,"* he said. *She will be fine now. Just don't let her go where he caught her. They linger on there.*

Jehangir agreed that Farzana needed to stay at home, although he didn't believe in the spirits but in the doctor's earlier diagnosis that the mountains had poisoned his sister. She was not to work at the slopes, and he asked her to sleep on the mezzanine floor, with his family. He would watch over her. Shakimun had asked friends to look for a match for Farzana. Until then, she would keep Farzana home and teach her to cook.

And yet, often, when they called her down for tea in the mornings, Farzana was not there. They were not sure when she had climbed down the steps, opened the door, and left. Even the goats, tethered at the door, had not bleated, Shakimun noticed. Friends told her they saw the Khaadi ka Bhoot on the slopes, before daybreak. Farzana bought vada pav, samosas, tea at the mountains or ate at the restaurants near the municipal office and stayed out all day.

Shakimun sent Jehangir, Alamgir, Sahani, or whoever else she could find to bring her back. But Farzana was never at the mountain they heard she was at. She had left with emptied garbage caravans, getting to clearings before trash arrived at them. Her growing collection of charms dangled off her. Anyone at home, who went to a shrine, brought one back to add to it. Slowly, Farzana began sleeping through the night. With a progress as slow as the aging mountains moving out of the city, the Shaitan began to leave.

On July 27, the consultants presented their plan to shrink the township of discarded desires to Mumbai's municipal commissioner, Ajoy Mehta. Through April and May, they had walked mountain slopes with municipal officials. They had collected samples and drawn up reports that laid the mountains bare, and the toxic halo that seeped in and settled into those who lived around. They had gone over the rules that bound the mountains, considered the municipality's brief, and made a plan for a plant that would shrink them and produce power for the city.

The mountains' noxious halo had thickened, data the consultants collected from the municipality's air quality monitoring laboratory showed. Hydrogen sulfide, a poisonous, flammable gas known for its rotten egg smell, had more than tripled between 2010 and 2015, as had methane, feeding the ever-burning fires. Carbon monoxide, which could cause headaches and dizziness, was five times higher. Rag-picking could cause confusion, laceration, indigestion, and hazy vision, among other illnesses, the report said.

The consultants proposed clearing a section out of the 132-hectare township, where, eventually, more than half the 5,100 metric tons that garbage caravans delivered every day would get fed to the plant. At first, it would be segregated, passing through a metal screen and then a magnetic screen to keep out larger bits of garbage. The rest would be spread on the incinerator floor, where hot air would blow from below, "causing the waste to bubble and boil, much as a liquid, allowing intimate interaction between the waste and the fuel and facilitating drying and combustion," the report said. The heat would produce electricity, which would get supplied to the city—although often less than the municipality's brief of 25 MW of power, it would be enough to power thousands of homes.

The burning incinerator would spew smoke over the mountains and the communities around, and the consultants planned for three rows of trees around the plant to absorb it. The trees, whose verdant pictures they stuck in the report, could reduce ammonia released from the plant by more than half and absorb most of the dust thrown up by the incinerator, the consultants said. The plant and its border of flowering trees would "improve the aesthetic of Deonar," while saving more than 8 million tons of carbon dioxide and other greenhouse gases over two decades. Without it, Mumbai would need the Deonar township to double in size to accommodate the city's trash, by 2021, they estimated.

The future they laid out was utopian, so close it hovered in the room: as it shrank the mountains, and the trees soaked its halo, the plant would create better jobs in the lanes. The twenty-two separate diseases they could give the pickers would fade away.

Soon after the presentation, officials and political leaders from the Shiv Sena, the party that controlled Mumbai's municipality, had begun meeting executives from India's largest power companies informally. The waste-to-energy plant they had planned at Deonar was to be among the world's largest, they said. The contract to make it would be given through an international bid. There was a lot of interest, they said. Large foreign waste-to-power companies were keen on the project. They coaxed power company executives to bid for it. Being in Mumbai gave them a moral responsibility to make the plant that would clean the city and its air.

They would invite bidding in a few weeks. And then, the mountains, their halo, and their spirits would finally leave the city.

SIXTEEN

AUGUST 15, 2016, INDIAN Independence Day, was also the first birthday of Alamgir's son Faizan. Farzana had begun saving for it soon after her own birthday. As dusk fell, Farzana and Farha stood on 90 Feet Road, as they did every year, and watched bikers whizz by waving flags. They collected the chocolates and sweets the bikers distributed, and soaked in the patriotic songs playing on loudspeakers installed in the street. They walked back through their lane to more such songs floating softly out of homes.

Farzana changed into a long, white lace kurta with dark green piping on its edges. She put on a deep red lipstick, powdered her face, and pinned back some of her long, loose hair. In a photo studio nearby, she held Faizan in her arms and posed against a leaf-green curtain, her fingers digging into his pudgy cheeks. The pressure to smile led only to two intent stares in the photographs. As the flash popped, Faizan burst into tears.

When Farzana woke up the next morning, the rain of the previous evening had abated, leaving an overcast sky. She put on bright blue leggings, a parrot-green kurta, a black jacket, and a large white handkerchief around her hair. Carrying her gumboots, she left unnoticed while her parents lingered over half-filled tumblers of tea. Farzana stopped at Jehana's house to pick up her sister, and the two walked over to the mountains to work. It was a little before 10 A.M. and the sun traveled slowly across the sky behind gray clouds. It was a mottled day.

After the fires, the municipality had created a new trash hill toward the creek, across from the *gobar*, or prawn loop, which was officially called loop one. Pickers called it the new loop one: trucks were increasingly sent to empty on it, and pickers followed them to the rising slopes. It had quickly developed a reputation for being slippery and precarious, but they had stayed on, hoping its craggy slopes would smoothen as trash settled on them.

That morning, with the clouds threatening to erupt, Farzana and Jehana thought the new loop one was their best chance at finding trash before the weather made it impossible. As they walked up the slope, they saw yellow and orange bulldozers and forklifts buzzing fitfully against the gray skies. Trucks had already been here. Pickers were at work, several in black jackets like her own, Farzana noticed.

They watched trucks come in through the gate, pass the municipal office, and grind slowly up the slushy slope toward them. As the trucks got to the clearing, pickers fell on them, working quickly. Farzana put on her earphones and reached for the pick of trash before the bulldozers moved in and began pushing it down the slope. As bulldozers reversed to flatten the clearing, she retreated, moving to the rhythm of the music and the machines. It was always songs of infidelity, from Hindi films she hardly ever saw. Absorbed in this intricate dance, Farzana barely looked up to see the skies rumble. More than an hour went by in the mucky, frantic scrambles to fill her bag with plastic bottles. Farzana barely felt it.

A truck drove up, and Farzana dived into the scramble to sift through its contents—wire, mushy paper, lurid colored cloth, and vegetable peels—to pick out her squashed plastic bottles. Tangled clumps fell into her bag. She would sort through it at home, Farzana thought, as she reached out for more. Jehana worked close by. Emptied, the truck was driving downhill when it got stuck in the muddy track. It revved up, noisily, trying to move ahead. Farzana looked up quickly, watched it struggling, and returned to fill her bag. It stayed stuck.

In a little while, she looked up and saw a bulldozer on the slope down below. It was moving backward and uphill toward the clearing. Farzana saw it get closer. Pickers rummaged around her. She waved lazily at the driver and went back to filling her bag.

Then she heard the bulldozer again and looked up. It had stopped and then restarted and was moving back up the hill toward her. She saw some pickers scatter to get away from its path. She took a step forward too and nearly tripped and fell into the slimy trash around her. Surprised, she looked down and saw a wire entangled around her ankle. She banged her foot on the clearing to free it but the wire only pulled tighter, cutting into her. She twisted her foot around in the air. The wire stayed stuck. The bulldozer moved closer. She sat on the clearing and struggled to untwist the wire from her foot. It would not come off, and the bulldozer was now moving closer and closer.

She stood, carefully, and waved at the driver to warn him that she was stuck behind him. The wire pulled her back awkwardly and she nearly fell again. Farzana picked up stones and threw them at the driver to get his attention. They didn't reach him. She yelled at him to stop moving back but he kept backing up slowly toward her.

The bulldozer was nearly at the clearing, and Farzana was still rooted to the spot. She screamed and craned, trying to catch the eye of the driver inside the cabin. She was close enough to see that he had earphones on. He was probably listening to music—her voice could not reach him. She waved at him frantically. Still, the bulldozer moved closer. She noticed he was wearing sunglasses. He could not see her, she thought.

That is when Farzana tripped and fell faceup on the slushy mountain clearing. Hyder Ali believed it was the Shaitan who had gripped her and pulled her down. The bulldozer drove over her left thigh as she lay on the ground. Screaming and flailing, Farzana tried to pull herself up from her stomach from underneath the bulldozer. It shoveled up a load of trash and moved forward again. Farzana fell back in agony.

Nearby, pickers were gesticulating and screaming wildly at the driver too. They were not sure which of the black jackets was under the bulldozer and called out different names. As the bulldozer drove back downhill, pickers tried moving closer to see who had been crushed under it. The bulldozer dropped its load of trash downhill and began moving back up again. The driver did not notice the frantic waving around him.

He drove back slowly, rolling over Farzana a second time. This time, the bulldozer went all the way up the left side of her body, nearly to her chest. Jehana and some of the other pickers were shouting, trying to get the driver's attention. Finally, catching sight of the commotion, he stopped the bulldozer. A skinny young man with a straggly mustache jumped out of his cabin and walked back to find a bloodied mess under one of his tires. Farzana's bloated face emerged just in front of it. Most of the rest of her was underneath the vehicle. Her eyes had nearly popped out of their sockets and stared at him, startled. Blood trickled out of her ears and nose. The driver turned and ran away. Some pickers chased him downhill. Fear kept him ahead of them. In a few minutes, they gave up and turned back to check on Farzana.

Jehana, and others, huddled around Farzana. They stared quietly at the swollen head and crushed body, spattered in bits of flesh, blood, and muddy trash. The relentless pursuit of garbage had suddenly halted. Pickers were not sure what to do. Jehana heard the people around her saying that this was Jehangir's sister. She watched municipal officials walk up from their office nearby, having heard the commotion. Pickers called out to Jehangir. She joined them. Someone had seen him buying trash nearby, a little earlier.

When Jehangir heard Jehana's voice calling out to him, he thought Ramzan, their youngest brother, had missed school again and was up to no good at the mountains. He followed Jehana's voice uphill, thinking of how he would drag Ramzan back home and give him a thrashing to make sure he didn't dare venture back. Instead, he saw a small crowd milling around. He looked under the halted bulldozer and saw a battered person. Green and blue clothes peeked out brightly under a black jacket. As he got closer, he saw flesh hanging loose, a bone protruding, a swollen face streaked with blood. Blood soaked the trash around her. In her right hand, she clutched a half-filled bag of plastic bottles. Jehangir realized it was Farzana that they were calling him to see.

Jehangir got into the driver's seat, Jehana recalled, and drove the bulldozer off his sister's body. Scavenging birds swooped down, forming shadows over Farzana's ripped-open flesh. Her insides spilled out on the mountain. A milky, white bone jutted out of her calf. Blood trickled down from her bulging eyes. Jehana stared, not knowing what to do.

Pickers suggested Jehangir take Farzana to Shatabdi, known officially as Madan Mohan Malaviya Shatabdi, the municipal hospital, not far from the mountains. He hailed a garbage truck that had just emptied. Friends helped him pick up the broken Farzana, carefully, in his arms. He laid her down on the back seat, in the driver's cabin, and directed the truck through the mountains' slushy tracks toward the highway. When Sahani arrived at the clearing, moments after they had left, she could still see Farzana's outline pressed into the trash.

One of Jehangir's friends, who had come with him in the truck, turned to look at Farzana in the back seat. "*Uska haath dekh Jehangir bhai,*" he said, staring at the blood and torn flesh spilling out of her left arm. *Look at her arm, Jehangir brother.* "*Usko dekho,*" Jehangir replied, wryly. *Look at all of her.*

At Shatabdi, Jehangir wheeled Farzana on a stretcher through the back door that opened across the emergency department. Jehangir pushed his way through the sick, waiting restlessly outside. The doctors he managed to stop recoiled at the sight of Farzana. They told Jehangir they did not think she would make it, that there was not much they could do for her. Their hospital was not equipped to deal with such grievous injuries. They asked him to take Farzana to Sion Hospital, officially known as Lokmanya Tilak Municipal General Hospital, one of the city's largest and busiest public hospitals.

Jehangir demanded an ambulance to move Farzana there, so treatment could begin. Doctors called for it and bandaged Farzana loosely, for the ride. As Jehangir waited outside for his parents, for the ambulance to arrive, and for the money they would need for her treatment, Farzana's life hung by a thread.

When Jehana came home and told him what had happened, Hyder Ali knew the Shaitan had struck. He had haunted Farzana for months, Hyder Ali said, and had trapped her and tripped her at that moment when she had faced the bulldozer. *"Vo uska nuksaan karne ke liye hi aaya tha,"* he said. *He came to harm her and now he has.* Hurriedly, he scraped together some money from friends and neighbors. When they arrived at Shatabdi, the ambulance that would transfer Farzana to Sion Hospital had still not arrived. Together, Farzana's family and their neighbors hounded doctors and staff.

When the ambulance finally came, they inched slowly through the highway. Afternoon traffic was piled up in light rain. Farzana had heard the doctors. *"Bhai mein bachoongi nahi,"* she told Jehangir. *I won't survive.* Her breathing was labored. "Don't worry," her brother repeated. "Don't worry."

At Sion, Jehangir pushed her stretcher through the frenzied emergency department. Doctors drew the curtain around Farzana's body to make a small examination room. They put on an oxygen mask: the long and painful breaths she drew to get even the tiniest bits of air suggested the bulldozer had punctured her lungs, which were filling with air.

Her left arm and leg were filled with broken bones and open wounds. Her left calf bone stuck out of her leg. Lumps of dark clotted flesh spilled out of her left thigh. Her right calf was wounded too, the doctors wrote in their examination report. Her left arm was broken. Scans revealed her liver and intestines were injured and there was fluid, most likely blood in her abdomen. Her back and pelvis were fractured. There was hardly a part of Farzana's body that was not injured, their report suggested.

Doctors moved a flashlight near Farzana's eyes. When they brought it close to her, Farzana could follow it with her right eye, but not with her left eye. It was her distended face with a contusion and head injury that had worried the doctors at Shatabdi the most. They thought her brain might be swollen or injured. She was so badly injured it was hard to know where to begin fixing Farzana.

There isn't much hope, the doctor said to the crowd of mud-splashed family and pickers waiting outside the examination room, but they would try their best to treat her. The next three days would be crucial. If Farzana responded to treatment they could begin treating the rest of her injuries. Jehangir's glass business and private garbage clearing had nearly ground to a halt since the fires. But he went home and emptied his savings and deposited them at the hospital. Then he left for the Shivaji Nagar police station to file a complaint about Farzana's accident.

Farzana's sisters and brothers crowded around her, crying. They bent low to hear her repeat, "I won't live long." She whispered that she was sorry for all the troubles she had caused them. Yasmeen and Sahani told Farzana they would pray for her. "*Tu theek ho jayegi,*" Sahani said softly into her ear, teary and unsure. *You'll get better.*

Doctors moved her to intensive care, the corridor outside filling with hundreds of pickers in their muddy clothes and oversized gumboots that left trails on hospital floors. Some were neighbors and friends, others were not even sure who was inside. It could have been any of them, the people whose lives existed in the flash between trucks emptying trash and bulldozers moving in to shovel it away. Farzana's was the kind of accident they tried to push out of their minds while they worked. It brought back memories of a lifetime spent under trucks, ferreting out garbage, jumping onto moving vehicles, dodging bulldozers as they picked trash and stepping aside just as forklifts moved to scoop them up with the trash. They had held tight to tipping trucks and turned away from bulldozers just when they got too close. Some had crushed fingers, others had limps that came from failing to escape as truck tires approached. As they waited to hear about Farzana, they shared stories of their narrow escapes and unspoken nightmares.

The doctors began with inserting a tube between her ribs to help her breathe, blood transfusions to make up for the blood loss and sending her for brain scans. That evening, Farzana was recovering when a police officer arrived to record her statement. Doctors had recorded most of her injuries as grievous in the medical report they submitted to be attached to the police complaint. The officer spoke to Jehangir, Jehana, and Shakimun instead and recorded their statements. Other officers had visited the mountain clearing and spoken to pickers who had seen the bulldozer roll over Farzana. They filed a complaint against the driver for causing grievous injury by accident and rash and negligent driving. If he was convicted, it would lead to a maximum of a couple of years in prison and the driver's license being revoked.

Police got the plate number of the bulldozer from the registers at the mountain gate where it had entered that morning. The driver's name was Mohammed Hashim Khan. Pickers who had seen him that morning described him as a slim, young man with an intent stare. By coincidence, he lived in the same sprawling complex of buildings that the police station had recently moved to, occupying a white, multi-storied building at the entrance. The elevator did not work and there was nowhere to eat close by. But it was a relief from the constant smell and the knee-deep, murky monsoon waters that had periodically filled the squat old police station near the mountains.

Officers walked through the tightly packed complex of one-room tenements to his apartment. The complex, which took up a vast tract between the mountain communities and the highway, was a step up from living on a street. People constantly arrived from the flimsy settlements that filled Mumbai's pavements and rail tracks, claiming their first concrete homes, their first address. Hashim's older brother opened the door and told them Nanhe, or the little one, as they called him at home, had not returned from work that day. Police parties searched for him through the night.

On August 18, he walked into the police station and turned himself in.

An officer recorded Hashim Khan's statement. He said he had come from his village five years ago to live with his brother and sister-in-law. He was twenty-six years old and had worked as a bulldozer driver for several years on the mountains. He had started work at his usual time of 7 A.M. that day and had been shoveling trash on mountain slopes all morning. A little after noon, a truck had emptied out garbage at a clearing near him, he said. While going down the mountain slope, the truck had become stuck in the tracks, which were muddied by rain. Khan was driving his bulldozer back to help clear the way so the truck could move.

He had been struggling to shovel away mud and trash for a while before he saw ragpickers waving and yelling in his rearview mirror. He stopped and got out as soon as he heard the commotion and found a girl under his bulldozer. She had headphones on that had drowned out the sound of his bulldozer getting closer, he said. He thought the pickers had waved at her too, to warn her, but she had stayed in place, not responding to them or his approaching bulldozer. He ran back to his cabin and drove the bulldozer forward, from over her body.

He had been so frightened of the pickers that he ran away from there until he reached near the mountain gate. He sat outside the municipal office under the old banyan tree that marked the end of the vanished *cuchra* train track that had settled their township, turning the swamp to the mountains. He watched the usual hum inside the small, single-story municipal office. He caught his breath and then walked home. He had come to report the incident on his own, he told the police officer. They arrested him.

On the mountains, work ground to a halt. Some pickers joined the vigil at the hospital, while fear and anger paralyzed others. Guards patrolled zealously to keep away those who still came to work. Older pickers spoke to staff at the nonprofit that gave them informal identity cards. After Farzana's accident, rage—that had been simmering for years while they stayed invisible to the city that relied on them to clean up after it— had boiled over. The pickers planned protests and met municipal officials. Any of them could have been crushed like Farzana, like the garbage they picked. They pressed officials to punish the driver, to compensate Farzana's family, and to protect them while they worked on the mountains.

The accident took place on municipal land. Farzana should never have been there. Jehangir, who had filed the police complaint, had appropriated a tip of the mountains, and was liable for punishment. It was a painful reminder to the pickers that they lived in an unofficial world of shadows, less people than intruders.

Officials had seen Farzana's accident and probably noted it in the daily registers they kept at the mountains but they seemed to be lost. No one, other than Nanhe, the little one, was responsible for what happened to her.

Hashim was produced in court the day after he turned himself in at the police station. His brother, Azad, posted bail and he returned home. Pickers heard Azad did house calls as an electrician. He had apparently borrowed money to post ₹20,000 as bail. Hashim put out word for new jobs to pay back the money, while the police built a case against him in court.

Meanwhile, Farzana's family prayed and waited through the longest three days of their lives. Hyder Ali sat in the filigreed gold corridors of Makhdoom Shah Baba's shrine, praying. He brought back a rose that he placed under Farzana's pillow in the intensive care unit. Jehana kept her company by her bedside, while the others waited anxiously outside. Nurses used eye drops to shrink Farzana's staring eyes.

Every day, the pickers waited in the chaotic and teeming corridors of Sion Hospital to know Farzana's fate. Yasmin was often in the crowd. Every time the doors to the air-conditioned intensive unit swung open and doctors came out, to a gush of cool air, she felt a gnawing pit in her stomach. Each time, she could not help thinking that the doctors had come out to tell them that Farzana had gone.

SEVENTEEN

AFTER THE THREE DAYS were up, the doctors told her family that the swelling in Farzana's brain was receding. They would begin the long and arduous part of putting her body together again. Hyder Ali believed it was the intercession of Makhdoom Shah Baba, tugging his daughter back to the land of the living.

Days turned into a haze, as surgeries went on. Farzana drifted in and out of consciousness. Her painful cries ebbed only when her swollen eyes, shrinking gradually back into their sockets, closed in a sedative-induced sleep. She awoke too soon, cold in her metal hospital bed, howling with pain.

At times, Farzana seemed to drift back to their world, asking for friends, or something cold to drink. At other times, hearing her scream, Jehana felt, Farzana spoke from the world of the spirits that pulled at her limbs and had dragged her down under the bulldozer. Looking at Farzana's broken body, Jehana wondered if she may already have slipped into some kind of underworld where she was unreachable. It was as if the world of the living and the world of the dead battled within Farzana. Jehana kept her covered with a blanket.

Farzana remembered waking up in long corridors, outside operation theaters, waiting for them to be free. She waited for hours, alone, afraid and crying. Later, attendants arrived and sent her back to the ward: there were too many surgeries lined up at the theater. She returned to wait outside operation theaters for days before finally making it in. Farzana woke up from surgeries to find herself increasingly bandaged. Her chest was held in a brace. So was her left leg, to draw her calf bone back in. She could barely move.

To keep the surgeries going, Jehangir dipped into his savings, carefully accumulated over years from his trash business, his own mountain clearing and from Javed's patronage. When it all fell short, he sold the motorbike that had helped give him a glow of success in their lanes. He was sinking fast, but all Jehangir could think of was Farzana. With nothing else to fall back on but the fickleness of mountain luck, love in the shadow of the mountains acquired an intense, burnished glow. Through the precarious turns of their lives, it was often the only constant. It was all they had when they had nothing.

When Jehangir's money began running out, Hyder Ali walked up to Farzana's hospital bed and took off the earrings she wore, as gently as he could, and sold them. "*Jab ladki hi nahi bachegi to sona leke kya karenge?*" he later explained. *If she doesn't make it, what good is the gold?*

At the mountains, pickers kept away, or were kept away by guards. They protested everywhere they could, trying to get help for Farzana and to make themselves visible. They heard a local corporator owned the bulldozer that had run her over. They protested outside his office. He was not there to meet them. Later, they learned he didn't own the bulldozers after all. Still, they kept up their protests, finding new spots for them. They had spent decades trying to stay invisible to the municipality, the police, the city, to trucks, and to bulldozers. But something had changed with the fires, tightening security and Farzana's accident. Now they fought to return to the world of the visible. For someone to see them. Someone to avoid them if they got too close. And someone to be held responsible for running them over.

AT THE MUNICIPAL office, officials were consumed in their own battles. In the plant's schedule, made to match Oka's deadline, September was the month for pre-bid meetings. They would confer with interested companies and take in their suggestions before inviting first bids in October, little more than a month away. Consultants had suggested that only companies with years of experience building large waste-to-energy plants be allowed to apply. But if Deonar's was to be India's largest waste-to-energy plant, no one had made anything like it before. Through August and September, rumors circulated that municipal officials had met companies from China, South Korea, and Brazil. They would partner with Indian companies, it was said.

In meetings, though, these company officials voiced worries Tatva's troubles could return to torpedo their plant too. They too could be stranded without garbage to incinerate, without the land lease, funds to construct the plant, or the municipality's support. The specter of the failed project, the continuing arbitration with the municipality, haunted the proposed project, dampening interest. Back at the mountains, pickers' frustration was growing. They looked for the bulldozer owner, whom they later found and brought to Hyder Ali. Farzana should not have been on the mountains at all, he said. The bulldozer was nearly as big as his room. Why had she not moved away as it approached? Was she crazy? They had heard that she was.

Sahani heard that bulldozer owners had told municipal officials that they would not work on the mountains if people came under their bulldozers and they were asked to pay compensation. They knew their bulldozers would have to keep moving for garbage caravans to keep arriving from the city, and the contents to be pressed down onto hills as they always had been. This shouldn't be our problem, Sahani heard bulldozer owners had said to municipal officials.

HYDER ALI DECIDED that Jehana would stay with Farzana at the hospital while the others would return to work so they could look for money for Farzana's treatment. He mostly stayed at home. He cried too much when he saw his daughter's broken body, and Jehana would have to send him away.

After several surgeries, Farzana was moved out of intensive care to the hospital's E ward, lost in a haze of pain and semi-consciousness. More than thirty female patients, and the smell of their sickness, filled it. Jehana walked through it, looking at patients she dryly called *bhayanak*, terrifying. They were all recovering from accidents or burns.

But no one cried like Farzana did when doctors came on their morning rounds, to change her bandages and dress her wounds, every few days. Jehana turned away as they unwrapped the long, gauze bandages to reveal Farzana's raw, pink body, barely held together. The doctors checked to see if her wounds were drying up, sprinkled powders, rubbed ointments, and wrapped new bandages on. "*Poora kamra sar pe utha leti thi,*" Jehana often recalled, with a wry smile, about dressing days. *She had the eyes and ears of the whole room.*

When they left, Farzana often fell into a deep, exhausted sleep, while Jehana got medicines or test results. She chatted with relatives of other patients, who asked why Farzana was so bandaged-up. At night, when Jehana was sleepy, Farzana was awake, crying in pain. Bony and austere, Jehana had the firm air of being the oldest of nine and the mother of six. On the slopes, she had often been able to make the intrepid, unstoppable Farzana follow her terse instructions. But in the hospital, she could only watch Farzana mumble and shriek in the darkened ward. She could not bring Farzana back to her senses, as she always had.

Later, Jehana would say that she thought the spirits had finally left Farzana as she lay under the bulldozer. But in those unending nights, Jehana thought it could only be the Shaitan flailing within. As lights went off in their ward, Jehana felt a fog rolling over Farzana. When she closed her eyes to sleep, Farzana found herself in front of the bulldozer on the cloudy, gray mountains that morning. She called out to the driver to stop moving back. She was behind him, she shouted.

Farzana called out to their mother and God to get her away from the approaching bulldozer. Sweat soaked her body as she saw it move closer. She called out to someone called Riyaaz. Jehana thought Farzana could see someone invisible to her and wondered if it was the spirits within her who spoke and who Farzana saw through her sleepless eyes. Her mouth felt dry. Jehana got her plastic packets of fruit juice. Farzana sucked the cool juice hungrily, struggled to curl up her long limbs and sleep without tugging at staples or wounds. If she turned the wrong way, or too quickly, the pain could make her howl for hours. Jehana, who slept on a sheet she laid out on the floor, cried softly, waiting for sleep to come over Farzana, usually as dawn broke.

One afternoon, Sahani, the sister after Jehana, arrived. The two chatted while Farzana slept. *"Vo to naram kachre mein giri to bach gayi, nahi to . . ."* Sahani trailed off. *She fell in soft trash so she got saved, else . . .* If the bulldozer had found Farzana on the road instead of the mountains, the outcome could have been worse, she suggested. Jehana asked if she knew who Riyaaz was. Sahani reminded her that there had been a boy in their lanes, around her own age, called Riyaaz Shaikh. He had left school to come to work on the mountains when his father's hand was injured and he could not work anymore. They had not seen Riyaaz for years.

When Sahani left, Jehana found Farzana awake. She didn't remember calling out to Riyaaz or the bulldozer driver in her sleep. But Farzana reminded Jehana that they had known him, in the years before she came to work on the slopes all day. He too came to pick trash in the afternoons and usually stayed on after they left.

On a stormy August morning in 2009, the sisters had seen a small crowd, on a hilltop, as they made their way up the slopes. They watched pickers standing in nearly knee-deep mud and soaked in rain. Jehana and Farzana had walked up and seen them huddled around Riyaaz, lying, pressed into trash, his face and body flattened. Thick tire marks ran over him. One of the oversized bulldozers the municipality used in the monsoon season must have rolled over him, pickers figured. They had taken him to Rajawadi hospital, but he arrived there cold and long dead. He had probably been lying amid the trash through most of the rain-soaked night.

Farzana heard his mother, Shakila, had walked the soggy slopes all morning looking for him. Maybe he had stayed the night on the slopes because evening had come before he'd found enough trash, she thought. Maybe he had tired of looking, and not wanting to return with an empty trash bag, had waited for trucks filled with valuable trash to arrive from hotels and slept on the slopes. Shakila asked pickers if they had seen her son sleeping in trash. He was in brown trousers that may have faded into the muddy slopes. She had gone to the hospital when she heard someone in brown trousers had been taken there. Riyaaz's death certificate had said his was an accidental death. That gray morning swam in Farzana's eyes. She saw Riyaaz's flattened, tire-marked face when she tried to sleep, she told Jehana.

Riyaaz's father had sat by his son's grave, all day, for months, while Shakila had walked adrift, in Banjara Galli. She seemed like half a person, gaunt as a ghost, tears never far, never leaving the lane, except to take loans to run a small corner shop with which she sustained her three younger children. There had been weddings in her village, her mother had fallen ill and died but Shakila had not left. *"Usko yahaan chhod ke kaise jaoon?"* she would say. *How can I leave him here? "Mujhe dhoodne aaya to?" What if he comes looking for me?* she would ask, even a decade later. Riyaaz wouldn't leave Farzana either.

JEHANA KEPT UP her tired vigil as Farzana drifted painfully between the world of the living and dead. As dusk fell every evening, Alamgir's friend Nadeem came into their ward, the shimmery pompadour in his hair just a little paler than the golden sun, deepening outside. The crowd of pickers had thinned out but he still came. Jehana often sent him to get painkillers, or asked him to help prop Farzana up on pillows. The sides of his head were buzzed to make his pompadour seem taller and win him a few extra inches of height. He came in, taking long, hurried strides, as if to make up for something: his lack of height and for having been away all day.

He became Farzana's shadow. His arms moved as if they were her own bandaged, immobile ones, massaging her head and her swollen feet, until she slept. He fiddled gently with her bandages so they didn't tug painfully at her and make her cry. He moved as if he was her still-broken legs, bringing water to drink, or a blanket. He perched himself next to Farzana, on the bed. Jehana could not hear what he spoke, softly into her ears. But sometimes, she saw it bring a weak smile on Farzana's face.

Jehana had first seen Nadeem in the crowd of pickers in the early days, when their lanes had poured into the hospital's corridors. Most people she knew from their lanes were there and she had barely noticed him, passing by while looking for Jehangir or Alamgir. At first, when Farzana was moved to the ward, Nadeem began coming in to see her with Alamgir, and then by himself.

Every evening, as the sun faded and the lights came on, Farzana tossed restlessly in her bed. Nadeem arrived, muddy from work, his pompadour wobbling, nearly falling to make gold streaks on his face, and sat at Farzana's bedside. Jehana saw them bicker and talk. She was not sure he should have been there. But he offered to bring any medicines she had run out of, or juice from the cafeteria. Jehana began to leave him to watch over Farzana while she took short breaks from her bedside.

She paced up and down the corridor outside, watching night attendants walk by hurriedly, holding bedsheets and woolen nightcaps. For the first time in the day, she thought about her children, wondering if they had been given dinner. Trying to scratch something together for them had taken up her evenings for years. Now she barely thought about it. Jehana had tried to get her husband to work. But the card games, and the gossip, alcohol, and drugs that went with them, around the mountains' rim, had filled his mind with stories of suspicion and conspiracy, making him lash out at Jehana. In his mind, she was always with someone else. He chased trucks desultorily and earned enough only for his stash. He searched carefully for the jewel-colored bottles of alcohol steeped in the trash, and stayed late on clearings, emptying their sour, leftover dregs.

Jehana's husband and his friends, their hair slicked back with gel, eyes lined with kohl, their bodies emaciated, had reoccupied the abandoned sheds made of dried leaves of the sort that Farzana and her friends had once built for their parties on the mountains. Their minds and bodies had shriveled by their intoxications that fueled suspicion, uncontrolled fits of rage and violence. They poured it all out on their women.

Jehana had tried picking trash to keep the house going but time and again her husband's jealousy had pulled her back. Tears ran down her eyes as she thought of long evenings planning dinner, around an empty stove, with him circling outside to ensure she didn't step past the threshold. Eventually the children would ask her for a few rupees to buy a bag of chips or biscuits. She would tell them to get it from Hyder Ali's house.

Her days with Farzana had been painful and sleepless. But they had taken her away from the constant anxiety and failure to produce meals at home. Farzana's struggles had lulled her own, given her something to think of other than her own troubles. She thought of Farzana's endless nights of crying and moaning, as she paced the corridor. Jehana realized, Nadeem, which means companion, was the name she took the most in her nightly mumblings. It was that Nadeem, the little man elongated by a gold pompadour, who had visited to care for Farzana, who had become her shadow, who had turned his limbs into hers.

Nadeem offered to bring the dinner Shakimun cooked every evening to the hospital. Even looking at it made Farzana nauseous. Jehana insisted she eat, and the two sisters squabbled over Farzana's barely touched dinner. Nadeem stepped in to broker a truce. He made little morsels and fed her.

Farzana, whose stomach had churned at the sight of food for weeks, began finding it bland. Suddenly, she wanted something spicy. One evening, he arrived with dinner from his own home. He had got his mother to make a *saalan*, a deep and rich lamb curry, with rice.

She tried fighting, feebly when he was late. He sat with her all night, watched her cry, helped her turn over, and spoke softly until she slept. Jehana and he watched her scream in pain, at the smallest movement. When Farzana finally fell asleep, just before sunrise, Nadeem left for work. A little before dawn broke, he rode garbage trucks as they began their rounds of the lightening city, filling them with its debris and emptying it on the mountains.

EIGHTEEN

TOWARD THE END OF September 2016, Farzana had returned home to the ebbing rains. The season of fires would begin on the mountains again. Warm, dry winds would soon bluster against the scorching sun of Mumbai's returning summer, blowing up dust, making a haze above them. In the haze, new guards appeared. They stood on watchtowers—freshly built by the municipality to police the hilly township of trash—and surveyed its edges with binoculars.

Carefully, Jehangir and Alamgir had carried Farzana in their arms from the entrance of their slender, long lane and laid her down on the floor at home. The doctors had finished her surgeries, Hyder Ali had claimed some expenses from a government insurance scheme and used up all his money to have her treated, but after a month and a half in the hospital, Farzana had hardly healed. Yasmeen and Rakila learned to change her dressings at home, to avoid the arduous and expensive journeys back to the hospital. She still cried until the neighbors arrived, to see what was happening. Shakimun sat hunched over her daughter, chasing out boys who strayed in to collect cricket balls and soccer balls from games in their lane and gawked at Farzana's still disfigured limbs.

Through September and most of October, municipal officials had presented potential bidders their plans to mend the mountains and shrink their halo. They had elicited suggestions from companies and offered to tweak their plans accordingly. But the troubles with Tatva, its continuing court cases, loomed over the meetings. Who would want to take on management of the township, with its fires, its shadowy army of pickers that stalked slopes, its messy past? Could the place ever really change, they worried.

As the date to begin submitting bids came closer, the specter of fires came to meet them. The municipality had hired the Maharashtra State Security Force (MSSF)—a commando force that was trained by police and could be hired to guard installations, companies, and wealthy people— to secure the mountains.

Hyder Ali stood by the wall watching these new guards dressed in army fatigues, baseball caps, dark glasses, looking bigger than anyone he had ever seen guarding the mountains before. He squinted against the afternoon sun to crack their patrolling schedule. When did they take breaks for lunch? When did they walk to the far end of the mountains' long, looping periphery so he could get in? When did their shift end? Someone always seemed to be there. The new guards were to rid the mountains of old ghosts, of fires, of encroachers, and prepare them for new suitors.

One evening, Hyder Ali returned home late from analyzing the new guards' ceaseless patrols, and he saw Farzana standing up. The stick they had found for her to use as a crutch lay abandoned on the floor. She was leaning against Nadeem instead. Hyder Ali had heard people speak about Farzana, in his walks to the mountains. Would she be scarred forever? Could she ever get mended? Most of all, they asked, who would marry her? Could she have children? They had heard all her bones were broken.

They had heard she had come back from the dead. Is this how the rest of her life would be? Hyder Ali had evaded Nadeem for months. Everything about the young man meeting with Farzana was inappropriate. If being seized by spirits, crushed by a bulldozer, and left for dead were not enough, news of his unmarried daughter, being visited by an unrelated man who had not been selected by her family, at night, would strangle her marriage prospects entirely. And yet, here was Nadeem, day after day, bringing Farzana to life again.

That night, Hyder Ali decided he had to know more about Nadeem. He called Alamgir, sprawled and nearly asleep, on the floor near Farzana. He came out, wearing a stiff, sleepy air, and was followed by Nadeem, who then left for home. Alamgir told Hyder Ali, Nadeem was from Padma Nagar, the last of the communities that hugged the mountains, said to be settled on a swamp of lotuses. His father had been a mason, who had earned well as the city inched its way toward Deonar. For a time, he had built a life away from trash, even if living in the mountains' shadow. He enrolled Nadeem and his brothers at a private English school nearby. At several city hospitals, he sought treatment for his daughter, the youngest of the children, who was born with a heart defect. As she grew older, they discovered she could neither hear, nor speak. He began retrieving Nadeem and his brothers from the mountains, where they were skipping class. His disappointments mounting, he transferred the boys to the municipal school. There too, all three boys soon dropped out. Alamgir had seen them on the mountains ever since.

Nadeem's father had died in April 2016, losing his battle with cancer. Days later, with debts to clear from the treatment, Nadeem had begun working as a garbage truck cleaner, washing trucks and helping fill them with trash. Often, he was assigned to the ones Alamgir drove. They sped through empty streets as dawn lightened the city. The early morning breeze blowing over them, they hardly noticed the stench their gradually filling truck emitted. They did the rounds of the central suburb of Kurla, filling the truck with sooty remains from one of the city's longest stretches of spare parts stores and car garages. The cutouts of cheap rubber soles from the city's shoe-makers and fish food from aquariums, emptied into their truck. They watched a mall rise over the stunted skyline and tall buildings stretching up from the far end of a swamp to make a gleaming new financial district. They drove on to Saki Naka and then Powai, where low-slung lakeside homes were giving way to condominiums, call centers, technology start-ups, and softly lit coffee shops. Nadeem kept things aside from the trash for himself and Alamgir to sell later. As Alamgir drove on, Nadeem leaned over to watch. Somewhere between filling the old Kurla and Powai and bringing it to the Deonar mountains, the two had become friends.

Alamgir often kept his headlights on, even in the day, to get to the more distant edges of the still smoky, burning, curving township. The fires had upended life on the mountains. Fresh trash fell on the old and charred. Hidden treasures surfaced from under burned layers. Around then, for the first time, Nadeem had noticed a tall, slender girl pulling out bottles, glass, and metal wires from his emptying truck. She was beautiful, unstoppable in the melee of pickers—and paid him no attention at all. Friends told him it could only be Farzana, Jehangir, and Alamgir's younger sister. Hadn't he seen her before?

Jehangir was Javed's man, rising on the hills with his restless energy and lispy chatter. Nadeem needed to learn driving from Alamgir if he was going to follow his route to a garbage truck driving job. Neither of the brothers could be messed with. Farzana was trouble. And yet, on days when he didn't see her brothers around, Nadeem watched Farzana edge into garbage scrambles and turn into a blur.

One afternoon, Nadeem was returning to the city, his emptied truck winding slowly down a slope. He spotted Farzana standing below, with

Farha. Could he help, Nadeem stopped near them to ask. Farzana recognized him as Alamgir's long-haired friend who always wore brightly colored net vests that peeked out of half-open shirts. As Farzana and Farha clambered into the back seat, conversation froze. They watched the trash hills pass by outside, in silence. Nadeem deposited them at the *katas* near the municipal office so they could sell their trash and left.

After that day, Nadeem thought he saw Farzana watching him at garbage clearings. One afternoon he noticed her speak to her friends and giggle. She seemed to be pointing at his long, poker-straight hair, which gave him a slightly electrocuted air. Nadeem's heart sank. A few days later, when Nadeem's truck arrived at the clearing, his hair was buzzed at the sides, and the pompadour had appeared atop. When she saw him, Farzana nodded tightly to approve, turned around, and burrowed herself into the trash shower erupting from his truck.

Another truck cleaner approached Farzana on a clearing, days later. His friend Nadeem liked her. Did she like him too? "*Sochoongi,*" she had replied, returning to fill trash into her bag. *I'll think about it.* She began staying buried in trash scrambles around Nadeem's truck, avoiding his gaze. She used the proceeds from the trash she sold to buy Chinese bhel, crispy fried noodles mixed with sliced cabbage, hot sauce, and Indian spices. It was a blend of two Eastern cultures that left Farzana and Farha orange-tongued and teary eyed. In the middle of getting their fix, Farha often nudged Farzana to show her: Nadeem was standing behind them, across the street. Farzana felt his eyes on her.

Farzana heard his calls ring, wherever she was. When she and Farha got home, Farzana often dug out, from her little sister's bag, the phone Farha had collected from the mountains and had repaired. She checked for Nadeem's calls and hid it again, sorting the day's trash, hoping Jehangir or Alamgir had not seen it. Sometimes, when Farha pushed Nadeem's ringing phone in front of her, Farzana spoke to him, airily, for a bit, and quickly hung up. Weeks after Nadeem had asked through his friend, Farzana finally took his call to say she liked him too.

Fires still simmered on the mountains. Drones hovered over slopes and television crews walked them. The mountains began closing in on them. Farzana waited at clearings but Nadeem's truck often got sent to the Mulund mountains instead. On other days, he looked for her at clearings when she had already been sent home by the guards. They fought over their increasingly averted meetings. Farzana kept trying to make it through the fires, smoke, and security. Fevers raged in her, talismans filled her arms, but nothing could keep Farzana home when she had plans to meet Nadeem.

In the evenings, Nadeem began following Alamgir to his *kata* to help organize the trash, weigh it, and pay pickers, except the fires had slowed business and there wasn't much to do. They locked up early and moved on to Alamgir's house to chat. Farzana hung around, usually ignoring them, occasionally turning to tell them their information about the guards, friends who had been beaten up or others who had paid to get in and work nights, was wrong. What did truck drivers know about pickers?

When they did make it to the same trash clearing at the same time, Farzana and Nadeem walked together furtively, concealed in the still rising smoke. The blazing sun parched Farzana's mouth, the smoldering mountains scalded the soles of her feet, peeling the skin off of them. Smoke made her cough and her throat and chest itch. Nadeem began bringing bottles of water for her.

One afternoon, when Nadeem arrived, Farzana was waiting for him with a small, transparent plastic pouch in her hands. Nadeem looked up at the smile that lit her face, then quizzically at the bag. It was her gift for him, a grain of uncooked rice. "*Dhyan se dekh,*" she said. *Look at it carefully.* "*Zyada,*" she repeated. *More carefully.* She had had their names inscribed on the rice grain at the Haji Ali shrine. Nadeem and Farzana, united forever on a grain of rice.

With Farzana's eighteenth birthday, rains had cleared the fires and smoke, hills began filling with moisture and rising again. Adulthood had arrived, and Farzana spoke to Nadeem in the glow of the phone, after everyone had fallen asleep, asking him to meet her parents, speak about marriage. They were looking for someone. She had hung up green bangles at Mira Datar's shrine. She would be married to someone else, if he did not come to see them soon. Nadeem was often at their home, avoiding her parents, avoiding Jehangir. He was waiting for his driver's license, for the job that would come with it and that he hoped would impress her brothers. She slept fitfully and worked before dawn.

Alamgir's wife, Yasmeen, was already suspicious. *"Naak to uski pakode jaisi hai,"* she told Farzana one afternoon, asking indirectly about the short man who was always at their house. *His nose looks like batter dropped into hot oil to make a pakoda.* She had not had any luck getting information from Alamgir, who only said Nadeem was new on the truck and needed to learn how to drive. Did he like her, Yasmeen asked Farzana, eliciting no reply. *"Naata hai vo,"* she said, scrunching her nose. *He's too short for you.* Farzana was the tallest of the six sisters, and Yasmeen thought she could do better than Nadeem.

ONE MORNING, NADEEM had come to the mountains, riding next to the driver, in a garbage truck, his water bottle rolling under his feet. Farzana waited for him. When she was done picking from his truck, Nadeem handed her the water. It dribbled down her long neck as she drank thirstily, chatting and giggling at the same time, barely pausing to breathe. When he returned from his round in the city, late in the afternoon, he didn't see Farzana or the usual crowd collect around his truck. A picker told him that the others had taken someone who had been crushed by a bulldozer and left for dead in the clearing to the hospital. They would be back soon. The victim was unlikely to survive.

The mountains were filled with stories. Nadeem had heard about children getting eaten by mountain dogs while their mothers whirled within garbage scrambles. He knew gang rivalries led to stabbings on quiet mountain peaks. A gangster had hidden, rolled up in a discarded carpet, for days, to avoid police. Cocooned within, he had been reformed, and when he emerged he had become a cleric at a mosque close by. It was hard to say which of the tales that filled the mountain air were true and which ones were not.

Then Nadeem heard it was Farzana who had come under the bulldozer. He left the truck midway through his shift and hung around in hospital corridors for days, unable to see her. Their friends had slowly returned to work but Nadeem had waited outside the swinging doors until Alamgir told him that Farzana had called out for him. Even as the doctors gave their dire prognosis, Nadeem heard, she had mumbled his name. For weeks, Nadeem spent nights at the hospital and days on the truck, keeping his household running and his head in a daze. As the days wore on, both his mother and Hyder Ali thought Nadeem would stop coming to see Farzana, that he would return to his own home at night. But Nadeem had kept returning to hospital corridors, the ward, and then later to Hyder Ali's home.

Speaking with his son that night, Hyder Ali realized it was Nadeem that Farzana had worked through the smoke-induced fevers and coughs for, and whom she had called out in the hospital for. He immediately asked Alamgir to call the young man. Hyder Ali asked Nadeem, why did he come every day? He knew how mangled Farzana's body had been. How scarred she still was. Nadeem told Hyder Ali he hadn't stuck through the long nights at the hospital only to leave Farzana now. He wanted to marry her. Tears welled in Hyder Ali's eyes.

For weeks, his friends had told Nadeem that Farzana could be deformed for life. It wasn't the only problem: his older brother had told him to keep away from mountain girls. *"Love shove shuru ho jata hai,"* he said. *They start love affairs on the slopes.* "*Bhai tu door hi reh,*" he warned. *Stay away, brother.* But Nadeem had given his word to Farzana and then to Hyder Ali. Jehangir, too, had wanted a match who would take his sister away from the mountains. But he knew, word traveled fast in the marriage market. Who would marry Farzana as she was? Besides, she would not budge. "*Usse nahi karoongi to mar jaoongi,*" was all she would say about it. *If I don't marry him, I will die.*

The plans were put in motion. Nadeem told Hyder Ali he would bring his mother to approve of Farzana. Then he would have to bring his uncles over, from the village. As the elders of the family, even though they had never lived together, the uncles would have to endorse the match. Hyder Ali charged Alamgir with taking Farzana's marriage proposal to Nadeem's mother, as is custom. Enduring, unchanging rituals of arranged marriages would replace the promises made between Nadeem and Farzana, two young souls on the shifting, rising trash peaks amid wafting smoke.

MEANWHILE, THE MUNICIPALITY also advertised for a match for its intractable mountains. Interest in prebid meetings had remained tepid. A municipal engineer said they had often been sent for seminars on what makes a good tender, how to write it so it would work well, so it would elicit bids. They had tweaked this one. But finding the balance between what worked for the municipality and what would attract an eligible suitor for its trash township was hard. The company that made the plant would have to pay a large deposit that it would get back only after five years, to ensure it kept the plant in good running order. An Indian partner was to operate the plant, but such a big plant had never been run in India. Companies worried the city's terms were too hard to meet.

Potential bidders worried also about the messy fallout with Tatva, the allegations that the municipality had not met the terms they had agreed on, the ongoing arbitration. Then there was the mountains' army of pickers that despite so many efforts to evict them, had never left. "It is true that we have never really been able to build a wall" around the mountains, a municipal engineer involved in planning the plant said. But without the wall to mark it as theirs and keep out the army of mountain denizens, how could a new company settle on the slopes, potential bidders worried.

On October 25, 2016, the municipality issued invitations for bids to make the waste-to-energy plant at the Deonar mountains. On November 9, Sanjay Mukherjee, Mumbai's additional municipal commissioner, was upbeat, telling reporters that "this will be one of the largest plants in the world."

The Hindu festival season ended days later, leaving the winds on the mountains drier and fiercer. They would soon wither the plants, turning the mountains brown and squeezing out any rain left within, deflating them again. As warm winds traveled through slopes, they could hit gases emanating from the slowly putrefying mountains or trash boiled by sun, and erupt in fires, even while bids were open. Guard patrols stayed tight. Hyder Ali watched pickers make their way slowly up slopes, guards gather around, batter them with sticks, and turn them back. He hoarded and relayed these worrying stories to friends who dropped by at home in the evenings. They recounted their own. A chill ran down their lanes.

Ragpickers from far ends of the city came before daybreak and worked in deep, unpatrolled mountain recesses. Days later, as guards discovered them, pickers scouted for new places to trawl for trash in. The secret spots shrank rapidly. Hyder Ali heard of more friends working nights, returning home before guards arrived in the morning. The guards began patrolling at night too.

On his bench outside, Hyder Ali pulled his knees up, resting his chin on them. He stared at the silvery gray remnants of a fire that Sahani and Yasmeen had made with scavenged wood scraps to cook meals on. The family's life lay suspended between Farzana's illness and the fading mountain luck. Hyder Ali had not bought cooking oil for the stove inside in weeks. The soap operas that had wafted out of the television all day, had been silenced after he stopped paying cable bills. Shakimun's sewing machine and the blender had sputtered out too. Sahani brought a mortar and pestle and ground chutneys to eat with chapatis they cooked on the silver-ringed fires. Hyder Ali had been getting property tax bills for three years—this was the municipality's acknowledgment that he lived here—but he had not paid any of them. *"Bhar doonga. Ayenge hatane to bhar doonga,"* he said. *I will pay if they come to evict me.*

The municipality planned that the bids were to be submitted by January 2017. Work would only begin after April. The plant would then take nearly three years to build, making Justice Oka's June 2017 deadline impossible to meet. But by making a little progress, officials hoped to keep the mountains going for just a little longer.

NINETEEN

NADEEM'S MOTHER, SHAHEEN, HAD waited for weeks for the arrival of the marriage proposal. She knew that Nadeem had stayed out nights on end because a friend's sister was in the hospital, after an accident. When he asked her to cook for the girl, who didn't like hospital food, Shaheen's neighbor had asked if she knew she was cooking for her prospective daughter-in-law. She watched him fix his hair endlessly in the small mirror stuck on the wall, and figured it was for the girl in the hospital.

When Alamgir finally appeared, in December 2016, Shaheen told him that their house was unlike Hyder Ali's. Theirs had been the first plinth of brick and stone in a lane of trash-made homes, marking them as one of the more prosperous families in their settlement. It rose over the rainwater that flowed down the mountains through their lane. The house had risen in fits and starts above this foundation. When Shaheen had been a bride, it had only two side walls. Fierce monsoon winds and rain blew through the house. Alone at home, while her husband was at work, she had sat at the front opening, with a stick, to keep the Shaitans out. Nadeem's father had slowly built a front and back wall and then a second floor. But unlike Farzana's flimsy house, which Shaheen had heard of, this one was solid, all brick. Farzana would be marrying up.

It was agreed that Shaheen would come to inspect Farzana a few weeks later. When Hyder Ali heard this, he paced Banjara Galli all afternoon, fretting about the tests Farzana would have to pass. It was for Nadeem that Farzana had forced herself out of bed, dragging her leg painfully, to walk. It was with him that she would have the life that others thought she could never have. If only she could make it through the bridal inspection. But how could she? he worried.

A few weeks earlier, he had watched fairy lights getting strung in their lane, glinting past his house toward the mountains. They ended at Parveen Shaikh's house. For years, the bespectacled, petite, and dour Parveen had taken pride in saving up from picking trash to push both her sons through high school. She had checked their pockets, every evening, to make sure gangs didn't lure them away with money or drugs. *"Khaane se zyaada to maine fikar khayi hai,"* she would often tell Shakimun. *I ate worry more than food when my boys were growing up.* Shakimun was never sure how to respond: aside from the youngest, Ramzan, her sons had never seen the inside of a school.

Parveen's oldest, Ismail, collected payments for a cell phone company while her younger son worked as a tailor and passed on scraps for her to sell. A few days earlier, when Parveen was cooking dinner, Ismail had walked in with a bride, a girl from work he had secretly married. Parveen's dreams of finding a pliant girl from their village had crumbled, but faced with a bride at home, she planned a wedding ceremony and reception, and had lights fixed in the lane.

Farzana had grown up with Ismail; he was only a few months older than her. She decided she had to go to the reception. Besides, she wanted to see the bride, who had upturned Parveen's carefully nurtured plans.

Everyone in Banjara Galli was talking about her. Farzana said she would go early, before her parents, and not stay long. The reception hall was at the lane's entrance. Hyder Ali could not bring himself to say no.

Farzana picked out a long blue skirt and top, sewn with gold thread work, to wear. Sahani helped her dress up. As she fixed her hair in the mirror, Farzana thought her throat bulged out awkwardly, making her face look frozen and distorted. She wrapped her blue dupatta with gold tassels tightly around her face to cover her neck, and powdered her face to brighten it. When she came out, Hyder Ali saw a skinny, drawn shadow of the old Farzana.

As she walked slowly down the lane to the wedding hall with Farha, Hyder Ali settled down with a tumbler of tea on the bench jutting out of the house. He heard Farzana crying. It was all he ever heard these days, Hyder Ali thought. But her crying only got louder. He put his tumbler aside and craned to look down the lane. He saw Farzana limping slowly back with her arm around Farha. Tears smeared her whitened face, crumbling the glowing excitement she had left with. Sahani helped her into the house, sat her on the floor, and tried fiddling with her dress.

They had only walked halfway down the lane, Farha explained, when a long, metallic thread from the scallops embroidered on Farzana's skirt had caught on one of the sutures that held her calf together. Farha bent down and tried to get it unstuck but tugging at it threatened to reopen the wound, Farha thought. Farzana could feel her leg throbbing. The lane spun in circles around her.

Farha cried with Farzana. Her palms got clammy and slipped on her sister's skin. She had stood up, wrapped Farzana's arm around her shoulder, and brought her home, hobbling. Farzana's screaming filled the house as Sahani and Farah tried disentangling her skirt from her calf. Hyder Ali cried helplessly outside. He heard them ask her to stay still so they could unfix the gold thread.

Then the room fell silent. She must have got out of the dress, he thought, relieved. The silence stretched on. She must be asleep, Hyder Ali thought, sipping his by then tepid tea again.

Then, Farzana stepped out again, this time in a baby pink salwar kameez. She had fixed her hair and her face again and was ready to leave. She had missed the wedding already but would not miss the reception for anything, she told him. It really was the old Farzana, Hyder Ali thought, as he watched her walk down Banjara Galli again.

Nadeem came over in the evenings. Farzana took slow steps forward with her hand on his shoulder. Was she taller than him, Yasmeen asked Farzana. Is that why her hand sat so comfortably on his shoulder? He was bending for her, Farzana said, bending a bit herself. She stopped in the middle of their walks, inside the house, on most evenings, turning to ask him what he would give her as a wedding gift. She would have to wait to know, he said. The wedding suddenly shimmered ahead. She had to get to it.

FARZANA JOINED KHULA Aasman, a free soccer class for girls in their lanes, to try to fix her limp. Mehrun and some of the other girls all tried to finish up their chores: cooking, fetching water, and embroidery by the afternoon, so they could play in a small and tilting open space. Farzana, with her limp, was sure to make any team she was in lose. The others begged her to sit out the games and just watch them play. But Farzana wore her baby blue t-shirt with "Khula Aasman," or "Open Sky," emblazoned on it and was there before the game began, twice a week, waiting to be picked. Doctors had told her to get some exercise, she told them. She loved coming home exhausted, having tried to run.

She tried walking down the lane, to her sisters' houses, then farther, to friends' places. That would heal her limp before Shaheen came, she figured. One afternoon, as she was walking down 90 Feet Road to a friend's house, she looked down to straighten her knee. When she looked up, a bulldozer was rolling slowly toward her. She watched it approach. Its growing rumble rang in her ears. She stood in place. It came closer. Tears streamed down her face. There was nowhere to go, Farzana thought. It was coming at her, as it did in her dreams.

A neighbor had seen Farzana standing in front of a bulldozer, crying. It was retreating by then, pressing down molten concrete, to fix the road cratered by rain. The neighbor walked her home. Farzana had sobbed through much of the afternoon. "*Vahi cheez thi*," she told Nadeem that evening, as they walked inside the house. *It was the same thing.* He kept her walking.

When he left, she massaged her knee to reduce the pain and swelling. Wanting to be married, looking like she did, walking like she did, did she want too much? Farzana fretted. But Nadeem came every evening. They bantered, Nadeem softly, Farzana more loudly. His soft voice making her brighter. He egged her on to stand, to walk, to move.

Farzana had no memory of being possessed and had never been sure about the spirits—or of anything that held her back. But with Shaheen's visit coming up, she let Hyder Ali and Yasmeen fiddle with her amulets and have new prayers read into them, to ward away any leftover spirits that they thought trembled in her hand and dragged her leg. Farzana worried about what she would wear and how best to sit and sip tea without her hand quivering. She got Sahani to buy lime green glass bangles to match the rose pink salwar kameez embroidered with small, lifelike rosebuds and roses, their bright green stems and leaves in place. She would wear it the day Shaheen came, hoping she would see Farzana not as she was, but as she could be.

WHEN OFFICIALS HAD presented their plans to the court committee, some members had worried they were too ambitious. The plant might not make money even after the concession of the company that was to run the plant ran out after twenty years. Could they begin with a smaller plant? Besides, the incinerator would have to be fed dry waste that would burn well and produce electricity. But only unsorted tangles came out of homes to fill garbage trucks. Wealthy homes, which produced the most valuable trash, sometimes didn't even have trash cans at all, their owners unsure about what happened to their possessions after they were done with them and handed them to household staff to dispose of. Everything— from food to shoes, to razor blades, used batteries, injections, tablet strips, and diapers—came to the mountains mashed together, and would make the incinerator less effective if fed together. But less than 10 percent of Mumbai's waste got separated, surveys showed.

Since the 1970s, waste incinerators had been installed at Deonar and one in the city even predated the mountains. But as the incinerators had failed, pickers collected what emptied from trucks turning *cuchra*, or trash, into *bhangaar*, scrap or raw material for something else, for some-one else. Phugawlas had trawled for plastic, Chumbakwalas for metal, Chindiwalas for scrap. They had brought it to their lanes, sorted and resold them to be remade.

Officials stepped up their campaign to get household trash separated. The municipality asked building managers to separate and compost the biodegradable waste in their compound and send only dry waste in trucks that left for Deonar, Mulund, or Kanjurmarg. If they didn't, the managers could get fined or lose their building licenses. At the mountains, consultants had planned for screens and magnetic segregators to separate the trash instead of pickers, so they could feed the right kind of things to the plant. The mountains' invisible army would be replaced but there would be better jobs for them at the plant, or in their cleaned-up lanes.

SAHANI DIDN'T KNOW how to tell Farzana that the more she tried to walk, the more her leg dragged. The evening before Shaheen's visit, Sahani climbed up the shaky metal stairs to the loft where Farzana lay awake on the bed. She wore a blue salwar kameez, her head demurely covered. Sahani threw away the quilt and lifted up her sister's loose-fitting salwar to look at the pink wounds that began a little above Farzana's ankle, traveled up her left leg, and ended at her buttocks, which were caved in from being stitched up over missing flesh. Long stitch marks ran the length of her arms too. Sahani jabbed at Farzana's swollen knees and ankles. "*Kaun isse shaadi karega aise,*" she asked, agonizing over the test that lay ahead. *Who would want to marry her like this?*

The following day, Shaheen walked up the stairs in Hyder Ali's house to meet Farzana. She had a plump softness that might have come from never having worked on the mountains, never having scrambled for garbage. The two spoke little but felt they knew each other. Nadeem had told his mother that Farzana could not carry heavy things or squat to wash clothes. "*Mil ke ghar chalaenge,*" she told the bride-to-be. *We'll run the house together.* She came down and gave Hyder Ali her assent for the marriage. "*Nahi to bachon ka dil tootta hai,*" she would later recall. *I would have broken their hearts if I didn't.* She told Hyder Ali that Nadeem's uncles would come for a final approval when they visited for his father's first death anniversary, next April.

Hyder Ali walked up the stairs to tell Farzana. She had waited weeks to hear this news. But he found her asleep, exhausted from making sure her leg did not drag, that the gauzy dupatta did not fall off her head, that she did not speak, from being the observant, pliant, and protected girl for the marriage market. It had worn her out, but a life with Nadeem lay ahead.

Hyder Ali came back downstairs, thinking about how he could stall the wedding without canceling it. Shaheen had told him that this was the first wedding in her family, since her own. Much of the groom's large and extended family would come. Hyder Ali could barely even pay for his half of the wedding. There was no one he could ask for money anymore, not even Jehangir, who had borne the brunt of Farzana's hospital expenses.

HYDER ALI FIXED Farzana's wedding for June 2017, nearly eight months later. He desperately needed money, but work on the mountains remained erratic. Guards had not let pickers work since they began finding money in the trash a few weeks before. Hyder Ali heard that someone had found a burlap sack full of notes. As word spread, police arrived, took the cash away, and told them most city notes were worthless. On November 8, 2016, the prime minister had banned high currency notes in order to prevent terrorists from printing fakes and undermining India's rising economy. Notes stashed secretly in the city for years had begun arriving at the mountains. They had suddenly turned to rubbish. Pickers sold them for less than the printed amount until guards and policemen blocked their entry into the mountains. Why was it that when money arrived at the mountains, packed in bags, it was useless, Hyder Ali thought.

"Pradhan Mantri hamare liye i-card bhej rahe hain," he told Badre Alam, his cousin who lived in their loft, as they chatted at home one evening. *The prime minister is sending us identity cards.* He would work at the mountains only when the cards, which let him walk the mountains officially, came. The guards would not be able to drive them away, if he had the prime minister's card on him, Hyder Ali thought. It was how he had understood the new solid waste rules that volunteers had told him about, the ones that said pickers were to be included in managing the city's waste.

The cousins chatted about reviving the embroidery workshop before Farzana's wedding. Hyder Ali softly let on that despite his resolution, he had gone to work on the mountains yesterday.

He had collected ten kilos of squashed plastic, he told Badre Alam, looking toward the black bags in a corner of the room. Badre Alam threw him a befuddled look. Hyder Ali just threw his hands up. What was he to do? Farzana's wedding was only months away.

Ten-year-old Ramzan, the youngest of the children, walked in. "*Isko kabhi nahi bhejoonga,*" Hyder Ali said. *I'll never send him to the mountains.* His eyes shone as he spoke of how Ramzan was the only one of his children who woke up on his own, made his tea, and left for school by 7:30 A.M. Ramzan's school tie and bag hung on a wall hook, along with Farzana's back brace. Ramzan responded saying he loved going to the mountains. Hyder Ali stared in mock horror. "*Bagule marne jata hoon,*" Ramzan reassured his father. *I go there to kill storks,* using the Urdu equivalent of "shooting the breeze."

As 2016 came to a close, the strange harvest of currency notes had left the mountains as trash had continued to fill them. The gray market for the old notes shrank, new pink and orange notes arrived on the market. Pickers gave up on waiting for their official identity cards. Security eased and they had returned to picking trash. Officials waited nervously for fires and prepared to quell them. The deadline for the plant tenders was in January 2017. Not a single bid came.

TWENTY

LATE ON A BREEZY January evening, Yasmin returned to her house after a medical trial. She paid rent with the money she brought with her and moved back into the room that she had vacated before she left. The children returned, bringing back bits of their home, which had been stored at *katas'* and others' places during their mother's absence. Mehrun resettled the family, folding everyone's clothes into the metal cupboard and lining up dishes along the kitchen counter while Yasmin dozed off.

The following afternoon, a long line of people blocked Banjara Galli's entrance, wanting a consultation at the free health clinic that had opened across the slim entrance. Perched atop the clinic was a board with a bicycle painted on a background of green and red, the symbol of the Samajwadi or Socialist Party. Elections for Mumbai's municipality, said to be India or Asia's wealthiest, were weeks away. Mumbai's election machine was moving through their lanes, glinting in them. But its promises barely reached Yasmin's house, dark in the mountains' shade, teetering at the edge. Inside, Mehrun, who was always home, was graduating from the cusp of teenage straight into adulthood.

The faintly sweet smell of rice Mehrun was steaming filled their room. Some of the women had not made it through the tests, Yasmin, in a sunflower yellow salwar kameez with pink and gold flowers scalloped at the edges, told Sharib, her older son, and Mehrun. So they had to be sent home. But she passed the tests and felt nothing after she took the drug, a contraceptive; Yasmin beamed. In a few weeks, she would return so doctors could check if the medicine had any side effects, earning her another month's rent and expenses.

The kitchen counter darkened and Mehrun turned to see her brother Sameer, who was two years older, standing at the door, blocking the light. The sun streamed around him, framing his edges with a gold rim. Coated in a patina of dried mountain mud, he looked like a sepia-tinted photograph, except for the blood trickling down his legs. Mehrun served Sharib, the older of the brothers, who looked up with a sour expression, aimed at Sameer.

He had been walking to work in the morning, Sharib told them, when he heard screaming. He turned and saw guards raining their sticks down on a picker whose long body curled up tightly under their blows. As their sticks swung back up in the air, he uncurled to breathe, and they kicked his stomach, curling him up in pain again. Pickers stood around and along the slope, watching. As Sharib, breathless, drew near, the guards stopped and the dusty figure uncoiled beneath them. It was Sameer.

Sharib had pled with the guards to let Sameer go. He would never come back, Sharib promised, retrieving Sameer. The two had walked down the slope, until Sameer veered, limping toward the market to scour the overflowing dustbins that garbage trucks hardly reached. He eventually returned home, trickling blood that Yasmin asked him to wash off before Friday prayers and Arabic class.

Whenever she returned with money from trials, Yasmin repraised her efforts to push her children out of the mountains' shadow. Sameer ate the rice Mehrun served, then messed through the clothes she had laid out in the cupboard, nearly missing prayers, until he found a dark, mismatched set and left with Sharib.

Mehrun tidied the cupboard and settled to fill a long saree border with gold flowers, when Hera arrived. She was followed by her mother-in-law and sister-in-law. Her sister-in-law wore a red salwar kameez topped with a red and green dupatta with a bicycle motif, as if the board above the clinic had draped itself around her shoulders. Mother and daughter had spent the morning walking through their lanes, campaigning for the Samajwadi Party.

The Party's traditional vote base was among the Muslim and Yadav communities in Uttar Pradesh, where it ran the government. Its roots had spread in the mountains' shadow as pickers came from the state to fill it, and these lanes formed the Party's stronghold in Mumbai. The city's major parties—the Bharatiya Janata Party (BJP) and Shiv Sena who had controlled the city and its wealth for almost two decades—mostly stayed away. Instead, they mounted furious campaigns in the city; after years as a junior partner, the BJP had taken control of the central and state government, and had now set its sights on one of India's largest and richest cities. Devendra Fadnavis, Maharashtra's young chief minister, smiled out of campaign hoardings across Mumbai. Among the promises splashed on them was one to make electricity from the waste at Deonar. The tender dates had passed by without any bids coming for the project at Deonar, but the promise remained, unwavering.

The Samajwadi Party's councilors had opposed the plant, saying it would sicken the lungs of their constituents, weakened by years of inhaling the city's detritus, without giving them the jobs the pickers had waited for. With the municipality controlled by the Shiv Sena and BJP, who represented the city that sent the waste to the unseen mountains, the plans were finally approved. The plant would come to the mountains, if only someone would bid for it.

IN YASMIN'S HOUSE, the city arrived, a little through official means, but more often through unofficial routes, couched in stiff officialese. While the women chatted that afternoon, gang payment collectors waited at the door to collect payments for the power they had illegally connected to homes in their lanes. Mehrun asked them to come back in a little while. She would borrow money to pay them.

Within days, Yasmin had nearly run out of the money she brought from the trial and returned for another. An angry red rash began growing across Sharib's back. It stretched and reddened in the sun, as he constructed a house near Ashra's school. Watching it grow, the boss had sent him home, where Sharib laid on the floor in pain, turning on one side and then another.

In charge of the house, Mehrun planned days around bringing back the free municipal water supply. She would have to walk down their long lane to 90 Feet Road, slip into the loud, slippery gaggle for the municipal water tanker, then make sure she ran into someone to help her bring back water cans. She could also buy water from a neighbor who had surreptitiously connected his pipe to the water supply. But he asked for a fee she could not pay.

Through the afternoons, she stayed buried in fixing flowers on women's sleeves, worrying her brothers would ask her what was for lunch when she had nothing. Yasmin returned, sooner than expected: she had tested as anemic and been rejected from the trial. She had begged them to take her anyway. She needed the money, but had been turned away only with travel expenses. The early winter dusk often set in before Mehrun could buy supplies and light up the stove to cook. Over these long, quiet afternoons, Mehrun embroidered beads, her hazel eyes getting larger, her face thinner. The gold flowers she stitched floated in her eyes and her empty stomach.

The only topic that made her seem like the twelve-year-old she was, was the collection of discarded dolls, accumulated from the mountains, now lost in the many moves in and out of the same house. "*Vo log ub jaate hain na,*" she said. *The owners must have gotten bored of them, right. Theek hai. Tabhi to hamein mila. It's okay. That is how we got them.* This too, was how the city arrived at their house.

AS THEIR LANES filled with party flags, Yasmin searched for work in the election industry. A friend had taken her along to a campaign rally in the city, where she heard their state representative say he had brought water to the lanes around the mountains. She knew it hadn't reached their house but Yasmin clapped on cue. Later, she heard that the rate for filling crowds at rallies had gone up to ₹800, far more than her first visit. If she went to a few rallies she would not need to go for a medical trial for a month, Yasmin thought. But she could not get any work, too many people wanted the well-paying jobs as crowd fillers at rallies.

Yasmin used the last of her notes for ointment to shrink Sharib's rash and handed Mehrun more embroidery instead. Late one afternoon, Mehrun and Ashra stuck tiny gold crystals onto a black burqa, making lengthening trellises on it. "*Bhook nahi hai,*" Mehrun said to Ashra, and almost to herself, *I am really not hungry.* Ashra soon left, unable to focus on work. Mehrun stood up, holding up a gold saree border that was longer than she was and would buy them a meal.

Explaining why she left Mehrun to fill the intricate borders and sleeves, Yasmin would explain that the medical trials had weakened her.

She knew people in her lane talked about her long absences, with Mehrun locked in the house, her odd hours and irregular, mysterious earnings. She knew that they thought it was why Moharram Ali had left her.

YASMIN WANTED TO enroll Sameer for a drug rehabilitation program. She suspected his foggy mind, slow, halting speech, and fitful head rolls were clouded by more than just the *gutkha*, or chewing tobacco, that had stained his teeth. But he also pulled out money when she could not find it anywhere else. She put off his treatment until after she had gotten Mehrun out of their lanes. Stuck in the mountains' shadow, Mehrun had stayed out of school, scrounging for meals, struggling for water, getting quieter and more translucent by the day, even as creditors crept closer. Yasmin wanted her out.

One afternoon, Yasmin decided to go to Mehrun's school to explore if she could return for classes or get a leaving certificate so she could enroll her elsewhere, far away from the mountains. Mother and daughter covered their heads with dupattas they held tightly at their chest, wore their slippers, and turned to close the house door behind them. Yasmin began to giggle, seeming childlike. *"Aadmi ghus sakta hai,"* she pointed out: the bottom plank of the door had come off, leaving a hole. *A man could get through it.* Mehrun placed the plank loosely in place so a potential intruder would think it was a full door, then turned to leave, looking nearly like the young woman she was becoming. The two walked out along their lane.

The newly built orange and green school building was across from a public park and had a large foyer with pictures of national leaders, most of whom Mehrun could not recognize. They walked up the stairs, painted with signs asking the children not to litter, in Marathi and Urdu. There was a poster showing pictures of children breaking stones in a quarry, with slogans encouraging them to go to school rather than work. But Mehrun's guess was as good as Yasmin's. She could not read it, although she had studied in Urdu until middle school. At every landing, the views of the trash mountains streamed in through the geometrical grills in the wall. At every landing, the reluctant Mehrun asked to go home. Yasmin kept her going.

As they reached the fourth floor, Mehrun looked breathless and relieved. It was Friday and school had closed for the day. They walked back downstairs, Mehrun telling Yasmin this was the first time she had come back to her school since she left more than a year ago. She had told her friends and teachers then that she was moving to a private English school. She would only speak English the next time they met, they had teased her. Since then, they had moved on to the next class and learned more Urdu and more English. "*Main unse kya kahoongi?*" Mehrun said. *What will I say if I run into them?*

Outside, they joined the lane jammed with handcarts and shoppers they had seen from high up. A Friday sermon began to crackle over a loudspeaker as the two walked through the clouds of flies. If you do your *namaz*, your prayers, before you sleep, then you will never sleep alone. He will be with you, a voice called over the loudspeaker, rising above the din of shoppers, as they walked back home.

WEEKS LATER, THE Shiv Sena had nosed ahead of the BJP in the municipal elections, but didn't secure enough seats to elect its own mayor: again, the two parties would have to work to realize the city's rising aspirations together. As expected, the Samajwadi Party had won in the shadow of the mountains made by the leftovers of Mumbai's aspirations, and hardly made a dent in the rest of the city. The city and its mountains would stay in different worlds.

TWENTY-ONE

I N THE NEATLY DESIGNED schedule that municipal consultants had made in their project report for the prospective waste
plant, March 2017 was filled with blue blobs, showing the
months when the company, which by then would have been selected,
would finalize the design. By the time the court deadline came, in June,
the blobs in the report's table turned green and then orange, showing the
beginning of construction on their schedule for the project that would
finally burn away the city's trash. The colors moved forward like a rising
wave on the long schedule in the report, but no plant was underway at
Deonar. No bids had come. More than two months before the deadline
to close the township, the municipality was back in court, asking to extend
its life for four more years.

Raj Sharma, the activist, had filed his own petition saying that hardly
anything Oka had asked for, the boundary wall, the cameras, the lights,
and the cessation of dumping building debris, had happened. For
months, he had photographed people getting through the broken wall,

and seen debris fill roads within the township and top the mountains. As the security tightened farther around the mountains' border with the lanes, other court committee members had heard that pickers made rafts with the rubber and plastic they foraged, and sailed into the township through the creek. They had asked for barbed wire to be installed along the creek's edge. It had not been fixed yet either. Sharma opposed the extension of the deadline. The court set a date to hear both petitions, a week before the June 30 deadline to stop dumping garbage at Deonar.

Hearings began in the packed Room 13, a year and a half after Justice Oka had handed down the construction ban and set the deadline to close the Deonar township. Petitions filed in public interest, such as Sharma's, were presented in turn before Oka's ornate, elevated chair, forming a moving tableau of Mumbai's aches and wounds, of dreams that clashed as they rose. The concerns were varied: the city's cramped jails, the sound of the millions-strong orchestra that played day and night at festivals, residents cooking meats that their neighbors' gods prohibited them from even smelling, the smoke that wafted from unseen garbage mountains into its rising towers. Oka make space for endless dreams and needs in a city with little space.

Petitioners, lawyers, and an assortment of government functionaries squeezed past one another to recount these often years-long troubles to Oka. The only comfort in the courtroom's crush came from the air conditioning that had been installed when Justice Chandrachud had adjudicated on the Deonar mountains' fate, nearly a decade before. A deep thud sounded as Deonar's case papers, accumulated over years and in which the mountains' invisible army appeared only as fire-starters, landed on Oka's desk.

Why would Mumbai's garbage be emptied on the hills for four more years, he asked when the waste rules gave only two more to fix garbage dumping grounds around the country. Anil Sakhare, the municipality's long-standing lawyer on the case, said it had made substantial progress on meeting Oka's goals and the waste rules. It was Sharma who had an obstructionist attitude.

The diminutive Sharma stood behind his lawyers in his oversized shirt and high-waist pants and nudged his lawyer to point out that he had asked to visit the mountains officially. When the municipality had not set it up, he had got through the cracks in the wall, photographed the mountains, and written a report for the court detailing all the ways in which Oka's orders had not touched them. Oka asked the municipality to allow Sharma and his lawyers to inspect its mountain registers. He set the next hearing for June 29, one day before the deadline for dumping to end at Deonar.

As Sharma stepped out into the colonnaded corridor that ran along-side the courtroom, a municipal engineer pulled him aside, into a sun-filled courtyard, and chatted affably. The waste-to-energy plant they had planned for Deonar would take off this time, he told Sharma. He made no mention of the absence of bidders so far or that the deadline had been extended and norms relaxed, in the hope that it would help attract bids. Mumbai's waste could produce enough power, he said. It would just have to be dried several times, to reduce its wetness, before incinerating it. He bought Sharma tea from one of the tea vendors who walked around the busy court, steaming kettle in hand and little glasses stuffed in their pants pockets.

"We were born here and lived here our whole lives," he said animatedly, in Hindi. "We know what works in this city. I don't look at what is happening anywhere else." Swallowing the last dregs of his tea, he expanded on how the project would transform the city and the Deonar township. "People tell us Pune model, Pune model. We should look at the Pune model," he said, referring to the awards the neighboring city had won for managing its waste. "They have no idea how big and complex Mumbai is." They needed Sharma's help getting their project off the ground, he said—these court cases only soaked up their energy and delayed the plant. Sharma nodded.

Sharma's lawyers calculated that more construction debris than garbage had been dumped on the mountains over the last few months. He wondered why garbage traders were in jail for dumping debris illegally on the mountains, when the municipality was dumping excess amounts of the stuff itself. Municipal officials said they were doing this within permissible limits and that it was needed to quell fires, make roads to reach the township's far end and fix it.

AT THE NEXT court hearing, both legal teams waited nervously as Justice Oka grilled the lawyers representing the state in the preceding case. The newspapers had been full of the death a few days ago of Manjula Shetye, a thirty-eight-year-old female prisoner at Mumbai's Arthur Road jail, who had been serving a life sentence for murdering her sister-in-law in 1996. Her fellow inmates alleged that she was beaten brutally and left to die by jail staff, after she asked for eggs and bread that they were supposed to get for breakfast.

Oka looked down through his glasses, selected pages from the case papers, then looked up and read out the orders he'd given on improving the state's jails, months before. Had they done it? Lawyers said that much like at Deonar, a committee had been formed to improve prison infrastructure and reduce overcrowding in jails on Oka's instructions. It would submit a report in a few months. Oka interrupted, his voice rising. He didn't think progress would be made, even months later. For a few moments, the lawyers and petitioners in the courtroom looked up from their own case papers to take in his anger. Cases could stretch on in court but in the city, the delays could lead to abrupt, dark turns—the mountain fires, Shetye's death. Behind the cases, the courses of the lives they obscured sometimes turned, ended, or darkened forever, through accidents, fires, violence, and the lengthening shadow of the mountains.

The Deonar lawyers moved in for their hearing, Sharma's lawyers saying Oka's orders had not reached the township and the municipality's lawyers saying they had. They only needed to extend the township's life a little longer. Oka instructed Sharma's lawyer to suggest names of waste management experts who could visit the mountains and report back to the court on whether his orders had been implemented. He extended the deadline for halting the dumping till the next hearing, a few weeks later.

A few days after the hearing, Sharma began calling experts he had met as he traversed through Mumbai's waste world for years. He asked them to visit the trash township at the court's direction and report back to Oka.

AS THE COURT and the city attempted to tighten their grip on Mumbai's waste, it kept spilling from underneath them. No one seemed to know how much waste there was: one report estimated that the city generated around 9,000 metric tons of garbage every day, concluding that as Mumbaikars continued to move out to suburban utopias, their waste would follow them, growing only by 1 percent a year for the next twenty years. Deonar could almost absorb this; it seemed to suggest and it fitted the municipality's contention in court that the township could keep going for longer.

But another study, commissioned slightly earlier, which had formed a part of the thick tender documents for the waste-to-energy plant, estimated that the city generated 11,198 metric tons of garbage and 2,500 metric tons of construction waste every day.

Together, the reports commissioned by the municipality suggested there was not so much trash that the Deonar township would get further overfilled and have to close but there was enough for the plant to make a profit. Mumbai's garbage mysteriously swelled and deflated to fit its precarious plans to manage waste.

A scandal had also erupted over a garbage truck contractor who had sued the municipality for not paying his bills. The municipality's own investigation revealed that some of the garbage the contractor ferried, and billed for, never existed. Mud was mixed in with waste to add to the weight of garbage. He was paid for the increased weight and passed a portion of the payment to municipal officials. It seemed officials had colluded with him to make inflated claims for garbage, to get overpaid, over several years. The Lohiya report, the police department's investigation into the fires in January, had also found the weigh bridges at the township were fixed to show at least 10 percent overweighing of garbage so contractors could be overpaid. The artificially inflated garbage brought with it money for equipment that was not needed, fees for transporting and handling garbage that did not exist, and pay for contractors who were not needed.

Digital cameras and automated weighing machines were installed at the weigh bridges where garbage trucks brought in their load to ensure it was garbage that emptied from trucks, not mud. Payment registers started to be monitored carefully. But the problems seemed endless. "Can you ever repair a house while you are living in it?" an aging and retired municipal engineer who had managed the Deonar township mountains and the city's waste for years asked. "As long as waste keeps coming to Deonar, how will we fix it? And our waste won't stop coming."

TWENTY-TWO

I N APRIL 2017, NADEEM'S uncles had come to see Farzana. The day before, Hyder Ali had called his future son-in-law in a panic, asking how he should explain Farzana's scars, her limp, to them, and Nadeem had told him not to say anything. Tell them only that you sent a proposal through Alamgir, he had said. Hyder Ali had felt his nerves calm as Nadeem navigated the way forward. When Nadeem's uncles arrived, Hyder Ali talked about their families, their villages, and the journey both families had made to settle in the shadow of the mountains.

Farzana had come into the room before them and sat with her gaze lowered. She wore a peach and gold kurta, its long sleeves hiding her wounds. Her sisters had covered her head with a dupatta and stuck a hairpin to make sure it did not slip. Hyder Ali told the men she stayed home, had learned Arabic, and knew some verses from the Koran.

Nadeem's uncles approved of the match, asking only to advance the wedding to May, so they could attend. The wedding date was set for May 21, six days before the first fast of Ramzan that year. Most of Shaheen's family from Nasik, and her husband's family from farther away in Akola, would cram into hired SUVs and drive up for the wedding, she told Hyder Ali. He tried to dissuade her from inviting so many people. She called back later, only to tell him the number in their party had gone up.

Hyder Ali had hired the wedding hall at the entrance of their lane, and the next few weeks went by in a frenzied scramble to collect money for the growing wedding party. Jehangir, Alamgir, Badre Alam, and he borrowed from friends and worked nights on the mountains. He asked Yasmin, who said she had no money to lend. But she had friends with political connections. She took him to meet their state representative, who asked an assistant to hand over some money and a dress for Farzana's trousseau. Hyder Ali wasn't sure how these bits added together, in those last few days, but they did.

On the day of the wedding, Sahani and Jehana helped Farzana into a red dress embroidered with gold flowers that Shaheen sent. They draped a red dupatta over her head and topped it with a blanket of milky tuberoses and scarlet roses. The flowers framed her face and felt cool and velvety against her palm when she touched them. The heavy costume, topped with gold jewelry and the flowers, kept Farzana's movement so limited that no quivers or limps showed. She kept her head bowed and unsmiling as Jehana had asked her to, making Farzana a demure, fragrant, and glowing bride. In the wedding hall, Nadeem sat in a separate room, wearing his own flower blanket over a white and powder blue salwar kameez. A crescent paper moon was strung across his forehead, a flower veil hanging below it.

Banjara Galli had emptied into the hall that night. Yasmin came with the children, Ashra wearing the dress and skirt that Moharram Ali had bought for her at the market last Ramzan. They ran into neighbors and old friends from the mountains. And yet, Nadeem's relatives more than matched them. Together, they packed the rooms, the greatest sign of a successful wedding. The flame-colored meat curries began emptying out too quickly.

All evening, the men had pushed and edged toward Nadeem and the women toward Farzana. They paused to pose for pictures, in which Farzana's face was turned down, eyes on the floor and her new, gold hand-bag held up against her waist, facing the camera. After signing the marriage contract, Nadeem took off his veil, and he and Farzana met guests together. Nadeem's gold flecked pompadour was teased even higher to make him look taller. And yet, his bride inched over him. Later, both would insist it was her heels, Farzana pointing to her shoulder to show where she reached up to on Nadeem, the height for good brides.

Guests crowded around Farzana's trousseau. On a cot that was Jehana's gift, Shakimun had laid out clothes, oversized cooking dishes, and sandals, along with gold studs Hyder Ali got to replace the ones he had taken out of Farzana's ears while she lay unconscious in the hospital. Friends wanted to tell Shakimun to add their gifts but it was hard to speak to her. "*Meri maa poori shaam roi,*" Farzana recalled. *My mother cried all evening.* Five of Shakimun's children had married already, but letting go of Farzana was too hard.

Farzana moved to Nadeem's house that night. Two days later, they dressed in wedding clothes again and left for their daylong honeymoon in the city, accompanied by Nadeem's cousin, his wife, and their children. They went to Haji Ali, the white marble mausoleum that rose from the sea, where Farzana had bought the rice grain and had it engraved with their names. They walked along the slim, rocky pathway, with waves lash-ing its sides, Farzana making sure to walk behind Nadeem, as she had seen brides do. Groups of beggars lined the pathway, chanting softly, asking for money. Little stubs of limbs hung below their elbows or knees. Farzana drew back, turning away, as they edged closer. They could have been her, Farzana thought. She could have been them.

Nadeem and Farzana entered the mausoleum through separate entrances, gave flowers and a brocade sheet to be laid over the tomb to the Mujawars, the keepers of the tomb, who waved and then tapped peacock feathers on their heads to bless them. Then they walked out through the sun-filled courtyard, onto the windblown rocks, jutting from the waves, where Farzana sat and felt sea spray on her face. Nadeem asked his cousin to photograph him, leaning into the waves. Later, they would go to a photo studio where Farzana sat on a cardboard crescent moon with Nadeem's baby nephew on her lap. Nadeem stood behind them, amid the stars in the backdrop, holding the moon's strings for her.

WEEKS LATER, ON a sun-baked afternoon, Nadeem walked Farzana back to Hyder Ali's home. It was one of the last days of Ramzan: the rains had set in but that afternoon the air was warm, heavy, and humid. Banjara Galli wore a languid air. Most people had retreated into their homes to escape the heat, their energy dissipated by hunger.

Hyder Ali and Shakimun were at Yasmin's house, chatting about the Shaitan they believed they had beaten back from Farzana. "*Vo khoobsurat thi na, usne fasaya*" was Hyder Ali's only reply, as they discussed why the Shaitan had gripped Farzana and tripped her right as the bulldozer approached on that overcast August afternoon. *She was so beautiful, the Shaitan entrapped her.*

Nadeem and Farzana walked in; she was wearing a burqa for the first time. Shaheen had given it to her after she got married, Farzana said. She began unbuttoning it, revealing maroon, freshly made henna patterns on her palms, with Nadeem's name written in English. Neighbors had dropped in with Mehendi cones the day before, to prepare for Eid, she said, curling her palm shyly into a fist.

Hyder Ali basked in the glow of the triumphant wedding; his esti-
mate of guests ranged from five hundred to two thousand. He could hardly
afford any gifts for Farzana himself, and yet she had received thirty sets
of clothes, he said. Nadeem's driver's license would come through any day,
Shakimun piped in: he would graduate from cleaner to driver.

Their lives buoyed in the rising tide of destiny, Hyder Ali had an
explanation and it rhymed with Nadeem: *Naseeb*, or fate. He fiddled with
the cracked plastic phone screen in his hand. A man's deep voice rose,
filling the room with a slow-paced song inspired by Koranic verses, Hyder
Ali explained. On screen, the singer's callow, thinly mustached face gave
way to shots that panned through a row of dead bodies wrapped in white
shrouds, one being lowered slowly into a grave. He was singing about
Naseeb, Hyder Ali explained, even as Farzana looked away. How it
steered lives.

"Upar vala pahunchata hai apne naseeb tak." God takes us where our destiny
is. It was not me or her. Hyder Ali pointed at his wife. *"Naseeb ne use Nadeem
se milaya, shaadi karai,"* he said, enjoying the rhyme. *Fate, or Naseeb, had
brought Farzana to Nadeem, her companion.* It was her fate that helped him
pull off such a big wedding, with so little money and that helped her escape
the life he and Shakimun had worried she would have. It was her fate that
the wedding party had been so big that food ran dangerously low.

He fiddled with his phone. On the screen, the camera panned across
darkened graveyards and freshly dug graves, keeping Hyder Ali on the
subject of fate and destiny. Everyone has to go back into the earth, whether
the person was from a bungalow or from a place like theirs, he said,
explaining the verses. Only a few meters of cloth would go with them,
this was fate. All the stuff that filled up the mountains behind would stay
behind, he said, waving his bony hand at the hills that rose behind
Yasmin's house.

Hyder Ali had spent nearly two decades collecting trash on the hills,
and yet, they had only risen. The mountains would stay as people came

and went, he said, pulling up more videos featuring graveyards on his phone.

Sprawling graveyards of belongings had lingered on in New York City too, the struggle to close them nearly as prolonged. Things belonging to people long gone still filled a beach near Jamaica Bay. Dead Horse Bay, as the beach was known, had absorbed much of the city's trash in the thirties. Half buried in sand were switchboards, cups, dishes, and other things made of Bakelite. An early plastic, it was easily moldable, didn't break, didn't conduct electricity or heat and could be made cheaply into products, allowing people to possess their desires in forms that ranged from rotary telephones to lidded serving dishes. Unbroken but soon unfashionable, these had been discarded for new things and found their way to the beach. The landfill had been emptied out and moved elsewhere. But its remains, including tights that gave women a shimmery sheen as they began working in offices, had stayed entangled in weeds, their stretchy nylon filament lasting over half a century.

Indians had not been as wealthy back in Deonar's early decades. They reused what they could and sent mostly leftover food to the trash mountains, which would have rotted to make its soil fertile. Engineers who had studied mountain composition believed that only animal bones and bits of gold would have remained from the early years. But in the decades that followed, with growing wealth, trucks had begun emptying plastic takeaway containers, large cloth and plastic sacks that once contained grains, aluminum foil and plastic boxes for milk and juice, stretchy tubes to squeeze out toothpaste or sandalwood-scented creams. They had dumped metallic strips packed with tablets that pickers consumed, disposable syringes used by the growing diabetes patients that jabbed pickers, and other things that would never turn to soil. Mumbai's age of dizzying growth was leaving its own immortal trail.

In New York's Staten Island, the sprawling Fresh Kills garbage township, where the city's garbage had been sent for decades, had also endured as a monument to the country's golden age of consumption. It was a garbage city so vast that there were traffic lights to direct the city's garbage truck caravans through its towering trash hills. After the 9/11 terror attack, debris from the World Trade Center buildings was buried here, the city began closing the Fresh Kills trash township. At its entrance, there were crushed bathroom sinks and pots. They had been left to dry in the sun and would later get immersed in the ocean bed so oysters could breed on their surfaces. The name Fresh Kills came from the Dutch word for the fresh streams of water that had once flowed through here. Streams would run through the slowly detoxifying hills again, and fish would get reintroduced in them. Newspaper reports later said trees had mysteriously grown on the hills, though they had only a thin topping of soil over its core of decomposing trash.

At Deonar, where newly discarded and unmeldable things were emptied constantly on the hills, only pickers took new trash away to be remade into new things. But now guards asked for ₹100 to let them pick through the mountains. Hyder Ali didn't earn much more than that in a day. So, he mostly stayed home and watched videos like the ones about the graveyards. *"Aur hain. Aur achhe,"* he said, and sifted through the videos stored in his phone. *I have more. Nicer ones.* He continued, narrating their message. *"Vo bata rahe hain, kaise sab cheez jama karo par naseeb yahi hai ki jana akele hai."* *They tell you all about how you can accumulate everything, but destiny makes us leave the world alone.*

Nadeem shifted awkwardly. He had to get back for an afternoon shift on the truck, he said. He would take Farzana back with him. Shakimun wheedled him to let Farzana stay, promising she would get Alamgir to drop his sister home later, but Nadeem motioned at Farzana to leave. As Hyder Ali and Shakimun walked them to the end of the lane, Yasmin stayed behind to plan for Alvida Jumma, or the last Friday of Ramzan, the following day. The crescent moon that brought in Eid was likely to be spotted the next night, bringing in the luckiest day of the year.

TWENTY-THREE

AT THE NEXT COURT date, in July 2017, the case of Deonar's
trash mountains did not come up until it was almost
lunchtime. Raj Sharma watched the crowd in the courtroom
ebb and flow and thought his hearing would be quick. He had already
spoken to a waste expert to arrange a visit and report back to Oka on
whether his orders to fix the mountains had been implemented. When
the Deonar case number was finally called, Justice Oka asked the lawyers
if they had thought of an expert to visit. The municipality's lawyer said
there was no need for one; the township fell in the purview of the committee Oka had set up and included scientists. Why would the court look
outside for help in monitoring the mountains?

Sharma's lawyer said the chairman of the court-appointed committee
had resigned a few months before, after doctors had told him the mountains' halo could worsen health issues. The committee had remained
directionless ever since, and had not met often. The municipal lawyer
interrupted, claiming the opposite: another member had headed the

committee, while it looked for a replacement, and it had in fact met. Oka and Justice Vibha Kankanwadi, also on the bench, watched, with bemusement, as their committee died and came alive in the sparring between the two lawyers, while the mountains and their people hung in the balance.

The judges resumed their attempts to shrink the halo that had quivered but hardly moved from over the mountains and their denizens. Oka asked the court committee to visit and report back on what progress had been made. While Sharma had surreptitiously gotten through to photograph the mountains by himself, this time the entire committee would go. The day before the visit, in late July, one of the committee's two scientists pulled out. At the newly renovated municipal office at the dumping grounds, the others watched a presentation on the waste-to-energy plant that officials still hoped to attract bidders for, months after they first invited them. The group then left to inspect the hills, their stomachs churning as they bumped along the cratered road and inhaled the heady smell, unable to get to the far end. Garbage hills rose on either side, gray with monsoon water and Mumbai's broken detritus. A broken electricity pole joined one craggy hill edge to another. Security guards had kept pickers away, giving the dogs and swooping birds their pick of the garbage that fell out of garbage trucks that afternoon. The mountains looked like an isolated archaeological find, filled with the city's dated desires, ringed by rising new buildings of glass and steel.

A FEW WEEKS later, at the end of August 2017, Oka's court hit news headlines. Sharma had often watched proceedings on another petition, which asked for national regulations on silent zones, where the city's blast would be reduced to a whisper, to be met. Oka had ordered that any place within 100 meters of a court, hospital, or educational institution had to be a silent zone. Enforcing his order in a city where everything and everyone was jammed too close to something else would mean gagging the festivals, marches, whistles, horns, processions, protests, and music that floated incessantly through Mumbai, keeping it always on edge.

When new national guidelines let state governments mark their own silent zones, officials quickly sidestepped Oka's orders. Oversized drums from Mumbai's rambunctious festival season would soon roll into the city, loudspeakers would fill streets. But Oka persisted. The state's lawyers accused him of bias and asked for his recusal. The chief justice replaced him on the noise pollution cases.

Lawyers' associations organized packed protest meetings in support of one of the toughest judges they had faced, and he had to be brought back on the case. But Oka's victory was a Pyrrhic one. The state withdrew its opposition in the High Court only to appeal in the Supreme Court, days later, which scrapped his silent zones and restrained him from passing any further orders on the issue. Just as the mountains had stayed unmoved, Mumbai's messy orchestra would stay too.

Oka had spent fourteen years as a judge and more than two decades as a lawyer before that. His father, Sreenivas Oka, had been a lawyer in neighboring Thane's district courts and Oka had taken over his grandfather and father's busy legal practice. He had probably spent his career seeing things, growth, justice, waste plants, and even clean air, move forward in courts and nearly arrive in the city, only to turn and slip sideways at the last moment. He probably knew, cities such as Mumbai sometimes appeared to move only to stay in the same place.

THE WASTE RULES required that thin layers of soil, or debris, top garbage mountains in order to keep them stable and prevent landslides. In the summer of 2017, municipal officials had brought in larger than usual amounts of debris from the city, although within permissible limits, to fill the potholed roads that wound through hills. They dumped it into the waves crowded with trash and mangrove to extend the township and make internal roads so fire engines could reach its far end. They topped the mountains with debris to bury the fires burning within so the township could stay unseen in the city and Mumbai's garbage caravans could keep coming.

Fires, landslides, and other disasters were usually how garbage mountains became visible in other cities too. A few months before the committee's visit to Deonar that summer, there was an accident at the Koshe trash mountain in Addis Ababa, Ethiopia. The capital city's partly consumed belongings tumbled down in an avalanche and buried pickers and their sloping homes, as they hunted for things to resell. The authorities had struggled even to get ambulances and stretchers to the mountain crevices, and surviving pickers had fashioned stretchers from trash to bring down the injured and dead. The landslide of used belongings had probably killed more than a hundred people, although no one was sure exactly how many people had lived and died on the slopes of Mount Koshe.

At Manila's Smokey Mountain in the Philippines, garbage had erupted down in fires and landslides for years, burying pickers. Tired of the deaths and ensuing headlines, the city had ultimately razed it in the late nineties. Pickers simply moved to the Promised Land mountain, where the waste slopes inched higher and garbage landslides and quiet burials continued.

At Deonar, municipal officials knew the construction debris would augment the mountains' noxious halo. Fed to the incinerator, it would not burn well to produce power. And yet, it was all that could keep fires buried within the mountains. As the rains retreated that year, fires had still erupted in October 2016 and again in 2017, though they were not as fierce as the ones in early 2016.

AWARE THAT THE mountains were closing on them, their luck draining fast, pickers tried breaking away. But there was nowhere to go. The mountains drew them back. Through the winter of 2017, after Javed Qureshi had been arrested, Jehangir made several flailing attempts to find work away from trash. Javed had been arrested for being a part of Atique and Rafique Khan's organized crime ring, making it hard to secure bail. Jehangir met a private contractor who supplied people who traveled on trucks and emptied trash cans into them and asked him for a job. In a few years, Jehangir would graduate to municipal rolls, getting him an official identity card, salary and, he thought, work until he retired, a pension after that. It was one of the most vaunted jobs in their lanes.

Since the municipality had asked suppliers to stop hiring garbage fillers, unable to afford their gushing pipeline onto its already overfull rolls, the agent had fitted Jehangir into a job that had emptied a year ago. Jehangir hired a young boy to do his job for him, paying the boy part of his salary, part to the contractor. It left him with hardly anything and he tried sidling into the space the Khan brothers had vacated after their arrest.

He tried collecting parking fees on a strip of 90 Feet Road that the Khans had managed, until he began getting anonymous calls asking if he had a fee collection contract from the municipality. The Khans were said to have collected parking fees for that stretch of the road for years, even after their contract with the municipality had ended. Jehangir did not have one at all. He would get arrested just as they had been, the anonymous caller threatened. Alarmed, Jehangir yielded the parking zone and got out of trouble. His attempts at breaking away, both illegitimate and legitimate, foiled, Jehangir returned to accumulating glass and plastic on the mountains.

FARHA OFTEN WENT over to see Farzana at her new home in the afternoons, after work. She usually found her older sister watching movies on the television, its noise washing over her, untouched by the increasingly desperate hunt for trash that filled Farha's own days. She talked to Farzana about how she hardly saw Jehangir these days. *"Is baar kuch bada soch raha hoon, dekhna,"* was all he would say. *I am thinking of something big this time. You watch.* Farzana hardly made it back to the family home either. Nadeem was usually working and could not accompany her, and she was not to step out of the doorstep by herself, he had warned her, or she could end up at the mountains, pulled into their dangers again.

Only Nadeem could afford for Farzana to stay home, Farha thought. Jehana and Sahani both worked on the mountains, struggling to produce food for their families. Often, Farha saw Farzana in her rose pink salwar kameez with tiny rosebuds and green stems, the one that she had worn on the evening Shaheen had visited their home and given their approval for the wedding. She covered her head demurely with a dupatta and draped it around her neck, obscuring it from view. It was how middle-class women, away from the mountains' shadow, lived, Farha thought. Farzana—whom Farha had seen aglow in mountain sun, afloat in its breeze—had quieted and become cocooned in the candy pink walls of Nadeem's home. The mountains had drained out of her, Farha figured.

Sometimes, Farzana's dupatta slipped and Farha caught a glimpse of her swollen neck. It made her face seem bloated too, her eyes bulging. She looked a bit like she did when they had gotten dressed for Parveen's son's wedding. Her neck had seemed swollen then too, Farha recalled. Sometimes she saw it balloon on one side, pushing her face to the other. At other times, it looked swollen all around and her face shrunken and at still others, it seemed smooth behind her flimsy dupatta.

Shaheen, too, had noticed Farzana's ballooning throat with alarm. She planned to ask Nadeem to take Farzana to the doctor. But these days she only saw Nadeem at night—if at all. He worked ten hours a day ferrying city trash to the mountains at Deonar or Mulund. Weeks later, when Farha returned to Nadeem's house, she saw uneven bumps swelling around Farzana's neck again. Farha wondered if the wounds from her sister's accident on the mountain were reappearing from within her, bubbling under the surface of her skin.

IN OCTOBER, THE rains retreated, and the season of fires had returned to the township. Smoke rose from the mountains for days, filling the lanes, while fire engines doused the flames to keep it from drifting into the city. But the pickers still woke up hours before dawn, walking through the dark and empty maze of lanes of Rafiq Nagar, its shuttered shop fronts and gambling recesses rising gently uphill. Half asleep, they slipped through the cracks they had hacked in the wall and walked up trash slopes in the dark, trailing trucks, sifting for plastic bottles, gadgets and wires, flashlights in hand.

The lights Judge Oka had asked for time and time again had hardly been installed on the slopes yet, keeping the township's darkness that successive judges had tried to dispel for years. Cameras flickered. Pickers hid in dark crevices if guards passed by, or picked until guard patrols began, at daybreak. They walked back into their lanes, with the early pink light balancing garbage bags precariously atop their heads.

As the sun warmed over them, some of the women sat together and sorted through the bags they emptied in the lane outside their homes. They flicked away mud and dirt, making heaps of varying thicknesses of plastic and some glass all around them. They would have to sell it at *katas* farther away: the long stretch of deep and roomy *katas* that curved around the wall, and that had once been filled with trash by Atique and Rafique Khan, were bolted shut.

For years, this had been the Khan brothers' territory. Their cameras had lined these streets, and their grip had been fierce. But the women in Rafiq Nagar's lanes remembered them with fondness. *"Koi police ka matter rahega to vohi dekhte the na, nahi to hamari kaun sunega,*" one woman said, flicking things away from a muddy tangle. *They are the ones who helped us with police matters. Otherwise, who would listen to us?* The brothers had lived close by and had lent them money when they needed it, bought their trash, and employed their children for years.

It was that girl, Farzana, who was to blame for the constantly patrolling security guards and continually rebuilt wall, not the Khans, the women complained. "*Main thi na us din,*" one of them said. *I was there that day.* It had rained, she continued. The slopes were slippery. Her foot got entangled in something, so she was stuck. The bulldozer went over her slightly, she recalled. "*Zara sa,*" she repeated. *Slightly.* She touched her index finger to her thumb to show how slightly the bulldozer had gone over Farzana.

"*Ab to vo theek bhi ho gayi.*" Farzana was married and walking around. *She is fine now.* The mountains should not get shut down because of her. The women didn't seem to know of the court cases swirling over their township. Another woman piped in, saying she had worked there since childhood, that even her mother had picked trash. "*Ham kidhar jayenge?*" *Where else would we go?* It wasn't as if they were going to ask the municipality for anything, she said.

Moharram Ali dropped by with some friends and sat down to chat with the women, not letting on that he knew Farzana or her father from his days in Banjara Galli. He was new in these lanes, but these women were old friends from his years of night shifts on the mountains. He joined in, the group trading stories of cuts and wounds the mountains had given them. A broken tube light had once lodged itself in his calf, Moharram Ali chortled, lifting his pants to show them. He had hobbled home, bleeding. Later, he got fifteen stitches. Did they remember? He looked at the group expectantly. They didn't. The men lifted their trousers and pulled up their shirtsleeves to reveal their own calves and arms filled with scars and memories they laughed over. They exchanged notes on guard patrol schedules. Best to work before the sun arose and guards arrived, they agreed.

THROUGH MUCH OF 2017 Yasmin wasn't sure where Moharram Ali was. He hardly ever took her calls, only called occasionally to tell her he did not work on the mountains. He did construction work. He told her he traveled to Pune, Navi Mumbai, and other towns, farther away, building homes. He was away for days, he said. Then, a friend told Yasmin she had seen him emerge from one of Rafiq Nagar's lanes, slim as a crack in a wall, their openings obscured by shops, houses, and a thicket of hand-carts. He had melted into the crowd of shoppers and pickers before they could get to him. When she called to ask if it had been him, he told her he was working on the mountains only between construction jobs and would not be here for long. He was going back to the village. But the lanes around the mountains were filled with Muslims, Dalits, and others, with no land in the village, no cattle or anything to keep them there. Like Moharram Ali, who as a teenager had sat in a train and left, many of them had made the long journey away from having nothing.

Gaunt but still exuding his old charm, Moharram Ali told people that in the village he performed the rituals he had learned from his father. Villagers came to tell him of ailments that they believed only he could cure, he said, beaming. A friend had recently come late at night and taken Moharram Ali to his cow, who had howled all evening with labor pains. Moharram Ali said he had chanted his prayers, and in less than an hour, it delivered a calf. Most of all, he performed a powerful *Tohna* ritual, he said. As he recited the prayers, a sharp smell of mustard rose and filled up the rooms, he said. Everyone scrunched their noses, uncomfortably. In a few minutes, the smell abated, and with it, their troubles vanished too, he said. His rituals seemed to resolve most problems—except his own. Debts from his sister's wedding and from the city had accumulated, and he had sold the land he bought in the village with the gold chain he found on the mountains. His sister had committed suicide—although he believed her husband had murdered her. Moharram Ali had filed a police case, which only put him deeper in debt. He returned to the mountains, trawling for treasures already taken by city pickers. There was nowhere to go but back to the trash.

On his phone screen he showed friends photos of Hera with her baby son, his first grandchild. She only saw him from a distance, entering rickshaws or getting out of them. "*Kudrat ka keher gira hai,*" she told her mother when she returned home. *The wrath of nature has fallen on him.* Yasmin nodded reluctantly in agreement for the man whose shirts she had spent years keeping stain-free and whose deodorant she had kept replenished.

Moharram Ali tried working night shifts again. Sometimes, he said, when the guards spotted his tall frame in the dark, they hurled their sticks at him. The sticks gathered speed as they traveled through the air and hit his calves or the back of his knees, flattening him with pain. If only Farzana had not brought this on them, he complained.

AT THE OTHER end of the mountains' long, looping, and fragmented wall, in Padma Nagar, Farzana stayed curled in front of the television, her neck spilling into her face, her eyes glazed, bile rising in her throat. Shaheen waited for Nadeem to have an afternoon off and asked him to take Farzana to the nearby Shatabdi hospital, where Jehangir had first taken her after she was crushed by the bulldozer.

They waited for more than an hour in its heaving corridors to see a doctor, Farzana warm and itchy in her burqa, Nadeem in a hurry to make it back in time for his work shift on the truck. The doctor prescribed tests and the two left, realizing on their walk back that they had forgotten to ask about her neck. A few days later, Nadeem and Farzana returned reluctantly to the hospital. Pulling out the test results, the doctor told them that Farzana was pregnant.

The medical file Farzana took home said she had no previous illnesses. In the busy examination room, Farzana had told the doctor she had nothing to report. She believed that the mountains had retreated from her bones. There was nothing to say.

TWENTY-FOUR

THE HIGH COURT HEARINGS began again, early in 2018. It was more than two decades since the first petitions asking to close the mountains had been filed, and a decade since Justice Oka began hearing the case. It was nearly 120 years since the swamp at Deonar began filling up with trash. In that time, the municipality's attempts to shrink the mountains had sunk into their soft, towering slopes, which were mirrored in the growing mound of papers on Oka's desk on an early January morning. A fog had arisen in the court that seemed to match the mountain's immovable halo.

Oka looked at the case papers and asked the state government's lawyers if they had provided the two plots that had been promised to the municipality so they could establish a new trash township to replace Deonar. One was at Karvale, in Navi Mumbai, and the other at Mulund, where the old dumping ground close by was to shut. The state's lawyer nodded to say yes, the municipality's lawyer shook his head to say no.

The municipality's lawyer said that the city had paid the state an advance but could not accept the land at Karvale, offered more than a decade ago. Oka looked down and asked the state's lawyers to turn to paragraph three on a page of their submissions. He asked how the city could even begin dumping garbage at the plot when more people lived there now than when it had first been offered. The plot had come up in court time and again because the tribal people settled there had blocked officials from even surveying the land, let alone seizing it.

The state's lawyer said only a few of the thirty-eight hectares of grounds had people living on them. It could fence these settlements off and give the rest of the land to the municipality for dumping and processing waste. "But the encroached pockets are all over the site," Oka noted, pointing to more lines in the middle of its thick written submissions. He asked the state's lawyers to look into resettling the residents or finding other dumping grounds by the next hearing, scheduled a few weeks later.

AT THE NEXT hearing, on February 11, the municipal lawyer spoke of the gas pipeline that ran the length of the grounds. Waste heaps could not cover the pipeline, the rules said. Could the pipeline be re-routed around the plot? the lawyers discussed.

Oka moved on to another plot the state government had offered the municipality, near the existing and aging dumping site at Mulund, within the city. Some municipal maps already showed it as garbage dumping grounds. But when officials went to survey it, some years prior, the central government's Salt Commissioner's officers had blocked them. The land was filled with salt pans, they said. They owned it. The state government had been fighting for it, in court, for years. Unless they lost the case, salt commission officials would not hand over the land to the state government, which had already promised it to the municipality for new dumping grounds.

On March 15, the Supreme Court allowed construction to restart in Mumbai, even if there had been no progress at Deonar, a little less than two years after Oka had banned it. Without striking down his ban, it allowed a six-month construction window to "explore the possibility of [a] safe method of permitting certain constructions," bringing instant relief to the city's developers. Sharma and the monitoring committee, which still remained without a chairman, was charged with "preventing dispersal of particles through the air," by ensuring construction was allowed only after Mumbai's debris-filled caravans emptied at quarries far outside the city, not at the Deonar township. The last chairperson had left because mountain air could sap his health, the court was reminded. "Anyone will have this problem. They will have to visit," Oka said with a smile, and asked for names of possible chairpersons for the committee.

Then he turned back to the nearly two-decade-long search for grounds to replace the Deonar township. "Why this insistence on encroached land?" he asked Ramchandra Apte, the state's lawyer. He responded by saying the government would clear the encroachments at the Karvale grounds, buy the tracts it did not own, and hand it all over to the municipality soon. Oka pointed to a line in the submission stating there were seventy-nine houses on the land. "From your experience, Mr. Apte, how many lawsuits do you think that will lead to?" Oka asked. Lawsuits from evicted residents could drag on for years, adding to the fog in court and the paper hills, holding up the transfer of the grounds and stretching the Deonar township's life on indefinitely, he suggested.

Days later, on March 20, the familiar sight of the Deonar hills throwing up flames and smoke against the dark sky lit up television screens. It was the second fire in two weeks. More than a dozen fire engines sprayed water night and day. In spite of all the debris the municipality had topped the mountains with, fires still swirled within the decaying trash.

The municipality would soon get water tankers at the township to spray water to cool the constantly warming, often burning trash hills. Dr. Anurag Garg, a professor of environmental engineering at Mumbai's Indian Institute of Technology and a member of the court committee, had asked to spray foam on the mountain fires instead of water. The water would seep through the mountains, collecting trash, and flow into the creek, polluting it, he had said. A contract for foam was opened too. Until a supplier was found, fire engines would continue to spray water, dragging mountain trash into the creek.

OVER THE DECADES, Deonar's case had appeared to be on the verge of resolution several times. Oka had set deadlines—checked if they were met, pushing officials to meet them. Each time it seemed as though the mountains trembled on the brink of movement. The municipality had needed only a few more weeks, and then a few more months, and each delay had stretched the mountains' life precariously on. The mountains had stayed. Oka presided over a similar case to find a new home for the high court building, allotting land in a distant suburb, then near the new financial district. But the court too had stayed in place.

Meanwhile, in the spreading edges of Delhi, some trash peaks had risen so high—while court cases to fix them stretched out indefinitely—that they nearly touched the power lines looping into the city. When pickers on those mountains, immersed in the search for trash, brushed against the wires, they died, electrocuted. That summer, garbage had tumbled down in a landslide there, killing a picker, and bringing the capital's trash mountains into the Supreme Court's view, which asked its municipality to fix them.

At the next Deonar hearing on July 25, the fog around finding a replacement for the township was only growing. Oka began by reading the response the state government had filed, that morning. He read and then looked up, surprised. It said the land at Mulund had been rented out to a private salt maker, who harvested salt there and who had sued the salt commissioner, also in the Bombay High Court. This case too had gone on in the same rambling court building for more than a decade, unbeknownst to Oka. The tussle over the land that he thought was three-cornered had been four-cornered. Oka asked Apte, with rising indignation, what the chances were of the municipality getting the land. "Bleak? Very bleak?"

AS OKA PUSHED to fix the trash township in court, the distant hamlet at Karvale in Navi Mumbai, which had been allotted to replace the Deonar township years ago, had withered to a stub. Months after the hearing, it became a green expanse filled only with streams, empty husks of homes and the shadow of the Haji Malang shrine, perched on a nearby cliff. When Farzana had drifted between their world and the netherworld at Sion Hospital, her sister Afsana had gone to visit Haji Malang, said to be the saint of common people. She had brought back a bracelet and tied it to Farzana's wrist. That talisman had tugged her back into the world of the living, Afsana believed.

Just before Farzana's wedding, she, Afsana, and Afsana's in-laws had walked up the last stretches of the rocky cliff to the shrine. They thanked the saint for Farzana's improbable life. The sisters had sat at the edge of the cliff, soaking in the breeze, the last fragments of Farzana's single life and the unending stretch of green that lay ahead, slim streams shining through it. They didn't know then that their putrid mountains and their spirits could come to fill a patch of this green one day.

While Farzana conducted her pilgrimage to Haji Malang, in the hamlet below residents were meeting their representatives, who had promised to keep their homes in place. They thought of filing a court case but their representatives had told them there was no need. The city's end-less trash caravans would not make the bumpy two-hour journey to deposit trash here. Besides, they could hardly afford to pay for a lawyer, perhaps for years, and even getting to the court, hours away, would be hard from here. As Oka's indignation grew in court, the representatives had returned empty-handed. By late 2018, the police had evicted residents, forcing them into boiling tin-sheet homes that lined the edges of the plot instead.

NEARLY TWO YEARS later, in July 2020, Oka gave a video talk to law students. He had no memory of why he switched to study law, from studying math, nearly four decades before. As a young lawyer, he only got cases from litigants who could not afford better, cases with little hope of winning. "When you connect with such litigants you learn what life is about. After becoming a judge I realized . . . the real challenge before our legal system is not of docket (legal file) explosion but of docket exclusion." He went on, "There are certain deficiencies in our legal system that large sections of our population silently suffer injustice." While the unending pile of pending cases clogging Indian courts had often been spoken about, Oka suggested, the bigger problem was that people like Farzana and the inhabitants of Karvale, remained invisible to the courts that decided their fates.

As Mumbai's warm winter settled in the city, the question of whether its trash would continue to arrive at Farzana's mountain commu-nity or get sent to the hamlet in Karvale's green valley remained. Municipal lawyers had asked for more time. At a hearing during the court's Christmas break, municipal lawyers announced the city would need nearly five more years to reroute trash caravans away from Deonar. The municipality had extended the deadline for bids for the waste-to-energy plant at Deonar seven times, but none came. One of the reasons no company had bid to make the plant, a presentation by Tata Consulting Engineers showed, was that potential bidders had wanted Deonar's trash township without its mountains of garbage. Moving them would be too expensive and arduous, they had said, making their plant unviable. The municipality had scrapped the plan for the plant and decided to make three smaller waste-to-energy plants at Deonar instead and needed an extension until the first plant was built. The court extended the Deonar township's life until Justice Oka could hear the case, after the holidays.

TWENTY-FIVE

THROUGH THE SUMMER OF 2018, Farzana's stomach had swollen. Perched atop her ballooning throat, her face grew too. Fevers came and went. Most mornings, after Nadeem left for work, she spread a bedcover in front of the television and watched until sleep drifted over and shut her eyelids. Music from eighties Hindi action movies filled the room. Sidekicks died, lovers reunited, and credits rolled. Farzana woke up, switched channels, and stayed in place.

Shaheen had asked Nadeem to show Farzana's neck to the doctors whenever they went to Shatabdi Hospital. But somehow, Farzana was always too exhausted when she arrived in the room packed with pregnant women, and Nadeem had to turn back soon for his shifts. Twice, they were halfway home when they remembered her distended neck, carefully covered under her dupatta and billowing black burqa.

At home, Farzana's movements shrank as her belly and the growth on her neck swelled. Her neck had stiffened, making her face look stuffy and sour. Her arms itched, filled with long, pink scars from the stitches that covered her carefully held together bones. The next time she sat across from the doctor, Farzana unwrapped her burqa and dupatta to show her swollen neck. Then she pulled up her sleeve to show the doctor her arm, still filled with marks for stitches. *"Bulldozer chad gaya tha,"* Farzana explained softly. *A bulldozer ran over me.*

The doctor looked up, surprised. She asked Farzana to get her case papers from the treatment at Sion Hospital. At the next visit, she rifled through the thick file that Nadeem had asked Hyder Ali to send over. A heavily pregnant woman stood behind Farzana, waiting for her to vacate the shiny examination stool. Others in the queue outside poked their heads into the room. The doctor shut the file, and told Farzana to go back to Sion Hospital for a follow-up. Farzana was relieved to have avoided the inspection of old wounds. She returned to her spot in front of the television, absentmindedly scratching her arms.

HYDER ALI WOULD have to take gifts for Nadeem's family, to bring Farzana back to her parents' home, for child birth, as was the custom. He tried working on the mountains in order to save up for the gifts. But, running into Yasmin in their lane one afternoon, he told her how life on the mountains was not as it had been. Security guards crushed his trash bags under their vehicles, or asked for so much money in bribes to let them work and take away trash that there was nothing left after a morning's work. Yasmin had heard, Farha had found a gold chain while scouring for trash a few weeks before, but Hyder Ali didn't say anything about it. Farha had discovered it was fake anyway. It's all that comes to the mountains these days, she shrugged.

As mountain treasures shrank, Moharram Ali had traveled farther out in search of jobs, returning home empty-handed, to an empty house. His new wife had left him, tired of waiting for his get-rich-quick plans to work. He called Yasmin and asked her and the children if he could move back in. *"Phir chala gaya to,"* she asked Hyder Ali. *What if he leaves again? "Meri usse koi ummeed nahi rahi,"* she said softly, almost to herself. *I have no hope left in him.*

The summer of 2018 wore on and Nadeem stayed busy, traveling in garbage caravans through the nights and in the day. Farha began accompanying Farzana to hospital visits. Along the way, they walked beside the outer edge of the mountains' long, carious wall. They watched people climb through cracks onto the slopes where they had spent so much of their lives together, watching cricket games, evading the buffaloes wandering up the parched hills, and chasing garbage trucks. Farha now worked alone on the mountains.

They passed by the parking strip that Jehangir had relinquished. He seemed consumed by a new business, Farha told Farzana. All she knew was, this time, it was not in trash. He had told them he was going to do something different, something that would take him away from the mountains. He spoke constantly to his business partner, who sounded like a woman, or to his lackeys. Around the mountains, Jehangir and others nipped at the edges of the gang bosses' sprawling fiefdom of illegalities.

AS FARZANA'S TIME to give birth drew close, Hyder Ali worked desultorily and waited for Nadeem to bring her over. On July 8, Shaheen called to say the baby was on its way, and late that night Farzana gave birth to a baby girl. Waking up in the hospital in a haze of sleep and pain, she saw her sisters huddled over the baby, exclaiming over how she looked just like Nadeem. Shaheen draped a quilt she had made from patched-together cloth scraps collected from the mountains over the baby and relented, letting her go to Hyder Ali's house from the hospital.

At home, Shakimun ripped white cloth, filled it with cumin and turmeric, and tied it into two small bundles, tying one to the baby's wrist and the other to Farzana's. These would trap spirits within them, forming a shield around Farzana and the baby in these early months when they could fall prey to illnesses, sadnesses, or spirit possessions that could hold them in their grip forever.

They stayed wrapped together, mother and daughter. Farzana babbled to her baby all day and late into the night. She spoke endlessly until Guddi, meaning little doll, became Buddhi, meaning old woman. "*Tune suna Guddi? Tera kuch bhi nahi hai. Kuch bhi? Sab tere Abba se aaya,*" she whispered, wiggling the baby's nose or cheeks until she cried. *Did you hear Guddi? Nothing you have belongs to you. Nothing at all. It all came from your father.* Farzana picked up and swung the baby in her arms to calm her.

Weeks later, when Farzana went home, Shaheen had stitched more quilts from mountain scrap to wrap the baby in. She laid out the largest cloth she had and covered it with scraps in a deep shade that was called chocolatey in Marathi and Mumbai Hindi, and that could be maroon, brown, plum, or dark purple; emerald green, like the grass that grew on the mountains after the rains; and a pink so intense it could be purple. She edged the quilt with a slim border of baby pink. But Shaheen was alarmed to see Farzana upon her return. Her neck was so swollen that her face was frozen in place, and she had to look from the corner of her eye to see sideways.

DAYS LATER, FARHA called Farzana and asked her to switch on the news. "*Bhai hai.*" Brother's on. Jehangir's face, covered with a scarf, the voiceover giving his name, age, and address, flashed on television news. Police had busted a kidnapping ring of five, including him, and released a child they had held for ransom.

With a succession of businesses floundering, Jehangir had made one last ambitious plan to break away from the mountains. A friend from their lane had introduced him to a woman whose brother-in-law was a wealthy businessman in the city. Police would later allege, she wanted to kidnap his son for ransom, giving them a portion of the money.

On the evening, in question, it was claimed that she led the boy to Jehangir and his friend who covered his face with a scarf and bundled him into a rickshaw. The boy had cried the whole way to the garage in a mountain lane, where they planned to keep him until they got the money. They gave him cough syrup mixed into a cold drink so he would feel drowsy and sleep. When they unwrapped the scarf from his face, they discovered it was actually their target's thirteen-year-old, older brother.

This could get them more money, Jehangir thought. He rehearsed for the ransom call. But before they could make it, police stormed the garage, released the boy, and arrested Jehangir and his gang of conspirators.

Sanjay Nagar's lanes were abuzz with news of Jehangir's arrest. Pickers saw his covered face in the newspapers, on television, and in messages traveling through phones in their lanes. Hyder Ali did not have money to hire a lawyer or post bail. "*Hamein kuch pata nahi tha,*" he said, his voice turning hoarse with shame. *I didn't know anything.*

Days later, Shakimun and Hyder Ali arrived at Shaheen's house holding a cradle, with colored ribbons wrapped all around the metal frame. He had saved up to buy the gift and placed it against the wall where Farzana had spent her days slumped during her pregnancy. She had vacated the spot now, walking around, ferrying things for the baby, piling soiled clothes for her sister-in-law to wash, folding washed clothes, cradling the baby to sleep while talking to her the whole time. "*Guddi tu samjhi na? Teri naak kiske jaisi hai? Teri aankh kiske jaisi hai?*" *Doll, you understand, right? Who does your nose look like? Whose are your eyes like?*

A FEW WEEKS after Jehangir's arrest, Farzana, her throat spilling into her face, went to see Dr. Satish Dharap, who had headed the team of surgeons that had operated on her two years before. Now at BYL Nair

Hospital, deeper into the city, he looked at her yellowing case papers, went over her treatment and asked if she had done okay since then.

She nodded, unwrapping her burqa to show her neck, while holding on to the baby. As he gently pressed and prodded the bumps around it, Farzana winced in pain. She did get fevers, it was painful, she said, in reply to his questions. They would have to extract the fluid within and test it, he said. It could be cancer or perhaps tuberculosis.

Farzana returned a few days later for the procedure, Farha holding the baby while doctors took her into an operating room. A little later, the nurse called Farha in: neck wrapped in blood and gauze stained with yellow ointment, Farzana sobbed softly, helplessly, drooling onto her cheek and the rubber sheet that covered her metal cot. With her burqa gone, Farzana's legs and hands coiled tightly into spindly V shapes. Her pink lace kurta, lined with satin, puffed around her, glinting in the late afternoon light.

Farha watched and then slid the baby into her arms. Farzana's tears rolled onto her daughter's soft, nearly bald head. *"Budhi, teri aankh kiske jaisi hai?"* she whispered, breaking into a weak smile even as tears rolled down her cheeks. *Old woman, you know who your eyes belong to?* She babbled softly, holding the baby close, feeding her even as she cried.

Slowly, Farzana spread her palm to grip the bed and lifted herself up. She put on her burqa, lifted the baby, and set off for home with Farha. They waited at the bus stop across the street from the hospital, watching the late afternoon light turn dusky and then dark. It was an immersion day during the Ganpati festival. Outsized idols of the elephant-headed God came into the city for ten days every year and were then given over to the sea, as a lesson in material detachment. That evening, potbellied idols, in giddily happy colors, moved slowly through cars, buses, and drilling machines that dug into Mumbai's slim roads, turning them to dust in preparation for Mumbai's metro transit lines. The baby howled. Thumping from the outsized drums rose over the buzz of drills and horns, and was intermittently drowned out by them. Traffic stopped for construction, then construction stopped for traffic, both moving fitfully in a jagged dance to Mumbai's accidental symphony. Farzana stepped onto the street, baby in her arms, to look out for buses that would take her home. She saw them waiting in the distance, then move slowly toward her before turning away.

Nadeem called. Why had she not come home yet? She was still near the hospital? How could the bus take so long to arrive? Had she really gone to the hospital? It was nearly midnight by the time Farzana got home. The following day, Nadeem, sulking from the previous night, dropped her at Hyder Ali's house, with instructions to stay away from the mountains, their men, and their hazards. Farzana slept for days, the baby enclosed within her arms. She had tried allaying Nadeem's fears and stayed away from the mountains that loomed above, for the most part.

One afternoon, Shakimun sat at the mountains' edge and watched Farzana walk by with the baby. "*Kaam kaise karein?*"—*How do I work?*— she asked. Her son was in jail, her daughter sick. "*Fikar khaye jaa rahi hai,*" she said, inhaling deeply from her bidi. *Worry is eating away at me.* She thought of sending Hyder Ali back to the healer across 90 Feet Road as she watched the sun turn peach and inch into the hills.

WHEN FARZANA RETURNED to the hospital, alone with the baby, to hear her test results, the doctor told her she had tuberculosis. He told her he would prescribe medication: stopping it might mean the disease could turn deadly. It wouldn't respond to the same medicines even if she restarted them. Farzana interrupted him impatiently to say that she would go to a doctor near her house and begin treatment there.

Farzana knew tuberculosis haunted pickers. She had watched it whittle down Badre Alam, Hyder Ali's cousin who lived in their loft, until he left for his village, dangerously gaunt. They had not heard from him for more than two months, and Hyder Ali feared he had died until he reappeared, a week or so before, his cheeks full, his face shining. A healer's rituals and his wife's care had cured him, he said. But Farzana knew, not everyone returned as Badre Alam had. Some of her childhood friends had come to work on the mountains after tuberculosis had wasted their parents away, only to be consumed in their turn by the insatiable appetite of the peaks.

A FEW DAYS later, Farzana bundled up the baby, collected a bag filled with clothes and towels, and went with Alamgir to Arthur Road Prison to meet Jehangir. At every previous visit, Jehangir had instructed his brother, "*Farzana ka khayal rakhna.*" *Look after Farzana.* Alamgir teased him, asking if he had any other brothers and sisters? "*Hain . . .*" Jehangir trailed off. *I do.* When Alamgir broke in, "*Par tu usko hi sabse zyada chahta hai?*" *But you love her the most?* Jehangir would only say, "*Bhejna usko.*" *Send her to see me.*

Weeks later, Farzana was ushered into a room with a glass screen. Jehangir walked in and sat on the other side. "*Kaisa hai Bhai?*" Farzana asked, softly into the phone on her side. *How are you, brother?* Jehangir nodded, looking at the baby. Farzana picked her up and held her up against the glass screen. "*Teri beti hai?*" *Your daughter?* Farzana nodded to say yes. "*Achhi hai,*" he replied. *She's lovely.* The siblings looked at each other. They had both so nearly left the mountains and their shadow, but the slopes had lingered within them both, holding them in their grip, holding them back. The guards came in to tell Farzana it was time to leave. "*Tu theek hai na?*" Jehangir asked. *You are okay, right?* She nodded.

A few days later, someone from Nair Hospital called asking if Farzana had her medicine regularly and for her bank account details, so they could transfer the government subsidy for TB patients. She had stopped medication a while ago. It made her dizzy, Farzana said. It brought a darkness in front of her eyes. Instead she spent her days playing with the baby, whom they had named Ayesha, the wise one. Sahani later said that Nadeem had not bought any more medicine.

Farzana's fevers raged and abated, her neck swelled and seemed to shrink. But she stayed immersed in the baby, who was getting taller, plumper, and gave gummy smiles. *"Guddi, Guddi, tujhe pata hai na, teri hasee teri nahi hai?"* *Doll, you know that smile is not yours, right?* Farzana tickled her nose, making Ayesha break into peals of laughter. In Farzana's babbling, Ayesha grew from a baby to an old woman but nothing would ever belong to her. It would all come from her father, from the mountains that rose behind them and endlessly, in caravans, from the city.

"Tujhe pata hai na, teri naak bhi teri nahi hai?" *You know, right, even your nose is not yours?*

"Budhi, Budhi, tera kuch bhi tera nahi hai, theek hai?" *Old woman, old woman, nothing you have belongs to you, alright?*

POSTSCRIPT

I**N THE FIRST WEEK** of 2019, I walked up the court's grand, stone staircase to the second floor. Justice Oka's cases and room had been reassigned. The Deonar case had moved with him.

As I arrived at the dark landing, I saw a marble plaque engraved with the words of Bal Gangadhar Tilak, a freedom fighter who had been convicted of sedition against the British state in 1908, in the courtroom that lay behind the plaque. "There are higher powers that rule the destiny of men and nations and it may be the will of providence that the cause which I represent may prosper more by my suffering than by my remaining free," he had said after the judge Justice Dinshaw Davar had ruled against him.

By a quirk of fate, in 1897, Justice Davar, then a lawyer, defended Tilak against sedition charges while the plague raged through Mumbai and neighboring Pune, where Tilak lived. As the anger over the invasion of British troops into homes, lives, and bodies grew, Tilak had written a veiled attack on the British plague campaign in his newspaper *Kesari*.

Government lawyers had accused him of bringing tensions to a boil and inciting the murder of W. C. Rand, the chairperson of Pune's plague committee, and Tilak was sentenced to eighteen months in jail, which only inflamed the anger in both cities. A few weeks later, *cuchra* trains had begun ferrying Bombay's trash to the swampy dumping grounds at Deonar. The plague abated, prosperity returned, and its bounty was consumed, discarded, ferried, and eventually dumped into the distant marsh that began rising, unseen in the city.

In its 120th year, the attempts to deal with Mumbai's waste township, to shrink the toxic halo that spread over the city and the illnesses it created, continued in a courtroom farther down the corridor. I turned the corner into Oka's new courtroom, so outsized and empty, his voice came like a distant, echoing muffle, discussing a criminal case: "Where did they find the body?"

Then the familiar thud of the Deonar files fell on his desk. Had the officials who had avoided telling him of all the court cases around the new Mulund dumping grounds been punished yet, he asked? When would the land to make a scientific landfill get handed over? Most importantly, how soon could Deonar's township of trash close? It nearly had, the municipality's lawyers told him, sensing his now familiar indignation. The garbage caravans now mostly went to the modern trash hills at Kanjurmarg. I had seen them rising across the creek when I stood on the trash peaks at the outer edge of the Deonar township. Trash hills had been rising there for five years and would be taken apart next year, as compost.

On April 9, 2019, Oka passed an order: this would be the last year for the township of trash. No new garbage could be dumped there after December 31, 2019. The old hills would slowly begin flattening or turn to something else. The following day, Oka was transferred to become the chief justice of the high court in the neighboring state of Karnataka.

I continued to visit the mountains and the lanes around them, waiting for garbage caravans to stop arriving at Deonar's hills, for the contract for waste plants to be given out, for new trash townships to begin. Caravans had dwindled but not stopped. It was all about to happen, municipal engineers had told me. They had put out ads for the first of the three smaller waste-to-energy plants at Deonar they planned to make over the next few years.

At the mountains, I ran into Jehana. Had she heard about the township's final closure? In return, she asked if I had heard about Asif. Surely, I knew him, she said and I nodded, although I was in fact unsure whether I had met him. He went to school and worked on the mountains in the afternoons, pickers told me. He was fourteen. A little over a week ago he had been chased by a guard patrol. His friends had slipped away toward their homes but Asif had kept running, straight ahead toward the creek. The guards stayed behind, following him. Then he vanished from sight.

When his friends returned to Rafiq Nagar, Afsana, his mother, had asked where he was. He must be coming, they told her. Maybe the guards had detained him or he was hiding until they left. When dusk fell, she went looking for him, staying out all night. She asked at a guard post but they had not seen him. The next day, she complained at the police station. She had accompanied police officers to the slopes but they could not find Asif. The guards and police had looked for him, for days, but they had not found him. Did he escape on a raft, they asked. He didn't have one, she said. Soon after that, Asif began coming in her dreams. He smiled, he spoke to her, saying he was close by. She had to find him, she told me, when I went to meet her.

Every morning Afsana left for the mountains with the day shift pickers. She looked in the thorny bushes, leafless in the summer heat. She walked to older clearings where trash no longer emptied, she waded chest deep into the plastic-filled mangroves. She returned after the night shift pickers began working, having seen no sign of him.

Afsana borrowed money, hired a boat, and floated around the edges of the township to see if he had got stuck in the soft mud at the creek's edge, entangled in the plastic or the tree roots that swam in the water, or been washed farther away with the effluent that gushed into the creek.

Pickers had begun to say that he must have jumped into the creek to avoid the guards. But he would have washed ashore somewhere by now, Afsana thought. He might have been kidnapped by organ traffickers so they could harvest his kidneys, they said, as rumors about him floated around the mountains. But time and again Asif came in her dreams. She felt he was close. Afsana had to find him. For months, she left every morning, with his photograph, and returned only after dark. She showed me the picture of Asif in a beige salwar suit, his baby face, his still pudgy cheeks, his unrelenting smile.

IN MY YEARS of walking the mountains, I had found children's sandals with plastic sunflowers blooming on them, hand-painted canvas paintings and half-empty bottles of perfume that felt like gifts people had tired of. I wondered what part they had played in the lives of their owners, whether they had made the relationships far from the mountains deeper, the people who received the gifts more precious. But then I saw Afsana who had nothing, cling to her son. She walked the mountains with Asif's photo. He came in her dreams. He stayed close to her. She had to find him.

On one of my visits, I met Atique Khan, the younger of the Khan brothers, released on bail after three years in jail. He had nothing to do with the mountains or the fires he said. His acolytes had misused his name. The wall had always been broken, fires occurred often. "*Ham jhukte nahi na, to hame mohra banaya gaya,*" he said, speaking of himself and his brother, Rafique. *We don't bend to anyone, so we were made into pawns.*

Farzana was pregnant again. Sometimes, when her dupatta slid her swollen neck emerged. At other times, it stayed hidden, or perhaps had even deflated. Her doctors had seen the swelling at prenatal checkups:

they told her to take a test for tuberculosis. She returned only to deliver a baby boy.

I saw Jehangir only in court, where his children arrived in makeup and puffy clothes, as if visiting him were a festive occasion. *"Maine phone to kiya hi nahi tha to phirauti kaise hua?"* he would tell me, always looking for loopholes to get through. *I had not made the phone call, so how can they charge me with asking for a ransom?*

By then I only walked Banjara Galli to meet with the pickers—we had stopped giving loans there in 2016, once we observed our clients lurch from one crisis only to land into another. Illnesses, guards, weddings, or retribution from gang bosses could take away any cushion they created with loans and their earnings. Slowly we retreated from the rest of the city too, working in a rural part of the state where our easily consumable loans supplemented more lasting skills training.

When I walked through Banjara Galli, I sometimes heard my name and turned sharply to see a golden head peeking out sideways, grinning at me. Standing in the lane, blocking the sun, Sameer, Yasmin's younger son, dropped his head down to his shoulder to greet me in a characteristic gesture. He had kept working in the area's overfull dustbins, pulling much-needed money out of their depths. Moharram Ali had mostly disappeared for good. Yasmin had fallen at the railway station on the way to a medical trial, losing her front teeth and any remnants of youth. Then she developed tuberculosis, barring her from medical trials, and so had Hera. Mehrun had stayed out of school getting engaged, at seventeen.

One afternoon, I had turned a corner into the lane to find the fragrance of jasmines filling it. Salma stood in a huddle, collecting the blossoms from a woman who was giving them out to be strung into garlands that she would sell. We walked up to her house, matching her slow shuffling walk. Since her eye surgery, soon after the fires, bumps appeared in her eyes, every winter, she told me. Everything became hazy. How was

Aslam, I asked. "*Vo to do hafte pehle off ho gaya,*" she said, softly. *He went off two weeks ago,* she said, using the Mumbai expression for having died. For years, tuberculosis, alcohol, and other mountain addictions had swirled through him, never completely draining until they had consumed him. Soon after, Salma had moved far from the mountains but died weeks later. Her younger son could only describe the cause as Gabrahat, or mortal fear.

Vitabai had taken up several cleaning jobs in the city, taking loans from bosses to treat her children's illnesses, to get a grandchild operated on after he fell off the roof, and to fix the house when it collapsed. She had to keep working, keep repaying, keep borrowing more. It kept her movement frenetic, her eyes dancing, as they were when I first met her, although I watched her arms sag, her rolling walk slow down even further.

I often ended my walks at Hyder Ali's house, where he told me of his plans to raise money and post Jehangir's bail, hosting me with mountain finds. Once, he tried to get me to sit on a pillowy soft black leather couch that I imagined had come from the house of a wealthy young couple. Instead, I sat on the ground across from him, as always. He told me he was planning to sell the house to hire a lawyer for Jehangir. Where would they all live, I asked, thinking about the cast of generations that filled their home. At that moment, Jehana's sixteen-year-old daughter, Muskaan, walked in, bent over and halting. Like Farzana, Muskaan had shuffled between school and working on the mountains until they had drawn her into their grasp. She lay down on the floor and curled up beside me. "*Dekhenge,*" he replied. *We'll see.* Muskaan was recovering from tuberculosis, he told me. I remembered her, tall, feline, and glowing, from Farzana's wedding photographs.

The next time I visited, Muskaan was half asleep on the floor, where the couch had been. Where did it go? I asked. Hyder Ali laughed. Bedbugs from it had infested the house and bit everyone, and he had had to throw it out. First he asked for tea in a porcelain tea set, then for water from a crystal glass: both mountain finds. Yasmeen often stepped over Muskaan on the floor, as she lay there never fully awake nor asleep, to serve the tea.

The next time I went to their house, tea and water came in steel tumblers. The front section of the house had collapsed in the rain, delaying Hyder Ali's plans to sell it. Had I heard, he asked, that Muskaan had died three days ago. She had lost even the energy to get to his house, by then, and lay in Jehana's house at the mountains' edge, too drained to flick away the flies that buzzed on her. The late afternoon sun streamed in, drying her mouth. Jehana went to get Muskaan water to drink and when she turned back, her daughter was gone, Jehana said.

With work erratic, Hyder Ali had gone to his village. He returned with instructions: everyone needed to remember his grandfather's name. In December, the Indian government had passed the Citizenship Amendment Act that made it legal for Muslims who could not provide paperwork and proof of citizenship to be held in detention camps or deported. Muslims coming in from other countries were not to be fast-tracked to Indian citizenship, the new law outlined, and so they had to establish Indian citizenship. Outside Farzana's lane, I saw a banner: "*Vo kehte hain, Hindustan chhod dein ham. Batao, bhoot ke dar se makaan chhod dein ham?*" *They want us to leave India. Tell us, should we abandon our homeland because it is haunted by a ghost?*

At Hyder Ali's house, the front of the house had gone back up, the plan to sell and post Jehangir's bail revived. In her house, Farzana repeated her great-grandfather's name. No one was sure what was the information they needed to tell officials when they came asking, information that would turn them into legal citizens, since they were not sure they had the right papers for it. They learned what they could and prepared for an interrogation that might, in a single movement, make them illegal occupants in their own country.

AS THE YEAR wore on, Sharma worried that the court hearings to ensure the closure of the township had not yet begun. The case was never listed for hearing at the Supreme Court again. The six-month window for fresh construction in the city carried on without end.

In December 2019, hearings restarted in the Bombay High Court, with Justice S. C. Dharmadhikari presiding over Deonar's fate. It was not the job of the court to set deadlines, he said. The municipality was working on closing the township of trash. Projects such as the waste plant do take time, he said, as he stretched the life of the township of trash on. On November 6, 2020, the municipality passed a plan to make the first of three waste-to-energy plants that would consume 600 metric tons of waste at the Deonar township, a little less than half of what arrived there every day. The first one would take three years to build, they estimated. In February 2021, the Indian government announced a $40 billion plan to reduce the country's worsening air pollution by shrinking its garbage mountains or "legacy waste," managing its construction debris among other measures. The case against Hashim Khan (known as Nanhe), for negligent driving and causing grievous injury by accident to Farzana never came up for hearing. He remains out on bail.

ENDNOTES

INTRODUCTION

telemarketers from banks often hung up when they reached people in slums—Saumya Roy and Gargi Banerjee, "Loan Approvals Depend on Borrowers' Address," *Mint*, April 8, 2008, https://www.livemint.com/Money/f0Rtetble3Chhd5PoAZ2KJ/Loan -approvals-depend-on-borrowers8217-address.html.

mountains that were more than 120 feet high—The height of the highest mountains was said to be 120 feet in the project report made by the municipality-appointed Tata Consulting Engineers. They did drone surveys to arrive at these measurements. Tata Consulting Engineers, *Development of Waste-To-Energy (WTE) Project at Deonar, Mumbai: Feasibility and Detailed Project Report* (Mumbai, India: Municipal Corporation of Greater Mumbai, October 2016).

written of the "waste Everest," outside Moscow—Alec Luhn, "Moscow Region Protests against 'Rubbish Collapse' as Putin's Friends Look to Profit," *The Telegraph*, May 8, 2018, https:// www.telegraph.co.uk/news/2018/05/08/moscow-region-protests-against-rubbish -collapse-putins-friends/.

The mountains in Delhi were said to be nearly as tall as the Taj Mahal—AFP, "Delhi's Ghazipur landfill site to rise higher than Taj Mahal," *Mint*, June 4, 2019, https:// www.livemint.com/news/india/delhi-s-ghazipur-landfill-site-to-rise-higher-than -taj-mahal-1559643893169.html.

no state willing to accept it for burial—Interview with Carol Ash Friedman, regional director New York City Region, New York State Department of Environmental Conservation, at the time. Also, Emily C. Dooley and Carl MacGowan, "Long

Island's Infamous Garbage Barge of 1987 Still Influences Laws," *Newsday*, March 22, 2017, https://projects.newsday.com/long-island/long-island-garbage-barge-left -islip-30-years-ago/.

ONE

They stretched over 326 acres—The township's area varied from 270 to 326 acres in various official documents. After the fires the municipality was said to have dumped earth, extending the township further into the sea. Sudhir Suryawanshi, "Soon, City Will Have No Place to Dump Trash," *Mumbai Mirror*, November 30, 2010, and from multiple sources cited in Wikipedia's article "Deonar Dumping Ground," en.wikipedia.org/wiki/Deonar_dumping_ground.

TWO

wrote in the assiduously compiled administration report the municipal commissioner sent to London every year—"Other Phenomena" section in the health officer's account in the annual administration report of the municipal commissioner of Bombay for the year 1896–97 (P. C. H. Snow, William Forbes Gatacre, Sir., Bombay (India). Municipal Commissioner's Office, *Annual Report of the Municipal Commissioner of Bombay for the Year 1896–97* (Bombay, India: Times of India Steam Press, 1897)).

other than a small red welt—Gyan Prakash, *Mumbai Fables* (Noida, India: Harper-Collins, 2011). Prakash goes on to record the exodus of residents from Bombay over the next few months due to the plague and plague removal measures making it a "City of Dead."

France imposed restrictions on Indian passengers and trade.—Myron Echenberg, *Plague Ports: The Global Urban Impact of Bubonic Plague 1894–1901* (New York: NYU Press, 2007).

Officials believed the disease had arrived in the city with pilgrims returning from a religious fair in North India.—In his report (Snow, *Annual Report of the Municipal Commissioner of Bombay for the Year 1896–97*), Bombay's municipal commissioner P. C. H. Snow stated, "Dr Weir in trying to arrive at the probable causes of the epidemic lights on the theory of migration of people from plague stricken districts."

rats moving through the overflowing filth—Malini Roy, "Bombay Plague Visitation, 1896–97," *Asian and African Studies* (blog), British Library, July 22, 2020, https://blogs.bl.uk/asian-and-african/2020/07/bombay-plague-visitation-1896-97.html.

"There is only one measure from which any effect can be expected and that is quarantine," he wrote.—Snow (*Annual Report of the Municipal Commissioner of Bombay for the Year 1896–97*) quotes Weir recommending quarantine "or any other name by which inspection of traffic and restriction of communication may be called, stringent and careful examination of everyone entering Bombay and careful disinfection of every article, but the result to be expected from that measure is very uncertain."

kept their families in the hospital for weeks—Municipal commissioner's report for 1896–97 (Snow, *Annual Report of the Municipal Commissioner of Bombay for the Year 1896–97*).

afraid that they were being taken there only to die, alone—Health officer's account in the municipal commissioner's report (Snow, *Annual Report of the Municipal Commissioner of Bombay for the Year 1896–97*). Parsi women surrounded a Hindu boy to prevent officer's from taking him to hospital.

having walked a long way—Escape from ambulance. A pitiful case, in the municipal commissioner's report for 1896 (Snow, *Annual Report of the Municipal Commissioner of Bombay for the Year 1896–97*).

"You think we are like mad dogs, and you want to kill us as if we are."—Snow in the municipal commissioner's report (*Annual Report of the Municipal Commissioner of Bombay for the Year 1896–97*). Officers of the health department were charged with a brutal pleasure in dragging the sick from the homes and in killing them, and it was stated that our Sovereign Lady the Queen had demanded five hundred livers of the people of Bombay to appease the wrath aroused at the insult offered to her statue. Men have said to me, "You think we are like mad dogs and you want to kill us, as if we were."

"What can anything done outside this room, do for the people in their misery inside?" he wrote—From Snow's report (*Annual Report of the Municipal Commissioner of Bombay for the Year 1896–97*). The room, in Khara Talao, that held fifty-seven people was 111 feet in length and 18½ feet in width, with no ventilation.

patients walking city streets in delirium and lying beside the road—From Snow's report (*Annual Report of the Municipal Commissioner of Bombay for the Year 1896–97*), in the section Desire to Wander in Delirium.

Enforcing them would only accelerate the surge of leaving residents, they wrote.—From the municipal commissioner's report (Snow, *Annual Report of the Municipal Commissioner of Bombay for the Year 1896–97*), which states that "a number of influential citizens" wrote to him, on October 14, a week after the plague measures had been imposed. They said that if the measures were enforced, a "much larger number of inhabitants would fly from Bombay."

"a vast panic and exodus" from the city, Snow wrote.—Weir wrote of the night he and Snow met the police commissioner, with the crowds swirling outside. The police commissioner and the health officer "were of the opinion that our sanitary staff would make common cause with the rioters, nor was it possible to ascertain in a time of such wild panic and excitement how far the fine discipline of the Bombay Police would avail" (Snow, *Annual Report of the Municipal Commissioner of Bombay for the Year 1896–97*).

much less adopt a single preventive measure against the plague—Executive engineer's account in the municipal commissioner's report 1897–98 (Snow, *Annual Report of the Municipal Commissioner of Bombay for the Year 1896–97*).

The government acquired the land from its owner, Ardeshir Cursetji Cama, that May.—executive engineer's department report in the municipal commissioner's report for 1899 (Snow, *Annual Report of the Municipal Commissioner of Bombay for the Year 1896–97*).

The smell of garbage, it was thought, would make them gag.—Executive engineer's report (Snow, *Annual Report of the Municipal Commissioner of Bombay for the Year 1896–97*).

to keep the sea from seeping into the site, and garbage from flowing into the creek—The bund was completed on December 15, 1901, according to the executive engineer's report in the municipal commissioners report (Snow, *Annual Report of the Municipal Commissioner of Bombay for the Year 1896–97*).

". . . an unhealthy swamp, could be converted into fruitful agricultural ground," the report concluded—Executive engineer's account in the municipal commissioner's report (Snow, *Annual Report of the Municipal Commissioner of Bombay for the Year 1896–97*).

hand their settlements over to developers so they could build apartments and office towers— *Times of India* Proquest Archive. Among the stories dating back to the early sixties is one about the residents of a *chawl*, or tenement, near Vitabai's house in central Bombay. The municipality had ripped out the door and window frames and the tiled roof, and withdrew the power and water supply, while some residents battled in court to stay on, rather than move to Deonar. The court eventually asked them to move.

large workshops to house their small businesses—Lisa Björkman, *Pipe Politics, Contested Waters: Embedded Infrastructures of Millennial Mumbai* (Durham, NC: Duke University Press, 2015). Björkman shows how the slums around the mountains were planned and legally settled.

gases from hastily closed dumping grounds didn't settle for years—Shalini Nair, "Gases Spook Comps in IT Park Built on Dump," *Times of India*, April 2, 2007. Also interview with Amiya Sahu, founder of the National Solid Waste Association of India, who tested and found gases from trash floating in the newly made corporate offices.

THREE

In 1995, Bombay had become Mumbai.—The city is referred to as Bombay before 1995 and Mumbai after that in the text.

India's environment ministry had framed rules, for the first time, to manage waste— Ministry of Environment and Forests, Management of Solid Waste (Management and Handling, 2000 Rules), 2000, https://www.mpcb.gov.in/sites/default/files/solid -waste/MSWrules200002032020.pdf.

FOUR

"which show a film of gas over the waste," later court observations said—From court orders passed by Justice D. Y. Chandrachud on July 7, 2009, in the Bombay High Court. Dr. Sandip K. Rane v. Municipal Corporation of Greater Mumbai & Ors. (Contempt Petition 29 of 2008), https://bombayhighcourt.nic.in/generatenewauth.php?bhcpar=c GF0aD0uL3dyaXRlcmVhZGRhdGEvZGF0YS9vcmlnaW5hW5hbC8yMDA5LyZmbm FtZT1DT05QVzI2MDgwNzA3MDkucGRmJnNtZmxhZz1OJnJqdWRkYXRlPP SZ1cGxvYWRkD0mc3Bhc3NwaHJhc2U9MTAwMTIxMjIyNDIw.

constricting their breath—From the petition filed by residents of Shanti Park/Sorento against Municipal Corporation of Greater Mumbai (MCGM) in Writ petition 1138 of 1996, obtained through the Right to Information Act, from MCGM.

seven times more than the rules allowed—Shanti Park residents quoted the municipal submissions showing respiratory suspended particulate matter at Deonar was 2163Mg/m3, seven times higher than permissible limits (Shanti Park "Sorento" Co-Op Housing Society Ltd and Others v. Municipal Corporation of Greater Mumbai and Others (Writ Petition 1138 of 1196)).

brain damage in the children who breathed it in—Petitioners quoted municipal findings in their court affidavit showing that the lead content in mountain air was two and a half times the permissible limits.

The municipality's response at the time declared the mountains lit up in "spontaneous combustion."—Affidavit by Narayan Achrekar in the Bombay High Court. Other municipal affidavits from the time say the fires were a "natural phenomenon."

continually burning fires and their rising smoke—Petition by Shanti Park "Sorento" Coop Housing Society Ltd. and Others v. MCGM and others. They asked for police patrols, fire engines, and water tankers to curb fires and a telephone number to complain on, when the smoke increased at night.

interstitial lung disease, which would thicken the tissue around their lungs, consuming them within five years of breathlessness and coughing—Details on interstitial lung disease were given by Dr. Kumar Doshi, a chest physician, in a letter to Dr. Rane that was included in Rane's contempt petition. Dr. Vikas Oswal, a well-known pulmonologist who practices in the lanes around the mountains, confirmed that he saw more interstitial lung disease in these lanes than elsewhere in the city, and that half his patients arrived with respiratory diseases. Other doctors confirmed this.

the Triangle of Death—Men living near the illegal landfills in Campania province in Italy had a 35.9 in 100,000 rate of dying from liver cancer, compared to 14 in the rest of Italy. Women had a 20.5 in 100,000 rate of dying from liver cancer, compared to 6 in the rest of Italy. From a study published in *The Lancet* in September 2004. Kathryn Senior and Alfredo Mazza, "Italian 'Triangle of Death' Linked to Waste Crisis," *The Lancet Oncology* 5, no. 9 (September 2004): 525–27.

cleansing the murky air and water it spewed—₹10,500 crore landfill fixing project, taken from tender documents.

their homes inched into hills, and gangs fought for trash—Among project and tender details for this project, obtained through the Right to Information Act, were letters to this effect.

In a ward further away, by comparison, it was less than 1 percent.—Rajil Menon, "Gas Chembur," *DownToEarth*, November 30, 2009, https://www.downtoearth.org.in /news/gas-chembur-2658.

the haze was thick with the carcinogenic chemical formaldehyde—Findings of high levels of formaldehyde were communicated by NEERI to Dr. Rane in March 2009, according to court orders (Shanti Park "Sorento" Co-Op Housing Society Ltd and Others v. Municipal Corporation of Greater Mumbai and Others (Writ Petition 1138 of 1196)). Also referred to in the above story.

the authors looked at elsewhere in the world—Dipanjali Majumdar and Anjali Srivastava, "Volatile Organic Compound Emissions from Municipal Solid Waste Sites: A Case Study of Mumbai, India," *Journal of the Air & Waste Management Association* 62, no. 4 (2012): 398–407.

little more than half the lives that other Indians did—Human Development Report, by Municipal Corporation of Greater Mumbai (New Delhi, India: Oxford University Press, 2009).

". . . no serious attempt has been made to alleviate the problem."—Orders passed by Justice DY Chandrachud in the Bombay High Court on May 8, 2008—Dr. Sandip K. Rane v. Municipal Corporation of Greater Mumbai & Ors. (2008), https://bombay highcourt.nic.in/generatenewauth.php?bhcpar=cGF0aD0uL3dyaXRlcmVhZGR hdGEvZGF0YS9vcmlnaW5hbC8yMDA5LyZmbmFtZT1DT05QVzI2MDgw ODA1MDkucGRmJnNtZmxhZz1OJnJqdWRkYXRlPSZ1cGxvYWRkD0m c3Bhc3NwawaHJhc2U9MTAwMTIxMjIyNDIw.

FIVE

to see the forgotten world with his own eyes—From the May 8, 2008 orders passed by Justice Chandrachud in the Bombay High Court. Dr. Sandip K. Rane v. Municipal Corporation of Greater Mumbai & Ors. (2008).

they called it Tatva—Tatva means "elements" in Hindi, and "principled" in Marathi.

the tender process had material flaws—Ajay Saxena Committee Report on Public Private Partnerships. Ajay Saxena, *Inquiry Report on Public Private-Partnership Integrated Solid Waste Managements at Deonar, Mulund and Kanjurmarg Dumping Grounds*, September 2011.

SIX

so it could begin making the plant—From court orders passed in Tatva's plea for arbitration in the Bombay High Court, March 19, 2015.—Tatva Global Environment (Deonar) Ltd. v. The Municipal Corporation of Gr. Mumbai, https://bombayhigh court.nic.in/generatenewauth.php?bhcpar=cGF0aD0uL3dyaXRlcmVhZGRhd GEvZGF0YS9qdWRnZW1lbnRzLzIwMTUvJmZuYW1lPU9TQVJJCQVAyMj Y4MTMucGRmJnNtZmxhZz1OJnJqdWRkYXRlPSZ1cGxvYWRkD0yNC8wMy8yMDE1JnNwYXNzcGhyYXNlPTEwMDEyMTIzNDYzOA==.

Atique and Rafique were charged with her son's murder, Atique recalled—From the police charge sheet against Atique and Rafique Khan, filed in 2016.

slipping through holes in the wall at the far end of the township's official entrance—Atique Khan told me that Rafique's trucks were contracted by the municipality, brought only as much debris as permitted and emptied it where asked. The police had framed charges saying that Rafique broke the wall at the far end and brought in debris illegally.

begin making the plant, which would lead to the mountains' closure—From court orders passed in Tatva's plea for arbitration in the Bombay High Court, March 19, 2015—Tatva Global Environment (Deonar) Ltd. v. The Municipal Corporation of Gr. Mumbai.

the terms of the municipality's contract with Tatva—From Maharashtra State Assembly proceedings dated April 3, 2013.

hand over the township's lease and pay its dues—From court orders passed in Tatva's plea for arbitration in the Bombay High Court on March 19, 2015.

SEVEN

irregularities with the tender process—SK Goyal committee report submitted in January 2015 (S.K. Goyal and Shrikant Singh, *Report of SIT for the irregularities in Mumbai SWM Projects in Deonar, Mulund and Kanjurmarg*, January 27, 2015).

It took back the plans for the plant.—Documents showing the meeting at the municipal commissioner's office where that plant was scrapped; found at http://forestsclearance .nic.in/DownloadPdfFile.aspx?FileName=0_0_5114123712111AdminAppA-III .pdf&FilePath=../writereaddata/Addinfo/.

only six years into its twenty-five-year tenancy—Termination of Tatva's contract. While this forms the subject of ongoing arbitration between the municipality and Tatva, it is referred to in several documents, including the Achrekar Committee report to probe the fires, ordered on February 1, 2016, by the municipal commissioner (Kiran Achrekar, *Inquiry Report on the Cause of Fire at Deonar Dumping Grounds on January 28, 2016*, February 1, 2016).

and doodled when she was—A study conducted by the nonprofit organization Pratham and the MIT's Poverty Action Lab found that teachers taught according to the curriculum, while students—often first-generation learners—lagged behind. Known as Teaching at the Right Level, or TaRL, it was conducted in Ashra's ward (among others) in Mumbai, and encouraged teachers to take some time teaching at the child's level. The scheme was eventually taken across the country and to several other countries.

EIGHT

asking for fire engines—From the testimony of Rajan Anant Patil, junior supervisor. MCGM's Achrekar Committee report (*Inquiry Report on the Cause of Fire at Deonar Dumping Grounds on January 28, 2016*), inquiring into the January 2016 fires.

winding slowly through flaming trash hills—Deepak Ahire in the Achrekar Committee report. Other municipal officers have said 8:30 A.M. The fire department's inquiry report states that it received a call at 12:58 P.M. and reached the grounds at 1:35 P.M.

hydrants at the township—From the inquiry report on the fires in January 2016, conducted by M. N. Dhonde, Assistant Divisional Fire Officer, *Fire Investigation*

Report, February 15, 2016. Report obtained through the RTI Act. Tatva executives did not respond to several emails seeking comment.

the acceptable limit was 200—AQI measurement from SAFAR, the System for Air Quality and Weather Forecasting and Research.

it should have stayed below 80 micrograms—Measured by the Maharashtra Pollution Control Board, and quoted in the Lohiya Committee report: *Inquiry Report on the Cause of Fire at Deonar Dumping Ground on January 28, 2016* (submitted on May, 11, 2016).

the day the fires began—From "Contractor Asks BMC for Rs 36.19 cr to Return Deonar Dump Ground," *Hindustan Times*, February 11, 2016, https://www.hindustantimes. com/mumbai/contractor-asks-bmc-for-rs36-19cr-to-return-deonar-dump-ground /story-Tp4EeBQKp5eTIOm46X5qKN.html.

$5 billion had been committed to making iPhones in the state—From a story in *Mint* newspaper by Makarand Gadgil, "How Maharashtra Bagged the $5 Billion Foxconn Deal", *Mint*, August 13, 2015, https://www.livemint.com/Politics/VXNlQnXrncM9FR BO5xE2pK/How-Maharashtra-bagged-the-5-billion-Foxconn-deal.html. It stated that Foxconn, the contract manufacturer of Apple phones, would invest $5 billion over five years in a factory that would be a replica of its second-largest plant in China. The plans had languished for years and were officially scrapped in 2020 when Chinese and Indian troops faced off in Ladakh.

NINE

soaking into submission the fires that could have raged for days—"Major Fire Breaks Out at Deonar Dumping Yard again," *Business Standard*, February 15, 2016.

municipality's security cameras that did not work and was captured on the gangs' cameras that did—Raj Kumar Sharma's petition filed in January 2016.

Down the street was RK Studios—RK Studios was named for Raj Kapoor, the actor, director, and producer behind it.

the land was dotted with private homes and tribal settlements—From court orders passed in February 2016—Municipal Corporation of Greater Mumbai v. Pandurng Patil and Ors. Public Interest Litigation 217 of 2009, https://bombayhighcourt.nic.in /generatenewauth.php?bhcpar=cGF0aD0uL3dyaXRlcmVhZGRhdGEvZGF0YS9 qdWRnZW1lbnRzLzIwMTYvJmZuYW1lPUNDQUkyMjY5NzEzLnBkZiZzb WZsYWc9WSZyanVkZGF0ZT0zMC8wMy8yMDE2JnVwbG9hZGR0PTExL zAzLzIwMTYmc3Bhc3NwaHJhc2U9MTAwMTIxMjMyNjEw.

which made for most construction in the space-starved city anyway, could continue—Court orders say that new development formed only 18.7 percent of all proposals for construction in the city, which was banned, compared to 81.3 percent for the redevelopment of old buildings, which could continue (from January 1, 2014, to September 30, 2015).

They tried to revive a breathless baby who, newspapers later reported, died.—Press Trust of India; the parents of a six-month-old baby said he had suffered from breathlessness since the fires began in January and died during those in March. The AQI was 319, which was "very poor." Authorities said the baby had had respiratory problems since birth.

There were no cameras on the mountains.—From the statement of Dayanand Naik, junior supervisor at the Deonar Dumping Ground in the Achrekar Committee report (*Inquiry Report on the Cause of Fire at Deonar Dumping Grounds on January 28, 2016*). He said there were no cameras on the grounds. Others said that only four of the forty cameras were installed, and none of them worked.

TEN

while police settled a booth across it—Letter from MCGM to Tatva, on the wall at the far end of the township being broken.

veered away from her on hill clearings to this estate—This is backed up by the Lohiya Committee report (*Inquiry Report on the Cause of Fire at Deonar Dumping Grounds on January 28, 2016*).

blew toxic clouds into the air that the pickers barely noticed—An inspection by the Pollution Control Board had found biomedical was arriving by cycle, in unmarked vehicles and only one of its four incinerators working as required. It also questioned whether permission for the plant should have been given in the middle of the packed lanes. The plant was closed for a day before compliances were met and the plant restarted, in documents obtained through RTI.

on behalf of the lanes near where the city dumped its own garbage, endlessly—From records kept by Praja, a nonprofit organization that conducts research on urban governance.

they had been threatened, intimidated, beaten, or their vehicles impounded if they did not pay—From the police charge sheet. (Atique Khan had told me they gave up on the parking space when officials asked for such high bribes and they could not make a profit anymore.)

ELEVEN

seasonal inhalation and exhalation in the municipality's fire inquiry report, in Marathi—Madan Yavalkar in the Achrekar Committee report (*Inquiry Report on the Cause of Fire at Deonar Dumping Grounds on January 28, 2016*)—"pavsali hungamyat kachryat paani gelya mule tyache aaakarmaan vadhte va teevra unhalyat tyatlya panyache bashmi bavan zhalyane kami hote."

Maharashtra Control of Organized Crime Act (MCOCA), which allowed for long periods of imprisonment without bail—Bombay High Court orders passed on October 1, 2018. While the case had come up in a special court and then the High Court, these orders explain the police and Khan brothers' account of their role on the mountains and deny bail. They did get bail some months after this order, when the Khan brothers had spent more than two and a half years in jail, under trial. Javed Yousuf Qureshi v. The State of Maharashtra, Criminal Bail Application No 3020 of 2017, https://bombayhighcourt.nic.in/generatenewauth.php?bhcpar=cGF0aD0uL3dyaX

RlcmVhZGRhdGEvZGF0YS9jcmltaW5hbC8yMDE4LyZmbmFtFtZT0y
QkEzMDIwMTcwMTEwMTgucGRmJnNtZmxhZz10OJnJqdWRkYXRlPSZ1c
GxvYWRkD0yMi8xMS8yMDE4JnNwYXNzcGhyYXNlPTExMDEyM
TE2NTA0NA==.

or returned to their villages to escape attention—I later read that Jehangir had given a state-ment in the Lohiya Committee report: *Inquiry Report on the Cause of Fire at Deonar Dumping Ground* (submitted on May 11, 2016). He concurred with Javed Qureshi's statement, saying that younger pickers consumed drugs to keep working. They often burned wire to extract the copper, with the fires sometimes getting out of hand.

TWELVE

truly, in this there is a lesson for men of insight—From the well-known translation of the Koran by Abdullah Yusuf Ali. While Yasmeen was not sure this was the verse she recited that afternoon, she sometimes did read and recite it.

Shahenshah-E-Chembur, or the Emperor of Chembur, presiding over a kingdom of poisonous chemicals and disease—In September 2019 the Bombay High Court ruled that city dwellers resettled in the two colonies in the halo of these refineries were to be reset-tled and paid compensation. The court relied on medical and environmental studies that showed air quality in the area had deteriorated as these refineries and factories around them had multiplied. One study measured benzene at 88.67 Mu/m3 in these villages, increasing the cancer risk and health problems. An earlier study had shown benzene at the Deonar grounds to be 286 Mu/m3.

THIRTEEN

the shrine of Mira Datar, the patron saint of exorcizing spirits in Mumbai—I found Beatrix Pfleiderer's book *Red Thread* (Delhi, India: Aakar Books, 1994) helpful in reading on the history, legend, and rituals at the shrine of Mira Datar in Gujarat.

waste-to-compost plants and power plants around the world—From draft project report and environmental clearance documents made by Tata Consulting Engineers, *Development of Waste-To-Energy (WTE) Project at Deonar, Mumbai*.

higher than in most other cities the authors studied—From the Tata Consulting Engi-neers project report on environmental clearance; Tata Consulting Engineers, *Development of Waste-To-Energy (WTE) Project at Deonar, Mumbai*, http://forests clearance.nic.in/DownloadPdfFile.aspx?FileName=0_0_5114123712111Admin AppA-III.pdf&FilePath=../writereaddata/Addinfo/

FOURTEEN

money was due to her family—Based on documents where Yasmin gave her consent for medical trials.

to quell their stink—Obtained through a Right to Information (RTI) request.

FIFTEEN

the toxic halo that seeped in and settled into those who lived around—From the Tata Consulting Engineers project report on the waste-to-energy plant (*Development of Waste-To-Energy (WTE) Project at Deonar, Mumbai*).

feeding the ever-burning fires—From the municipality's Air Quality Monitoring office, quoted in the project report (Tata Consulting Engineers, *Development of Waste-To-Energy (WTE) Project at Deonar, Mumbai: Feasibility and Detailed Project Report* (Mumbai, India, October 2016)). Air quality data for after 2015 was obtained through RTI requests.

would get fed to the plant—A spokesperson from Tata Consulting Engineers did not respond to an emailed questionnaire. Tata Consulting Engineers, *Development of Waste-To-Energy (WTE) Project at Deonar, Mumbai: Feasibility and Detailed Project Report* (Mumbai, India, October 2016).

"…facilitating drying and combustion," the report said—From the Tata Consulting Engineers project report *(Development of Waste-To-Energy (WTE) Project at Deonar, Mumbai).*

SIXTEEN

The account of the accident and Farzana's medical condition was obtained from the medical papers released from Sion hospital with Farzana's consent, the police charge sheet and from interviews with family members, pickers, municipal officials, etc. The police charge sheet includes Farzana's medical report, Hashim's statement, and so on.

but they seemed to be lost—I had applied for these registers through the Right To Information Act but was not provided copies of the registers for the day of the accident and the weeks after.

SEVENTEEN

September was the month for pre-bid meetings—From the Tata Consulting Engineers project report (*Development of Waste-To-Energy (WTE) Project at Deonar, Mumbai*).

EIGHTEEN

that "this will be one of the largest plants in the world."—Vishwas Waghmode, "Deonar: Tenders Floated for Waste-to-Energy Project," *Indian Express*, November 9, 2016, https://indianexpress.com/article/cities/mumbai/deonar-tenders-floated-for -waste-to-energy-project-4365155/.

NINETEEN

one in the city even predated the mountains—Municipal commissioner's reports from 1897 (Snow, *Annual Report of the Municipal Commissioner of Bombay for the Year 1896– 97*) show that there was a Garlick's incinerator in the city. It was sold as scrap when the *cuchra* trains began ferrying garbage to Deonar.

Farzana's wedding was only months away.—A randomized control trial by Abhijit Banerjee, Cynthia Kinnan, Esther Duflo, and others at the MIT Poverty Action Lab had shown that micro-finance loans helped increase business investment, but increased profits only for those that were already the most profitable. Conducted in Hyderabad, the study found that loan-takers invested in growing their businesses, but those that were already profitable had grown the most. I too had found that the small profits they made were wiped out by sudden illnesses, weddings, deaths, or village trips. Hyder Ali, Moharram Ali, and others often stayed in this cycle of making small profits and then losing them to emergencies.

TWENTY-ONE

asking to extend its life for four more years—Draft project report by Tata Consulting Engineers for the waste-to-energy plant at Deonar, (July) 2016. (*Development of Waste-To-Energy (WTE) Project at Deonar, Mumbai*). The accounts of the court proceedings come from my own notes. I attended hundreds of hours of court proceedings, moving slowly from the back to the front to hear. I later read, in Dr. Rahela Khorakiwala's book *From the Colonial to the Contemporary: Images, Iconography, Memories and Performances of Law in India's High Courts* (New Delhi, India: Hart/Bloomsbury 2020), that this was known as "auditory autism." https://www.hindustantimes.com /mumbai-news/bombay-high-court-raises-a-stink-tells-bmc-to-identify-dumping -sites/story-Sfb9BRQlmSlI5K0uCDEz6M.html.

the cessation of dumping building debris, had happened—From R. K. Sharma's petition to Bombay High Court.

barbed wire to be installed along the creek's edge—Minutes of the court committee meeting.

more construction debris than garbage had been dumped on the mountains over the last few months—From Affidavit filed by R. K. Sharma in Bombay High Court.

growing only by 1 percent a year for the next twenty years—Report by All India Self Government Institute submitted to Bombay High Court (All India Institute for Local Self Government, *Scientific Assessment of Impact of Future Development in Great Mumbai on Generation of Solid Waste*, June, 1, 2017).

construction waste every day—CSIR-National Environmental Engineering Institute, *Studies on Quantification and Characterization of Municipal Solid Waste in Municipal Corporation of Greater Mumbai (MCGM), Mumbai Region* (Nagpur, India: May 2016).

some of the garbage the contractor ferried, and billed for, never existed—Chore Committee report, in *Indian Express*, July 12, 2017, https://indianexpress.com/article/cities/mum bai/show-cause-notices-to-4-officials-for-conniving-with-garbage-contractor-mum bai-4746554/.

10 percent overweighing of garbage so contractors could be overpaid—Lohiya Committee report (*Inquiry Report on the Cause of Fire at Deonar Dumping Grounds on January 28, 2016*).

garbage that emptied from trucks, not mud—"Deonar Dump's Garbage Collection Data Goes Digital: BMC," *The Asian Age*, December 17, 2016, https://www.asianage.com /metros/mumbai/171216/deonar-dumps-garbage-collection-data-goes-digital.html.

TWENTY-TWO

trees had mysteriously grown on the hills, though they had only a thin topping of soil over its core of decomposing trash.—William Bryant Logan, "The Lessons of a Hideous Forest," *New York Times*, July 20, 2019, https://www.nytimes.com/2019/07/20/opin ion/sunday/forest-garbage-trees.html.

TWENTY-THREE

within 100 meters of a court, hospital, or educational institution had to be a silent zone— Bombay High Court orders passed on August, 2016 (Narsi Benwal, "Ganesh Chaturthi 2017: August 2016 Order on Silence Zones to Prevail, Says Bombay HC," *The Free Press*, August 24, 2017).

restrained him from passing any further orders on the issue—Supreme Court orders passed on September 4, 2017.

no one was sure exactly how many people had lived and died on the slopes of Mount Koshe—Elias Meseret, "46 Killed, Dozens Missing in Ethiopia Garbage Dump Landslide," *Associated Press*, March 13, 2017.

even after their contract with the municipality had ended—According to the police charge sheet on Atique and Rafique Khan.

many of them had made the long journey away from having nothing—In their opening essay in *Muslims in Indian Cities: Trajectories of Marginalisation* (HarperCollins, 2012), Laurent Gayer and Christophe Jaffrelot quote the National Sample Survey data show-ing that Muslims' average monthly expenditure was just ₹800, equal only to that of Dalits and Adivasis. Dalits and Muslims make up nearly all those who lived around the mountains. Upper-caste Hindus spent ₹1,469. The data is from 2004–2005.

TWENTY-FOUR

a little less than two years after Oka had banned it—Orders passed in the Supreme Court on March 15, 2018 (Maharashtra Chamber of Housing Industry v. Municipal Corporation of Greater Mumbai and Others, Special Leave Petition (Civil) D23708 /2017), https://main.sci.gov.in/supremecourt/2017/23708/23708_2017_Order_15 -Mar-2018.pdf.

It was the second fire in two weeks.—Richa Pinto, "Fire Breaks Out at Mumbai's Deonar Dump, Spreads and Rages on," *The Times of India*, March 27, 2018, https:// timesofindia.indiatimes.com/city/mumbai/fire-breaks-out-at-deonar-dump-spreads -rages-on/articleshow/63472468.cms.

had asked to spray foam on the mountain fires instead of water—From minutes of the court committee proceedings obtained through RTI.

But the court too had stayed in place.—From Rahela Khorakiwala's *From the Colonial to the Contemporary: Images, Iconography, Memories, and Performances of Law in India's High Courts* (Oxford: Hart Publishing, 2020). The case for finding new space to build a High Court building was also reported in the newspapers.

brushed against the wires, they died, electrocuted—From an interview with the then chief executive of Tata Power, the electricity supplier in Delhi.

the Supreme Court's view, which asked its municipality to fix them—On July 10, 2018, the Supreme Court had passed an order saying that "mountains of garbage" nearly buried the city, and the civic administration needed to fix the situation, https://main.sci.gov.in/supremecourt/2015/31019/31019_2015_Order_10-Jul-2018.pdf.

Oka gave a video talk to law students—Talk to law students at the National Academy for Legal Studies and Research, July 5, 2020 (https://www.youtube.com/watch?v=BeTz72F8INc).

TWENTY-FIVE

giving them a portion of the money—Special court proceedings, news reports, and charge sheet against Jehangir.

POSTSCRIPT

he had said after the judge Justice Dinshaw Davar had ruled against him—Bombay High Court Archives (online)—https://bombayhighcourt.nic.in/libweb/historical cases/cases/1908%2810%29BLR848.pdf.

Tilak was sentenced to eighteen months in jail, which only inflamed the anger in both cities—Judgment of first sedition trial in Bombay High Court: https://bombayhigh court.nic.in/libweb/historicalcases/cases/ILR1898%2822%29BOM112.pdf.

No new garbage could be dumped there after December 31, 2019.—Bombay High Court orders on April 9, 2019: https://bombayhighcourt.nic.in/generatenewauth.php ?bhcpar=cGF0aD0uL3dyaXRlcmVhZGRhdGEvZGF0YS9jaXZpbC8yMDE5 LyZmbmFtZT1DQUkyMjY5NzEzMDkwNDE5LnBkZiZzbWZsYWc9TiZy anVkZGF0ZT0mdXBsb2FkZHQ9MDcvMDUvMjAxOSZzcGFzc3BocmFzZ T0xMDAxMjEyMzI2MTA=.

as he stretched the life of the township of trash on—Bombay High Court order, December 19, 2019. Municipal Corporation of Greater Mumbai & Others v. Pandurang Patil.

a little less than half of what arrived there every day—Vijay V. Singh, "Mumbai: BMC Panel Greenlights ₹1,100 Crore Deonar Waste-to-Energy Plant Plan," *Times of India*, November 5, 2000, https://timesofindia.indiatimes.com/city/mumbai/mumbai-bmc -panel-greenlights-rs-1100-crore-deonar-waste-to-energy-plant-plan/articleshow /79053083.cms.

ACKNOWLEDGMENTS

Castaway Mountain could only be written because the residents of Banjara Galli welcomed me into their homes and lives. I remember returning there early in 2016, not offering loans, but simply to hear more about them. Pickers went on to walk me through the mountains, take me into their homes, the clinics they visited, the schools their children attended, their embroidery workshops, and their *kata* shops, bringing alive their memories, their scrapes, and their festering aches.

I am thankful to all those who chose to be written about. Others, who were barely featured or chose not to be, helped out too, including Saabir Pathan, Miya Khan, Lilabai Pawar, Shakila Shaikh, Shiva Shaikh, Rauf Shaikh, Akhtar Hussain Mullah, Hussain Shaikh, and countless others.

Geeta Anand read and helped shape *Castaway Mountain* every fortnight, even when it felt like a stormy, shapeless cloud that I was stuck in. Soon after moving to Berkeley, she told me it was Farzana who glowed through my messy drafts. Remotely she mediated between us, so that

Farzana could say the things she could not bear to, and I could ask about them, hear them, and write about them. For helping channel Farzana's story through my hands, her wisdom, and her friendship, it will probably take me the Deonar townships' more than hundred-year-long lifetime to thank Geeta.

My thanks to Taran Khan for walking me nearly every day through my failings and stumblings, in the face of a story that was inextricably stuck within me and had to be told. Manu Joseph kept showing me the light—at the end of writing tangles, apparent publishing dead-ends and mangled Mumbai metaphors. *Castaway Mountain*'s hardest passes were traversed with Taran's and Manu's handholding.

Alessandra Bastagli, my editor, shaped the script it in ways that felt effortless to me but that took *Castaway Mountain* to an unscaled height. She helped tell Farzana's story so it would move readers worlds away from Deonar and make her feel their own. Cecily Gayford, my editor at Profile Books in the U.K., had taken on this project first of all, seeing it for being about Farzana's incredible journey, one that revealed as much about our world as Farzana's. *Castaway Mountain* is illuminated and elevated by the thoughtfulness, grace, and polish of my editors—Alessandra and Cecily.

Sophie Scard and Alison Lewis, my literary agents, kept guiding this project calmly through a worsening market. To them and Georgina Le Grice, my thanks for taking life in the trash-made homes of Banjara Galli to distant parts of the world, where castaway aspirations made more mountains and other lives. I hope their work will help augment the project to shrink desire and its long, dark trail.

R. K. Sharma was often my intrepid co-traveler in the world of waste. We frequently walked the mountains, visited waste plants, sat through court proceedings, and drank endless glasses of tea while ruminating about the fate of the mountains. For sharing my obsession, I offer my immense gratitude to him. I had turned to Dayanand Stalin when I figured that I needed data and documents to see the mountains, through their fog. For years Stalin helped me navigate the Right To Information application process, through which I collected thousands of pages of documents that brought alive the world of the mountains.

Jairaj Phatak, Ajit Kumar Jain, Bhalchandra Patil, Rajiv Jalota, M. R. Shah, Amiya Sahu, and more than a dozen other retired and serving municipal officials who decided to remain unnamed provided context and detail on life at the mountains, on the challenges in managing them and giving them a new life. While the information came from them, the analysis was my own. Chandan Singh and others processed hundreds of RTI requests regarding the mountains with alacrity and patience.

K. P. Raghuvanshi and Rahul Asthana, both of whom had chaired the High Court committee on Deonar, provided their insights.

Jennifer Spencer and her team at Praja provided health and education data for the ward around the mountains, which gave much-needed context to the lack of development in the area. Jockin Arputham, who passed away during the writing of this book, not only held Vandana Foundation in his arms but also provided great anecdotes on how the slums around the mountains were settled, demolished, and resettled. His mentoring and stories are sorely missed as are Rashid Kidwai's, who passed away weeks before this book first came out.

Vighnesh Kamath, from R. K. Sharma's legal team, provided documents and backed up my memories and notes from hundreds of hours of court proceedings. Rohit De and Rahela Khorakiwala helped me make sense of the court through their brilliant books and conversation.

Although Sukriti Issar had left Oxford to join the Sciences Po faculty by then, she supported my research at the Bodleian Library remotely, helping me trace back the Deonar township's history from 1927—the officially quoted date—to records in 1899. Nilesh Wadnerkar at the Maharashtra State Assembly Library brought out proceedings and newspaper articles on Deonar.

Dr. A. D. Sawant patiently deconstructed the mountains' toxic halo and its impact on health. Anjali Bansal, Devina Parekh, Asad Hussain, Sarfaraz Arzu, Tanvi Kant, Shivaji Nimhan, Abdul Rauf Shaikh, Rukshana Shaikh, Dr. Khalid Shaikh, Dr. Vikas Oswal, Birju Mundada, Kishore Gayke, and Prafulla Marpakwar provided invaluable help with research, while Kanika Sharma and Abhijeet Rane helped with legal processes.

The frail Sachin Tambe, who had collected loan instalments, kept walking with me through the skinny lanes around the mountains, helping me trace the pickers, their shifting homes and crumbling lives. Prashant Shinde at Vandana Foundation helped with sending, tracking, and collecting my endless applications for documents.

Biaas Sanyal helped with fact-checking my seemingly unending research. Ashlesha Athavale rechecked the Marathi documents. Both helped iron out my flaws.

Writing residencies helped transform all the interviews and research material that I had collected over the years into re-creating the world of the Deonar township on page. Two Logan Nonfiction fellowships helped me begin, and then nearly complete, *Castaway Mountain*. Pilar Pilacia and her team at the Rockefeller Foundation's Bellagio Center provided the warmest cocoon for writing, along with brilliant company and views that were as far from Deonar as possible. Blue Mountain Center gave me a quietness and calm that I had almost never experienced as a Mumbai-kar, allowing the world of Deonar to appear in slow motion in my mind, letting me capture it. I began writing this book at Sangam House. Note-books emptied onto the computer, with Arshia Sattar and Pascale Sieger's care and to the beat of Nrityagram's dancers, never letting me stop. My thanks also to Dora Maar House, where I was supposed to be when the pandemic hit and lockdowns shut travel opportunities, and where I hope to work later. Just as this book came from my being filled with the world of the Deonar township, it probably could not have been articulated without the distance of residencies, for which I am deeply thankful.

Residencies also provided the precious company of writers who had written books more achingly beautiful than mine. Lisa Ko and Kiran Desai talked me through their experiences over long walks at Blue Mountain and Bellagio, canoeing and ferry rides, long meals, and frantic emails. Suzannah Lessard, Adrian LeBlanc, and Suzy Hansen provided invaluable advice on finding my voice in the first person, when all I wanted was to turn invisible. Risa Lavizzo Mourey helped me make sense of Farzana's dire medical records, even as I saw her heal, as did Parina Samra Bajaj. Abby Seiff, Melanie Smith, Rana Rosen, Diane Mehta, Philippa Dunne, and Justin Kaguto Go provided long-distance advice on writing, art, cities, and looking at things a bit differently.

Marco Armiero at KTH, Stockholm, provided insights, anecdotes, and learnings about the Italian waste crisis. Rajesh Parameswaran and Markley Boyer were my companions through the world of New York's landfills, its waste, and the legends around it.

I am thankful also to Olivia Dontsov, Rachael Small, Sabrina Dax, Alisa Trager, Tiffany Gonzalez, Lisa Taylor, and the rest of the team at Astra House for their careful editing and support. Thanks to Rodrigo Corral Studio for the gorgeous cover design and to Jake Coolidge for the map.

Most of all, I would like to thank my parents and sister. My father ran the Foundation with me, while my mother and sister supported us— nudging me every day to feel our borrowers' troubles and pain better. Throughout the writing of this book their love inflated me during my failings and deflations, squeezed out my inadequacies, and poured out onto my computer when I stared, completely stuck.

ABOUT THE AUTHOR

Saumya Roy is a social entrepreneur and journalist based in Mumbai. In 2010 she cofounded Vandana Foundation, a nonprofit that provides microloans to entrepreneurs in the Maharashtra region. Soon she began lending to the wastepickers of Deonar, discovering their secret world and intrepid lives, and has stayed, chronicling them. She has written for *Forbes India*, *Mint* newspaper, *Outlook* magazine, wsj.com, and thewire.in, among others. While working on *Castaway Mountain*, Saumya received fellowships from Rockefeller Foundation's Bellagio Center, Blue Mountain Center, Carey Institute for Global Good, Sangam House, and Dora Maar House.